A Thread of Hope

I love you

Sis. Melinda

Books by Melinda J. Kaffer

The Women of Faith Series
Book One: The Crooked Path
Book Two: Whispers in the Night
Book Three: Hadassah's Cry

The Broken Dreams Series
Book One: A Thread of Hope

Non-Fiction
God Hears Your Silent Cry

A Thread of Hope

Book One of the Broken Dream Series

Melinda J. Kaffer

Library of Congress Control Number: 2016907432
ISBN: Hardcover   978-1-5144-9174-4
               Softcover   978-1-5144-9173-7
               eBook   978-1-5144-9172-0

Print information available on the last page.

Rev. date: 05/12/2016

To order additional copies of this book, contact:
Xlibris
1-888-795-4274
www.Xlibris.com
Orders@Xlibris.com
736589

Come unto me, all ye that labour and are heavy
laden, and I will give you rest.
Take my yoke upon you, and learn of me; for I am meek and
lowly in heart: and ye shall find rest unto your souls.
For my yoke is easy, and my burden is light.

—Matthew 11:28–30
KJV

Broken Dreams
As children bring their broken toys,
With tears for us to mend.
I brought my broken dreams to God,
Because he was my friend.

But then instead of leaving him,
In peace to work alone.
I hung around and tried to help,
With ways that were my own.

At last I snatched them back and cried,
"How can you be so slow?"
"My child" he said, "what could I do?
You never did let go."
—Unknown

PART ONE

1992

1

Peoria, Illinois

Todd sat on the couch searching for something to watch on TV, anything to drown out the noise that came from Maggie's bedroom. Maggie was his mom, at least according to his birth certificate. Truth be told, she was more like his best friend. He honestly didn't think he would want it any other way. She was cool. She gave him his space. She loved him the best she knew how. However, she was far from perfect. But hey, who was he to judge? Because he too was far from perfect.

After a few moments of flipping through the channels, he tossed the remote aside. "What's the use?" he asked himself. "There's nothing on, and it's not like we have cable."

He took a deep breath and allowed the stale smell of cigarette smoke to fill his lungs. He heard the sound of the small clock that hung above the couch tick away. He wanted to move the stupid clock to another location. To him, it looked completely out of place on the yellow stained wall. One lonely clock and nothing else hanging on the wall. Ridiculous. He even tried hanging a few posters on each side of the clock, but Maggie removed them. She claimed they looked too tacky.

What did she know about class? Really? She more than likely worked as a prostitute longer than most women in the city of Peoria. She lived a life of tawdry, and she didn't care who knew about her line of profession.

For the life of him, Todd couldn't figure her out, but then again, he gave up years ago. Not that he was that old, because he wasn't, although he was sure he had witnessed more in his twenty-one years of living than most people had in a lifetime.

He jumped to his feet when he heard the sound of footsteps. He wanted to get to his bedroom before Moe, Maggie's boyfriend, made his way to the kitchen for a beer. At least he claimed to be her boyfriend. Todd questioned how a man could call a prostitute his girl. He came to the conclusion that it takes all types to make the world spin around.

Moe had been coming around for as long as Todd could remember. He normally paid his weekly visitation on Sunday nights, but tonight was an exception. They were celebrating Maggie's thirty-sixth birthday.

Todd decided years ago to give Maggie some credit for at least trying to provide for him. Mostly because she was barely fifteen when he was born. After all, she could have aborted him or put him up for adoption.

He supposed he was thankful she ruled out abortion, but he was persuaded she should have put him up for adoption. Life would have been simpler for both of them. He would have been out of the equation, and she could have stayed in school. Who knows, maybe she could have gone to college.

Maggie was darn smart, and Todd had no doubts she could have had a bright future. With the proper education, she could have chosen a much better career. Anything would have been better than prostitution. He could easily see her as a secretary or maybe even a model. Even though she was his mom, he couldn't deny that she was one beautiful woman.

Fact is if he had a quarter for every time he witnessed a man looking her way as they walked in public with desire written all over his face, he would be rich. Maggie would simply smile and bat her big hazel eyes and keep walking.

Todd cringed when he heard her bedroom door creak. "Toddy, can you get Moe and me a beer?"

He rolled his eyes as he listened to Moe calling his name in a sarcastic tone. "Oh, Toddy, it's Saturday night, shouldn't you be out on the town with a girl?"

"Shut up, Moe, you know he's not like that—"

"Like what, Maggie? A normal twenty-one-year-old man—oh, I forgot, he's still your little Toddy."

Todd wondered if they even cared that he could hear the hushed words being spoken within the paper-thin walls.

"Whatever, Moe . . . just leave him alone. He's a good kid."

"Yeah, whatever you say, doll. Hey, Todd, are you going to bring us a beer, or do I need to come out and get them myself?"

"I'm on my way," Todd replied with a hint of cockiness.

He walked to the kitchen and grabbed two beers from the fridge. He paused for a moment, thinking he was ready for a drink himself. He tried not to drink until the sun went down. Somehow that made him feel like he had a handle on Jack Daniel's. He didn't like getting filthy drunk, but he did like feeling comfortably numb.

Todd opened the cupboard above the sink and retrieved a goblet. He then opened the fridge and allowed the cool foggy air to fill his lungs. The cool air felt refreshing in comparison to the stuffy apartment. He placed the goblet in the freezer so it would get good and cold. He planned to fill it with ice in about thirty minutes and then go to his bedroom for the evening. He would listen to some classical music and get lost in a good novel.

Later that night, Todd sat at his small desk reading a Stephen King novel, listening to some Beethoven, and sipping on his JD. Todd started drinking Jack Daniel's regularly at the age of fourteen. Maggie made sure there was a bottle stashed in the kitchen at all times.

Maggie never asked him why he drank every night, and he never offered an explanation. When he first started drinking, he would sneak a nip of the dark liquor while she was entertaining her clientele.

Todd could still see the look of complete shock on Maggie's face the first time she found him suffering with a hangover. Once he recovered from his hangover, she sat him down and made him promise he would never again keep a secret from her and that he wouldn't drink to get drunk. He promised, and from that day forward, she supplied him with Jack Daniel's, and he never suffered from another bad hangover. Sure, he had the shakes every now and then, especially if he went a day without JD flowing in his bloodstream.

He could hear the ice clicking as he rolled the dark liquid around in the goblet. He couldn't understand why people diluted such a good-tasting drink with Coke or Pepsi. Todd's way of thinking was why drink Jack Daniel's if you couldn't handle it on the rocks. The sound of Symphony No. 9, the "Choral," drowned out the sounds coming from Maggie's room. And for that, Todd was appreciative.

Todd savored the taste of his drink as he looked at the pages of his novel. He never really cared much for beer, and he detested cigarettes. As for drugs, well, he never could get into something that caused him to space out or hallucinate. Occasionally, he would drink wine with Maggie.

He was basically a good guy, and this was how he spent most of his time. He liked being alone. He learned a long time ago that there was safety within the four walls of his bedroom. He was raised in the two-bedroom apartment above the pool hall located on Main Street. This is where Maggie started her *career*, if one would call it that, when he was just a baby. Although here lately, he had been contemplating getting his own place.

Every now and then, he would go down to the pool hall to shoot some pool, but not too often because of the sly remarks made by the cruel losers associated with the pool hall. Their words were like a dull knife trying to penetrate his hardened heart.

Often times, he could hear the comments in the recesses of his mind. *Todd, your old lady working tonight? How much would she charge a poor guy like me? Are you her little pimp?* Since he really didn't care for people, being friendless suited him just fine.

Todd also enjoyed running and riding his Harley. He felt free when he ran and took off on his Harley—free from the cold reality that threatened to snuff out the small amount of life that remained in his soul. The cold reality that Maggie, his mom, was a full-fledged prostitute, and it plagued his mind that he had no clue of his biological dad. There were times when reality seemed to be like a lead blanket placed upon his shoulders, and for the life of him, he couldn't shake it off.

The thing is Maggie was good to him. She never beat on him or yelled at him; in fact, most of the time, she talked to him like he was a baby. Maybe it was because she felt guilty, or maybe she didn't want him to become an adult. After all, she knew all too well just how cruel the world could be. Her folks threw her out to the curb when they found out she was pregnant with him. Todd had no idea what it was like to have family. His only family was Maggie.

Todd would never forget the way Maggie smiled when he graduated from high school. She dressed up in her finest for his high school graduation, and she refused to allow the whispers and stares to put a damper on her mood. After all, they were used to being snubbed. Maggie was proud of him, and he saw it written all over her face.

Todd chuckled as he allowed his mind to replay the event. With legs that felt heavy as two ton weights, he walked up to the high school principal to obtain his high school diploma. Maggie whistled and shouted, "Way to go, Toddy!"

He supposed that his relationship with Maggie was established on one word. Honesty. Maggie taught him at a young age that honesty was always the best policy.

Even though her line of work was as dishonest as they come, she never tried to be someone she wasn't. Maggie Jenkins was a prostitute who knew how to keep her enemies at bay.

Todd even witnessed a few police officers stop by a few times for a short visit. Todd felt certain that the only reason the state didn't snatch him from her was because she stayed off the streets. Maggie refused to be sold over to a pimp because they were dishonest. She refused to walk the streets because she had no one to take care of him. So she simply pulled her tricks on her own turf, so to speak. Also, the fact that she knew a thing or two about many of the prominent folks in the city of Peoria kept her from losing him.

When Maggie felt Todd was old enough to understand, she explained to him why men came in and out so frequently. To Todd, it was just life. Did he like it? No. Nonetheless, it was the life God had chosen for them.

As for God, well, He was a whole other issue for Todd. He was sure he only believed in God because Maggie had drilled in his head the notion that God existed from the time he was a young boy. To him, all of it was kind of freaky. For the life of him, he didn't understand why Maggie believed in a God that allowed her to be thrown under the bus. But like he said, he couldn't figure her out, and he gave up trying.

It really troubled Todd that Maggie never once spoke of his dad. It's like the guy was a ghost. Maybe to her he was a ghost of her past that she would rather forget. Or maybe he was more like a demon from her past that threatened to haunt her for the rest of her living days.

Todd learned a long time ago that everyone had a tormenting demon, and either you control it, or it controls you. Whatever the case, to Todd, it was all a mystery. All of the unanswered questions ricocheted in his mind like a bullet ricocheting off a concrete wall.

Todd tried to get back into his novel, but he couldn't seem to concentrate on the story. He kept seeing Maggie's smile. Not that she smiled that often—she didn't. Truth be known, when she wasn't working or busy with him, she spent a whole lot of time crying.

It made him angry to hear her cry, so to keep from blowing up at her, he would write his thoughts in notebooks.

As a child, he could remember writing her stories. He always tried to make sure they were funny stories so he could hear her laugh. Her laugh was contagious. It seemed that her smile could easily light up the entire world.

Maggie always encouraged him to become a writer. She loved reading his short stories and essays. Todd actually thought seriously about writing a book. He even started a few novels, but he never got around to completing them.

Todd traced his hand over the book cover of the novel, *Gerald's Game*, and he asked himself why the book cover reminded him of Maggie. He supposed the answer was as obvious as the nose on his face. It was because of the handcuffs that dangled from the bedpost. Yep, Maggie was locked in her own prison. Todd only wished he could find the key that would release her to freedom.

2

Macomb, Illinois

Jenna yelled out, "The burgers are almost done!" as she flipped the thick juicy hamburgers on the grill. She loved cooking outdoors especially during the hot summer months. Her philosophy was why cook in the hot stuffy kitchen when one could enjoy nature? Sure, mosquitoes were a pain in the backside, but that's why bug repellant was invented. During the summer months, she kept a supply on hand.

She was celebrating the Fourth of July with her daughter, Tessa; her boyfriend, Grant; and Tessa's longtime friend Hunter. Jenna was grateful that Tessa decided to stay home rather than go to Argyle Lake with her friends. Of course, Hunter was Tessa's shadow. The two of them had been best of friends for as long as Jenna could remember. Hunter was one of the few people who never walked away from their tainted past.

Sure, she had Cindy's friendship, but she wouldn't allow her to get too close. Jenna could detect that it bothered Cindy, but Cindy was willing to accept Jenna's terms. She and Cindy had worked together quite a few years at Spoon River Junior College. Cindy's husband, Bob, seemed to get along relatively well with Grant, and for that Jenna was grateful. Jenna simply had a hard time trusting people. Mostly because of the way many of her so-called friends stabbed her in the back when Scott walked out.

Jenna couldn't help the fact that her ex-husband, Scott, ran off with a younger woman from the church they attended since Tessa was a baby. Scott left her and Tessa high and dry, so to speak. All in all, she was pretty proud of how well she bounced back. After all, she held a respectful position at Spoon River Junior College. She loved her daughter like crazy, and she loved her job.

She taught the adult education class, and for Jenna, it was rewarding to watch adults improving their future by pursuing a higher education. Most of her students had only a ninth or tenth grade education, but at least they were willing to wipe the dust off their backside and go forward by striving toward obtaining their GED.

Jenna was all for folks becoming productive, responsible human beings. In her opinion, there were too many people who blamed their childhood, society, and whatever else they could for their laziness.

Nonetheless, Jenna tried to see the best in all of her students, and she always tried to put herself in their shoes. She was no man's dummy; she realized there were some people who would try to take advantage of the system. Sad but true, for some people's way of thinking was if they got a better education, they may be forced to actually work for a living.

She was thankful her parents advocated education and that one needed to work for a living. Even though her dad was somewhat of a Bible thumper, he at least encouraged her to pursue college.

She could still hear her dad quoting scripture, "Study to shew thyself approved unto God, a workman that needeth not to be ashamed, rightly dividing the word of truth," and "But if any provide not for his own, and especially for those of his own house, he hath denied the faith, and is worse than an infidel."

Yes, he quoted scripture to her quite often, and as hard as Jenna tried, she wasn't able to forget the Bible verses she memorized as a child.

Jenna tried her best to raise Tessa with good moral values. Fact is she was extremely proud of her daughter. She may have struggled during her sophomore year because of Scott walking out of their life, but she bounced back. She graduated with honors, and for that Jenna was grateful.

Tessa planned to take her basics at Spoon River, and then she desired to go to WIU. She expressed to Jenna on more than one occasion that her dream was to attend Western Illinois University, and her ambition was to become a psychologist.

Jenna had to smile when she glanced over at Hunter and Tessa, footloose and fancy-free, throwing a Frisbee back and forth. She was sure Hunter's feelings for Tessa exceeded far beyond friendship. Nonetheless, Tessa insisted that she didn't want to ruin a good relationship by making him her boyfriend.

Later that evening, they planned to head off to Glenwood Park for the annual fireworks. Jenna was glad this year the holiday fell on a Saturday. She longed to spend some extra time with Grant. He had been putting a lot of overtime in at Bowers, and she missed having him around like crazy.

Grant had literally sweep her off her feet. To Jenna, he was simply the most charming man on planet Earth. There was not a day went by that she didn't forget to count her lucky stars for their paths crossing. For the life of her, she couldn't figure out why his first wife, Julia, kicked him to the curb. The way she saw it, it was Julia's loss and her gain. Some would say she was given a second chance at love. But Jenna knew otherwise; she believed they were destined to be together.

Grant was much more than her boyfriend; he was her best friend, her confidant, and her source from which she drew her strength. One of the things she admired about Grant the most was even though he was a Christian, he didn't try to pawn his faith off on her. It was as if they made a silent pact with one another. She would give him space to go to church and worship God, and he would give her space to live life free from Christianity.

Not that Jenna didn't believe in God because she did in her own way. She simply didn't believe in church, nor did she believe in having a so-called relationship with God. The way she saw it, God was a God afar off, and He was entirely too busy doing whatever it was He did to spend time with her. Sure, she taught Tessa the fundamental truths of the Bible, but that was about it. Yet for whatever reason, Tessa seemed to be more spiritually minded than Jenna had ever been. It was more than likely because of her grandpa Larry, Scott's dad.

Jenna could sense that Grant was ready to take their relationship to another level. In all honesty, she was ready to make a deeper commitment in their relationship. She loved him, and she had no doubt he loved her.

"Did I hear you say the burgers were almost ready?" Grant asked in an impish tone as he gently placed his hands on Jenna's shoulders.

At the feel of Grant's strong hands on her shoulder, Jenna felt her heart skip a beat. She quickly wiped her hands on her apron and turned to face him. "Yes, you did. And where have you been hiding?" she teasingly asked as she poked his chest.

"Hey, easy, darling. I've been busy working on the leak under the kitchen sink."

Jenna allowed her hand to rest on Grant's chest, and she reached up on her tiptoes to give him what her lips desperately craved—a big kiss—only to be interrupted by a couple of goofy supposedly young adults.

"Really, can't you two wait until Hunter and I are . . . like, somewhere, before you start acting all mushy?"

"Cut them some slack, Tessa. Hey, I'm going to wash up. Those burgers smell great!"

Jenna couldn't help but notice a hint of sarcasm in Hunter's tone. "Hunter, grab the potato salad out of the fridge on your way out. And, Tessa, you go wash up too, and grab the bake beans from the oven. Please."

Tessa mischievously walked over to her mom and placed a big kiss on her cheek. "Aren't my kisses good enough?"

"Oh, go do as I said . . . Oh, and be careful, the casserole dish will be hot."

"Duh, that's what potholders are for, Mother."

Jenna batted her cornflower blue eyes at Grant as she whispered, "Now, where were we?"

"I think you were about to give me a big smackaroo for saving you a bundle of green backs."

"Oh, well, if you don't mind me asking, exactly how did you save me 'a bundle of green backs'?"

"Duh, I fixed the leak under your kitchen sink."

"Oh, yes, that's right . . . now come here my plumber, and give me a big smackaroo."

Dinner went by with a lot of laughter, and before everyone knew it, it was time for them to head to Glenwood Park for the fireworks show.

They had just finished loading the lawn chairs in the truck when the telephone rang.

"I'll get it." Jenna ran to the phone and quickly picked up the receiver from the cradle, "Hello, this better be good because we're on our why out the door." She paused as she listened to dead silence on the other end.

"Jenna?"

Jenna shook her head, thinking maybe her mind was playing tricks on her. How long had it been? At least two years. *Why on earth is he calling?* "Yes, it's me. What do you need?"

"What kind of greeting is that? And when did you start answering the phone with 'this better be good'?"

"Look, Scott, we're on our way to the park. If it's Tessa you need to speak with, I'll have her give you a call later." Jenna felt her blood pressure starting to rise. *Who does he think he is? And what right does he have calling here with such an attitude?*

Everything within Jenna wanted to slam the phone receiver down as hard as she could in hopes he would suffer with a headache for a few hours. At least by doing so, she could presume she would be making a clear statement to the *jerk*. He was the last person she or Tessa desired to speak with or see.

They had been doing just fine without him. It was Jenna who made sure the bills were paid, and there was food on the table. She had yet to receive one child support check from Scott. Grant had encouraged her to take him to court, but she simply bit the bullet and continued to work her tail off.

Yes, at times money was tight. But wasn't it the hard times that defined the true character of a person? All in all, life was good. They didn't need the dark shadows of yesterday to remind them of the heartaches they both suffered when Scott intentionally stepped out on them for loose goose Mandy.

At the sound of Scott's squeaky voice, Jenna was brought back to matters at hand. She silently chided herself for not noticing the annoying sound of his voice before she tied the knot with the creep.

"Actually, it's you I need to speak with. Look, Jenna, it's Dad . . . He . . . uh . . . he passed away . . . this morning."

Jenna placed her hand over her forehead as she allowed Scott's words to reel around in her mind. She hated to hear Larry passed. He was a good man. Really he was. It was difficult for her to comprehend he played a part in parenting Scott. The two were definitely like day and night. Jenna never had the opportunity to meet Scott's mother. She passed away when Scott was only ten years of age.

Jenna supposed Larry overlooked many of Scott's behavioral problems because of the death of his wife. From what she had been told, Hazel was a real loving woman.

Tessa was going to be devastated because she dearly loved her grandfather. Larry always made sure he kept in touch with Tessa. He would pay monthly visits and come around for birthdays and holidays. He never mentioned Scott, and they never asked questions about his whereabouts. Jenna noticed he looked a little peaked the last time he paid them a visit.

Jenna heard the front door open, and she felt a peace wash over her as Grant stepped across the threshold. Jenna placed her hand over the receiver and whispered, "It's Scott. His dad passed." She reached her hand out toward him. She could tell by the puzzled look on Grant's face that he questioned Scott who exactly. Finally it dawned on him she was speaking of her ex-husband.

"Jenna, are you still there?"

"Yeah, I'm still here."

"Oh, I thought maybe I lost you."

You lost me all right. Over two years ago when you ran off with Mandy and humiliated me before the entire church. "So you're wanting me to tell Tessa?"

"I was hoping you would, and listen, I'll be sure to give you a call when I learn more about the funeral arrangements."

"You do that."

Jenna paused for a brief moment as she contemplated reminding Scott Tessa had graduated high school with honors. She relished at the touch of Grant's strong hand in hers. Really, to her, her marriage to Scott was nothing more than a faint memory in the recesses of her mind. What she had with Grant was real, and she wouldn't trade it for the world.

Before she allowed herself another moment to second-guess, she blared out, "You do know Tessa graduated this year? Oh, with honors, I might add." She heard the horn of Grant's truck blow from outside. "Look, I gotta go—"

"Look, Jenna, I got a card for Tessa—"

"Like I said, I gotta go." After she hung up the phone, she realized she never agreed to tell Tessa about her grandpa's death. Oh well, she guessed it was just one more plate Scott refused to step up to.

Jenna felt her world tilt as she fell into Grant's open arms. She wasn't ready for this. Tessa didn't need her dad back in her life. But it couldn't be avoided. Larry passed away. Tessa's grandfather. She didn't even think to ask Scott how he died. Did he have a heart attack? Or maybe cancer? Was the cause of his death really important? At the moment, all Jenna could think was it all seemed so unfair for Tessa.

"Baby, this is just another bump in the road." *Father, please show her that You love her with an everlasting love, in Jesus's name, amen.*

To Jenna, Grant's soft words floated around her mind like dandelion dust. Somehow, she realized this too would pass.

3

Jenna decided to wait until after the fireworks to tell Tessa about Larry's death. She replayed the brief conversation she shared with Grant as they walked across the park toting their lawn chairs. She came to the conclusion that he was right; Tessa was no longer a child, and she should be treated as an adult. But still, Jenna didn't have the heart to ruin her evening. The way Jenna saw it, why should both she and Tessa be down in the dumps?

Grant could discern the tension oozing from Jenna's spirit. He questioned if he should talk to her about trusting God. After all, doesn't death make one ponder on eternity? He couldn't seem to erase the look of despair on Jenna's face as she clutched the phone receiver as if she was holding a hot iron. He decided to take a leap of faith and let her know he would be praying for all of them.

He nudged her shoulder with his as he tenderly spoke just loud enough for her to hear. "Baby, I just want you to know I'll be praying for you and Tessa. Heck, I have been praying from the moment I saw the look on your face—"

Jenna abruptly interrupted him. "Okay, Grant, you do that." She could feel her blood start to boil at the very thought of God. "If it will make you feel better . . .," she trailed off for a moment as she tried to collect her thoughts, ". . . then you pray all you want." *Like God will answer your prayers.*

Grant could detect she wasn't opened to God, so he decided to steer her thoughts in another direction. "What do you say we go back to your place and play cards after the light show?" He gently traced his index finger up and down her forearm. "Uh . . . does that sound like a plan?"

Jenna felt her defenses coming down a notch or two. She secretly wondered how she could be so lucky to have such a good man. "That sounds like a plan. I think I'll tell Tessa about her grandpa's death after we play a few games of cards."

Jenna glanced over at Tessa and Hunter. They were both kicking back in their lawn chairs without a care in the world. She knew all too well the carefree attitudes would all change once they started college and once Tessa learned of the death of her grandpa.

೮ಛ

Tessa and Hunter lay across the railroad tracks on Brower Road gazing up at the stars. They were able to hear if a train was coming long before it made its way to their private spot. They had been coming to this spot to talk since their sophomore year in high school. It was their way of blocking out the world, and tonight, Tessa needed to do just that.

She silently wondered why she wasn't able to shed even one tear over the death of her grandfather. He had always been good to her, and it wasn't his fault her dad was a complete jerk.

"Tessa?"

"Yeah."

"You okay?"

"Sure."

"Well, then why are you so quiet?"

"I guess I have nothing to say."

"You bummed over your grandpa?"

"What is it with you? Why are you asking me so many questions?"

"Because I'm your friend."

Tessa allowed Hunters remark to play over in her mind. He was her best friend, and for the most part, he knew her like he knew the back of his hand. There were still a few things she kept tucked away in her heart. Maybe one day she will share her entire heart with him or someone special. She knew all too well what she needed to do. She needed to open up with her friend about what was bothering her at the moment.

"I guess I'm bummed. I mean, I loved Grandpa like crazy. It wasn't his fault my dad is a complete jerk."

Silence wedged itself between them like the darkness that blanketed the sky. The sound of night creatures softly singing a melody caused peace to fall over Tessa as she allowed her heart to open just a fraction. She longed to share with Hunter what had really been plaguing her mind.

"I'm sorry. This isn't about my dad. It's about the death of my grandpa."

"You're good. I mean, I can understand why you think he's a jerk. I have to admit, I not only think he's a jerk but he's also an idiot and an arrogant fool. He doesn't deserve to just waltz back into your life. I mean, after the way he walked out."

"Well, I don't exactly think he's trying to waltz back into my life. I mean, I guess he had no other choice but to call. After all, someone had to notify us about the death of Grandpa."

"I guess you're right. I just feel bad for you. I remember all too well how much he hurt you when he walked out of your life for that Mandy chick."

"Yeah, well, he didn't hurt me as much as he did my mom . . ." Tessa trailed off for a beat as her mind drifted back to the day her dad informed them he was leaving for good. She could remember him being away from home a lot, but somehow, when he packed up his belongings and walked away, it all seemed so final. She supposed in many ways, it *was* final. After all, she hadn't seen nor heard from him since that dark day.

"But that's all the past. I mean, I think we've done well without him. Mom is happy, and I'm getting ready to start a new chapter in my life." Suddenly, she realized Hunter was about to start a new chapter in his life. "I guess I should say we're about to start a new chapter in our lives."

Hunter avoided eye contact with Tessa. He didn't want her to see his true feelings. He was sure his eyes would convey how he felt for her. Sometimes he wondered how she could be so blind to the love he had for her. To him it was pretty clear his feelings for her exceeded friendship level.

"Yep, we sure are. Are you ready for Spoon River?" Hunter asked.

"Yeah, sure. Spoon River will be a piece of cake. I can't wait to start WIU."

"Well, time flies by pretty fast. Before we know it, we'll have our basics out of the way, and we'll be ready to start yet another chapter."

Tessa gazed up at the stars for a beat as she pondered on sharing her heart with her best friend. Finally, she decided, who other than Hunter could she be transparent with? When she opened her mouth to speak, she felt the words lodge in her throat. *What's the big deal? This is Hunter, my best friend.*

"We've been buddies for a long time, haven't we, Hunter?"

"Yep, we have."

"And you and me, we talk, don't we?"

"Yeah, sure. Why? Is there something you need to share with me?"

"Well, yeah, kind of . . . sort of."

"Shoot."

"Well, of course, I'm bummed 'bout grandpa passing and all. And the thought of seeing my dad makes me feel a mixture of anger and anxiety. I guess secretly I wish he was the one that died. I know, it's wrong for me to feel that way, but I gotta say it like it is. Plus I know it's going to be hard on Mom to have to see him and Mandy together—"

"I don't mean to interrupt, but I think your mom will be fine. I mean, she and Grant seem to be pretty tight."

"You're right. I can definitely see the two of them tying the knot."

There was complete silence for a beat until Hunter finally asked. "Are you okay with that?"

"Yeah, sure. I mean, I think Grant is a real cool guy."

"Okay, so what else is bothering you?"

"You know me to well, don't you?"

"Yep, I do."

Silence.

"Well, we've become adults. And I guess I'm thinking about adult issues. Did I tell you Brent has been calling?" Tessa knew very well she hadn't mentioned Brent to Hunter, but she liked using the question tactic.

"No, I don't think so. Are you talking about Brent Crawford?" Hunter asked with a hint of repugnance.

"Yeah, you don't have to sound so disgusted!" Tessa chided herself for sounding curt. "I'm sorry, Hunter. I realize you're only looking out for me. I mean, I know all too well what kind of reputation Brent has with the chicks."

"Tessa, listen to me. You're not just any *chick* . . . You're my best friend. And I won't stand back and allow a guy like Brent to take advantage of you. Trust me, he's trouble with a capital *T*."

"Maybe you're right, but still, like I said, we're adults. And maybe I'm ready to have a little fun. You know, experiment a little."

Hunter felt his heart drop to his stomach. He didn't like the idea of Tessa spending time with another guy. And he especially didn't want her experimenting with Brent Crawford. He could tell she was interested, but he was determined to defer her attention to hanging out with him.

"Hey, what do you say we do some canoeing out at Argyle tomorrow?"

"You don't want to talk about Brent, do you?"

"No, not really —"

"Hunter, do you feel the vibration?"

"Yep, a train must be heading our way."

"Let's lie here until we see it!"

Hunter laughed and simply replied, "I thought we're supposed to be adults."

"Whatever, Hunter."

∞

Jenna snuggled close to Grant, enjoying a glass of wine while listening to Miles Davis. He made her feel safe, complete, and loved. She loved the fresh clean smell of his cologne. It awakened all of her female senses and caused her intellectual mind-set to diminish. Nonetheless, she knew Grant was not a man who fooled around. He was a true man of faith, and he had high moral standards. The guy wouldn't even drink a glass of wine with her. He insisted on drinking water with lemon while she sipped on her white wine.

Truth be told, Jenna wouldn't want it any other way. Call it weird if you want, but the way she saw it, God's out there, and He's for some folks. He's just not for her. She could only cross her fingers that He's for Tessa. One thing she knew for certain, the man upstairs was for Grant. She supposed that made her feel secure in an odd sort of way. She even chided herself for doubting God would hear his prayers. Jenna was sure He heard Grant's prayers before one syllable came tumbling off his tongue.

Grant kissed the top of Jenna's head and ravished in the smell of her shampoo. She was a very striking woman, and he felt blessed to call her his girlfriend. He desired to take their relationship to another level, but there was only one factor that bothered him. Her faith. He was very much aware the Bible warns against being unequally yoked with unbelievers. On the other hand, he couldn't take away from the fact she did believe in Jesus.

One thing he was certain about was that he could never deny his love for her. He was sure God had caused their paths to cross. He had no doubt God wanted to use him to help bring Jenna back to her faith; yet for some strange reason, he hadn't felt released to talk to her about the Lord. Yeah, sure, there was small talk here and there, but he was able to discern Jenna had a wall built around her heart when it came to God, especially church.

"Are you comfy?" Grant tenderly asked.

"I am," Jenna purred.

"I think our evening turned out well."

"It did. And, Grant, thanks for your support. It really means a lot to me."

"Hey, you do know it's going to cost you?"

Jenna sat her glass of wine on the end table and tugged on Grant's T-shirt. She playfully whispered, "Oh, yeah?"

"Yes, well, I did fix the leak under your sink . . ."—he traced his thumb over the top of her lip—"I'm kind of thinking I've earned a big smackaroo and a home-cooked Sunday dinner."

Jenna moved unto his lap and gave him her most seductive look, "I think I can handle that."

"You think?"

"I do."

Jenna kissed his forehead with butterfly kisses and then ever so slowly brushed her lips across his. He allowed her to deepen the kiss as he drew her closer. She was so close, he was sure he could feel her heart beating against his own racing heartbeat. He felt waves of electricity flow through every fiber of his body. How many years had it been since he felt this place of ecstasy? He allowed their kiss to linger as he rubbed her back until finally, he broke away.

"Wow"—his voice was raspy, and he saw desire written all over her face—"that was some kiss."

"Well, you're some man."

"So," they both spoke in unison.

Grant smiled and whispered, "Ladies first."

"I was just going to ask you to come on by after your church service in the morning. I plan to have a good home-cooked meal whipped up that will be fit for a king."

He kissed the tip of her nose and replied, "I'll be here."

CଞÞO

The days following Larry's funeral went by in a complete blur for Jenna. She was thankful for Grant. He stood by her side throughout the entire event. She was also thankful Scott and Mandy kept their distance. Tessa seemed to have handled the death of her grandpa exceptionally well. Nonetheless, Jenna could detect the apprehension that projected from Tessa when Scott tried giving her a hug. To say the least, she was stiff as a board.

Jenna was also thankful for Hunter. The guy wouldn't allow Tessa to leave his sight. Jenna wanted to shout to her daughter, "Wake up and see the hunk of a man that's madly in love with you!" Nevertheless, she kept her lips sealed and trusted that one day, her daughter would see Hunter desired much more than friendship.

4

Todd had just finished running from one end of Peoria to the other. He was sitting on a bench at Riverfront enjoying the early morning sun. He liked running early in the morning. It gave him a chance to think, and here lately he had been thinking a lot more about moving away. He didn't want to move too far from Maggie. However, he longed to live far enough that he wouldn't have to witness her crazy lifestyle. He was sick of watching her being used by men.

He had read in the paper that Bowers was hiring. The factory was located in a small town by the name of Macomb. The way he saw it, living in Macomb would be perfect because he would be far enough from Maggie, yet he would still be close enough to pay her a visit every now and then. It was Monday, so Todd planned to make a trip to Macomb and check it out.

Todd's way of thinking was actually pretty simple. If he landed the job, then it was meant for him to move away. Nevertheless, if he didn't get the job, he would continue to apply at Caterpillar. Whatever the case, he was moving out. He was a grown man, and it was ridiculous for him to continue living with his mother.

Todd looked up at the blue sky and allowed the sun to beam down upon his face. He knew he needed to head home before people started buzzing around like a bunch of busy bees. Todd never did well around a lot of people, which is why Macomb sounded real good to him. Yep, he was ready to live in a small town. Not that Peoria was all that big of a city because it wasn't. Still, it was big enough for hookers to pull their tricks and for muggers to roll their victims.

Todd was sick of watching his mom dwindle away as she gave herself to one man after another. He had been pondering on moving for some time, and he was at peace with it. To him, his life was pretty much on a dead-end street. It was time for him to branch out and experience life a little even though he dreaded talking to Maggie about his plan. Todd stood to his feet and stretched, and then he set out on his quest to talk with his mom, Maggie. Secretly, he questioned if he was trying to convince himself that moving was a good idea.

When Todd stepped across the threshold, the smell of sausage and eggs lingered in the small apartment. He was surprised Maggie was up before noon. He decided he would take a quick shower before breakfast. He paused for a moment as he approached Maggie's bedroom. He was shocked that there was nothing but complete silence. The thought tugged at his mind that maybe she decided to get out of the stuffy apartment. Maybe she went for a walk or decided to pick up a few groceries.

He lightly tapped on her bedroom door and hesitantly called for her. "Maggie, you okay?" The silence was beginning to make Todd feel a little irritated. "Mags, you in there?" Todd felt his heart rate speed up. His mind started traveling down a dark path, one that haunted him in the midnight hours. What if she committed suicide?

Maggie spoke in a hush tone just when Todd was about to barge into her bedroom, "I'm okay, Toddy. I'm just a little tired is all. Your breakfast is in the oven. It should still be warm."

Todd felt a surge of relief flood through every fiber of his body—yes, all the way to his bones. Maggie was all he had, and he loved her the best he knew how to love.

He cleared his throat and replied, "Yeah, I smelled it when I came in from my run. Thanks for cooking it for me. You didn't have to, really. Look, I think I'll take a quick shower before eating." He paused for a moment, feeling like he needed to go into her room to check on her. "Can I get you anything before I jump in the shower?"

"No, Toddy, I'm okay. Like I said, I'm just a little tired."

"Okay, well, I'll see you in a bit."

Maggie traced her fingers over the old picture frame of her and Drake. She allowed her mind to travel down memory lane for just a while longer. Yes, this time, instead of suppressing the past, she allowed the memories freely to flood her soul. It wasn't often she opened this secret door she kept locked in her heart. But today, she simply couldn't resist.

She could remember the day the picture was taken like it was only yesterday. It was twenty-two years ago, and they were on the Riverfront enjoying the afternoon. Drake asked a gentleman passing by to snap the photo of them. They were so much in love. The two of them were soul mates, or so Maggie thought.

She knew she was pregnant with Todd, but she hadn't shared the news with Drake. She was sure he would have been ecstatic that she was carrying his child. Sure, they were both young as all get out, but they were exceptionally mature for their age. At least that's what Maggie kept telling herself.

Drake had promised her he would carry her off into the sunset and make her the happiest woman alive. Maggie learned real quick that promises like that were only made to be broken. As soon as Drake learned she was pregnant with his child, he hightailed it out of the state. The last she had heard he was living in California, but it had been at least ten years ago since she gleaned that little tidbit of information. What haunted her soul the most was she heard it from one of her regular customers.

In the end, Maggie learned who the mature one was; it sure wasn't Drake. Nevertheless, he would always be her shadow. She saw him every time she looked into her sons ice-blue eyes. Occasionally, she would allow her mind to drift back to him while entertaining her customers. To put it plain and simple, Drake Wilson would always lurk in the corners of Maggie's mind.

Maggie brushed the tears that trickled down her cheeks. She placed the picture over her heart, and she prayed the best she knew how. Yes, she poured her heart out to a God that had dealt her a bad hand of cards. This was just life as Maggie knew it. It is what it is, so to speak.

She had learned how to please her customers with the passion for which they longed and how to close her heart to love. The only person she loved besides God was Todd. Moe was just a convenient relationship. She refused to give her heart away. Maggie had vowed to never again believe one single promise because she knew all too well that promises were only made to be broken.

Todd poured himself a cup of coffee and tried to read the paper while enjoying his breakfast. The thought of asking Maggie to pack up and move with him kept bouncing around in his mind. He realized he hadn't even applied for the job at Bowers, but still, he would like to get her out of Peoria. He decided that he wanted her to go with him wherever the path of life may lead. He hated the thought of her living in this dungy apartment, so very alone.

Todd knew all too well that convincing Maggie to leave would be a big challenge. This was her way of life, and it was pretty much all she knew. Heck, who was he fooling, this lifestyle was all he knew as well. Nonetheless, he was ready for a change. He felt certain that in time, he could persuade his mom to pack up and leave dodge.

Todd was brought back to matters at hand when he heard the sound of Maggie's bedroom door creak open. He felt his chest restrict when he caught a glimpse of her. He could tell that she had herself a good hard cry. Todd was used to seeing her eyes swollen from crying, but it always ripped his heart out of his chest and at the same time made him angry.

"Hey, Mags. You doing okay?"

Maggie pulled at the belt that looped around her robe as she walked to the small kitchen. She knew she needed to avoid eye contact with Todd. His eyes reminded her to much of her shadow, Drake. Today, she was tired of crying, and the day had barely started. Today was simply one of those days that his shadow seemed to be hovering over her.

"I'm good, Toddy . . . yeah, real good. You doing okay? How's your breakfast? Your eggs still warm?"

"Yeah, breakfast is good. You didn't have to go through all of the trouble. I could—"

Maggie quickly interrupted, "Don't be silly . . ." She drifted off for a brief moment as she poured hot coffee into her cup. "You know I love cooking for you. Do you need some more coffee?"

"No, I'm good. I was just going to say I could have cooked my own breakfast." Todd contemplated if he should talk to Maggie about his plan. He came to the conclusion that now was just as good a time as any other. "Look, Mags, I was kind of hoping you could join me." Todd cleared his throat. He could feel a blanket of awkwardness falling upon them. "There's something I would like to talk with you about."

Maggie felt the sting of guilt rage through her heart. She hated to say no to Todd. Mainly because it was rare he ever wanted to talk with her. He normally kept himself locked up in his room, doing whatever it was he did. *Why today, Toddy? Today is not a good day for a talk. Today, your dad's shadow is haunting me.*

"Actually, I was thinking of taking a good, long bubble bath and then try to get some rest." She hated to disappoint him, but she knew it would hurt him to see her cry. Everything within her knew she would break. A woman knew her limitations, her breaking point, so to speak.

Todd realized Maggie was avoiding him. Sure, it stung a little. How often did he ask for some of her time? But that was fine; he also knew she couldn't avoid him for long. After all, neither of them rarely stepped out of the small apartment they called home. However, today he planned to jump on his Harley and take a little road trip to Macomb just so he could get a feel of the town. Todd would know it in his heart if Macomb was the place he could call home.

"That's okay, Mags. We can talk later. You go on and enjoy your bath."

"Are you sure?" Maggie's voice was just above a whisper.

"Yep, I'm sure." For a beat, silence threatened to wedge itself between them. "I think I might take a small road trip." Even to Todd, he sounded relentless, and for that he chided himself. He didn't want to inflict heartache on Maggie because she had experienced enough heartache for two lifetimes. "I'm sorry, Mags. I didn't mean to sound harsh."

"No, you're good, Toddy. Really, you are. So where are you planning to go?" Maggie could feel curiosity weaving its way around her heart. For the most part, the only time Todd left the apartment was when he ran. But every now and then, he did take off on his Harley.

"Macomb."

"Macomb?" she asked.

"Yeah, that's right, Macomb."

"Where's that?"

"It's a little town about seventy miles from here."

"Well, why in the world are you going to Macomb? Toddy, are you hiding something from me?"

Todd buried his face in the newspaper so Maggie couldn't see his smile. He got her attention, but he decided he would wait to talk to her, at least until after his trip. "Don't worry about it, Mags. Just enjoy your bubble bath, and I'll talk with you when I get back."

"Toddy, remember, no secrets."

He hated it when she whined and talked to him like he was still a child. He was a man, and he was ready to prove to the world he was a man. "Mags, stop talking to me like I'm a child. I'll talk with you later. Okay?"

Maggie felt the sting of his rejection. Nevertheless, she wasn't in the mood to argue. "Okay, if you say so."

"Look, I won't be gone for long. Okay?"

"Sure thing. Hey, maybe we can talk tomorrow . . ." She drifted off for a beat. "I shouldn't be busy."

"Yeah, sure thing, Mags . . . tomorrow sounds good." *Maybe I should make an appointment with you, Mags.*

5

Todd felt good about his plan, real good. He had already been to Bowers, and the receptionist working in the office seemed to be thrilled to no end about him applying for a position. To Todd, she was maybe a little too thrilled, but that was just his opinion. Who was he to say? So he filled out the job application and then set out on his quest to learn about the town.

He liked Macomb a lot. The town had a lot of quaint little shops around the town square, and the old fashion street lamps projected a coziness. He had been riding around for a while just admiring the quiet town. It was so unlike what he was accustomed to. In comparison with Peoria, it was so serene. He questioned if he could get used to the quietness. He came to the conclusion that he would adapt, but he highly doubted Maggie would. Oh well, he couldn't think about Maggie, at least not at the moment.

Todd felt his stomach rumble, and he realized it had been a while since breakfast. He was driving down East Jackson Street when he spotted a little café called Jo's Place. He slowed down, put on his turn signal, and pulled his Harley into the parking lot. The small café reminded him of someplace he had been before, but he couldn't pinpoint exactly where.

The smell of cigarette smoke filled Todd's lungs as soon as he opened the rickety door to the joint. He took a glance around and questioned if he made a wise choice. Without second-guessing, he stepped across the threshold and made his way to a booth. A young-looking waitress threw a worn menu on the stained tabletop and mumbled, "I'll be right with you," and abruptly walked away without making eye contact. He shook his head, thinking, *Maggie would most likely fit in here.*

Todd glanced through the menu and decided he would just get a tenderloin sandwich with the works. He drummed his fingers in a staccato fashion while he waited for his waitress to return. His day was going well up to this point. This joint reminded him too much of home. The waitress walked up to his booth, just when he was about to walk out.

"What can I get for you, sweetie?"

Sweetie? Really? Todd cleared his throat and mumbled, "I'll just have the tenderloin basket with the works on my tenderloin."

"Are you sure about that?"

Todd gave her a blank look and dryly replied, "Yeah, I'm sure."

"Well, you do know that includes onions and banana peppers, right?"

Todd rapidly blinked his eyes as he spoke in a punitive sounding tone, "Yeah, sure. I can read."

The waitress rolled her eyes and replied, "Okay, well, I'm just trying to do my job." She walked away mumbling loud enough for Todd's ears only. "Some people can be so rude."

Todd had to admit the tenderloin sandwich and home-cooked fries were pretty tasty. He was about to pay his check when a tall metal stand with free fliers caught his eye. He stood in a nonchalant fashion and walked to the stand to retrieve a paper. As he thumbed through the thin paper, the real estate page seemed to have jumped out at him. He was rather surprised at the cost of housing. The way he figured, if he landed the job at Bowers, he would be able to buy a house within no time. He chuckled at the thought of him and Maggie living in their own home.

Todd was brought back to matters at hand when the snotty little waitress came to his booth. "Can I get you a refill on your Coke? Or maybe some desert with coffee . . ." She paused for a moment as she fumbled through her tickets. "Folks around here say Jo makes some of the best coconut cream pie in town." She looked in the distance for a beat and then verbalized her afterthought, "Possibly even the entire state of Illinois."

Todd discreetly looked into the waitress's eyes, and for whatever reason, he felt compelled to ask for her name. "So do you have a name?"

Even to him, the question sounded lame. For some odd reason, she reminded him of Maggie. Maybe it was the dark shadows on her face, or maybe it was the emptiness in her hazel eyes. Heck, for all Todd knew, she could be in the same profession as Maggie. Yep, maybe her job as a waitress was just a camouflage.

The waitress absently patted around her collarbone and rolled her eyes. "Bummer, I forget my stupid name tag . . ." She paused for a moment when one of the old grungy-looking farmers called her name.

Todd couldn't keep his smile at bay "Sure, Donna. I think I will try a piece of that coconut cream pie and a cup of coffee—black."

Donna looked into Todd's ice-blue eyes, and then her eyes slowly moved to his lips. She allowed her eyes to linger on Todd's full lips longer than she intended. She could feel heat ever so slowly climb up the back of her neck as she whispered, "Yeah, sure. I'll just go get that pie, and coffee—black—no cream, no sugar, right?"

"Right."

Todd had to admit, the pie was probably the best he had ever tasted. He looked around the old café as he savored the last bite. He couldn't help but notice the yellow stains on the wall caused by cigarette smoke. He had to chuckle as he listened to the old farmers swapping stories about last year's crop and what they predicted for this year's harvest.

He silently thought it would be interesting if the walls to the old joint could talk. He was sure there would be a lot of chuckles at what they had to say, maybe even a few tears. But then again, wouldn't it be the same if the walls where he was raised could talk? Somehow, being here felt right. Todd took a long sip of his coffee while he glanced over at Donna. He felt his heart skip a beat because somehow, she too felt right.

CB&ED

Maggie must have scrubbed every nook and corner of the small apartment they called home. Why was her son going to spend his day in some off-the-wall town called Macomb? She did take the liberty to do a little asking around about the town. For what it was worth, she learned it's where Western Illinois University was located. She knew Todd would not be interested in going back to school.

The only question that continued bouncing around in Maggie's mind while she scrubbed floors was what in the world was Todd up to? Maggie couldn't bear the thought of Todd leaving home although she knew all too well he was a man. He was no longer her cute little Toddy, but he had grown into a handsome man. And Maggie was able to discern he was becoming restless.

Maggie jumped at the sound of the door squeaking. She must have reminded herself a thousand times she needed to oil the hinges. She had been in such deep thought she didn't hear the creaking sound of the steps that led to their upstairs apartment.

"Toddy, you made it home!" Even to Maggie, she sounded way too enthused to see her son walking across the threshold.

"What are you so jumpy about?"

"Oh, nothing. Hey, what kind of greeting is that?" Maggie rubbed her hands down the front of her old blue jeans. "I mean, I was worried about you."

"Well, you don't need to worry about me, I'm not a child."

"I know you're not, Toddy. So are you ready to have that talk . . . you know, the one you mentioned to me earlier?"

I wish she would stop calling me Toddy. "Yeah, sure, if you're up to it. I thought you wanted to wait until tomorrow."

"Oh no, really. I'm feeling a lot better. I think the bubble bath did me a world of good."

"Looks and smells to me like you've been on another one of your cleaning spells."

Maggie absently looked around the apartment. She opened her arms wide as she replied, "Oh, no big deal. I just rearranged a few things is all. Come on, and cop a squat while I pour us a glass of wine. Don't you think wine sounds good?"

The last thing Todd wanted was a glass of wine. It was almost time for him and Jack Daniel's to spend some time together. "Nah, Mags, I'm not up to wine tonight. But you go ahead."

"Okay, well, suit yourself." Maggie went to the kitchen to pour herself a glass of wine. She wished she had beer, but she's happy to enjoy some good wine.

"Hey, Mags, can ya put my goblet in the freezer? I plan to call it an evening after we talk."

"Yeah, sure, no problem."

Maggie realized that meant Todd would be locking himself in his room for the rest of the evening. At times, she did worry about him, but on the other hand, she really couldn't blame him for isolating himself. After all, who would want to live the life he had been forced to live? Maggie felt a pang of guilt stab at her heart as she thought of everything Todd had been exposed to. She literally felt like such a failure.

After a few moments of silence, Todd cleared his throat and looked over at Maggie. He figured there was no use in wasting time. Now was just as good a time as any to break the news to her. "Look, Mags, I might be moving to Macomb."

Maggie felt her heart fall to the floor. All she could think was this can't be happening. Somehow, she thought her son would always be with her. After all, he was her rock, her flesh and blood, and her only sense of normalcy. "What do you mean you might be moving to Macomb?"

"I applied for a job at Bowers, and if I get hired, I'll be moving there."

Silence crept between them like the darkness that overshadowed the earth. Todd reached for the only ray of sunlight that could possibly bring hope for Maggie. "Hey, don't worry. Do you honestly think I would just up and leave you here alone?"

Maggie felt her heart rate slow down a notch or two. She wanted to go to him and wrap her arms around him like she did when he was just a small child. She couldn't believe he would consider commuting back and forth to work, that's if he landed the job. "Really? You would stay here, for me?"

"That's not what I'm saying, Mags . . ." Todd trailed off for a beat, thinking he needed to walk softly. He knew he was treading on thin ice, and he didn't want to blow it. "Actually, I was hoping you would consider moving to Macomb with me. I mean, once I find a house and get settled and all."

Maggie sat in complete shock. She didn't know if she wanted to laugh or cry. She decided she had already spent enough time crying, so she did neither. She simply stared off into the distance as she contemplated how she would answer her son. She finally came to the conclusion that she needed to be straight up with him, yep, no beating around the bush. "What? Do you *actually* think I would move away from here? Honestly, Toddy—"

Todd abruptly interrupted, "Will you stop calling me *Toddy*?"

He felt a prick in his heart for raising his voice at Maggie. He hastily walked away and went to the kitchen to retrieve his goblet from the freezer. He was ready for a drink and some solitude.

Todd stopped dead in his tracks and shouted much louder than he intended. "Look at me! I'm not a kid! I'm a grown man, for crying out loud!"

Maggie squared her shoulders. She absolutely refused to give in to her tears. "You're right, *Todd*. You're a grown man! If you feel it's time for you to move out, then go! But don't expect me to move to some rinky-dink town with ya! This is my home, and this is where I'm staying!"

Todd rubbed his hands over his face as he allowed Maggie's words to play over in his mind. She was right. This was her life—all she knew—all she cared to know. His eyes started to blink rapidly fast. This was something they did when he was extremely tired or nervous or was on the verge of being extremely mad, and he was sure in this case it was the latter. He could feel his chest tightening with anger. He needed to get to his room before he did something he would regret. But before he did, he had just one more thing to say.

"You know, Mag, one can lead a horse to water, but one can't make her drink."

For a fleeting moment, Maggie stood in shock, but then reality set in like a cold winter night without a blanket. He was disdaining her. Yes, his taunting words were like a knife stabbing away at her already fileted heart.

"Yeah, well, you know, Todd, this *horse* put food on your table, a roof over your head, and Jack Daniel's in you cupboard." With that said, she retrieved her bottle of wine and moseyed off to her bedroom.

Later that evening, Maggie tossed and turned. As hard as she beckoned for sleep to come, she was far from finding rest. She couldn't help but think that she should have worked tonight. Yep, she should have taken up a few offers she received via telephone. Pulling a few tricks would have done her some good. Although she couldn't take her built-up anger out on her customers, she could have turned it into raw passion. But then again, wasn't it her line of work that was pushing Todd out of her life?

After a few hours of tossing and turning, she decided what she needed was a shot of Todd's Jack Daniel's. Yep, she no longer felt the effect of the wine. So she ambled into the kitchen and retrieved the bottle of dark liquid from the cupboard, and she poured herself a shot. She walked over to the small kitchen table with the bottle and full shot glass in her hand. At the moment, the two felt like her life support.

After she sat down at the table, she put the shot glass to her lips and allowed the smell of alcohol to fill her nostrils. She tipped her head back as she downed her first shot. The dark liquid felt like fire going down her throat, straight to her stomach. Nonetheless, by the time she took her third shot, old JD tasted pretty sweet.

6

Hunter and Tessa were sprawled out on a blanket stargazing on the rooftop of Tessa's house, when all of a sudden, Hunter realized he longed to know more about Tessa. Sure, they were best friends, and they spent a lot of time talking about school, friends, the opposite sex, and life. Nevertheless, he felt this overwhelming need to get to know her secrets buried deep in the dark corners of her heart.

"Tess?"

"Yes, Hunter."

"Do you have any fears?"

Tessa was able to see Hunter from her peripheral vision. She had to admit, she was a little taken aback by his out-of-the-blue question. He was serious, and she didn't like it when Hunter got in one of his serious moods. No doubt he would ask her about Brent, and then, for the umpteenth time, she would have to go through the whole rigmarole as to why she decided he was not worth her time of day.

Or maybe he wanted to talk about her grandpa's funeral. She most certainly wasn't in the mood for that type of conversation either. Somehow, talking about death while enjoying God's creation just didn't set well in Tessa's spirit.

Even though Tessa didn't attend church, she believed wholeheartedly in Jesus. She figured she would start attending church one day, just not any time soon. Tessa was kind of thinking that after her college days were behind and her career as a psychologist was in full swing she then would think about finding a church. She knew without a doubt by then she would be living somewhere besides Macomb.

Tessa began to feel a little ornery as her answer to his ridiculous question started formulating in her brilliant mind. "Yeah, sure, Hunter. I mean we all have fears."

"Well?"

"Well what?" she asked in a nonchalant way.

"You're not going to tell me?"

"Tell you what?"

"What's your biggest fear?"

"Oh, you didn't ask me that. You simply asked if I had any—"

"Okay, you got me there. Maybe I was a little ambiguous—"

"*Ambiguous* . . . Really? When did you start using such sesquipedalian words?"

"Well, remember we are adults now. I mean, high school is behind us."

"Whatever, Hunter. Okay, my biggest fear is standing before a class giving a speech with a big booger hanging out of my nose. And, of course, everyone sees it but me. To top it all off, my speech is supposed to be funny, so I think everyone is laughing because I did such a great job writing my masterpiece when all the while, they're laughing at me."

"Are you serious?"

"Hunter, I'm serious as a heart attack." Tessa couldn't keep her emotions at bay. She busted out into an uncontrollable laughter. She stopped laughing when she saw that Hunter was not at all amused.

"Tess, I really am being serious here."

"Okay, I gotcha. I can do this . . . be serious, that is. I guess my biggest fear is failing."

"Really?" Hunter asked with a hint of compassion.

"Yep, really."

"Tess, don't you realize that it's our failures that determine our character?"

"Maybe so, but you asked."

"Okay, that's fair enough. So what's your wildest dream?"

"Hmmm, my wildest dream would be to have my own private office practicing in the field of psychology. Oh, and a replica of Sigmund Freud would be one of my regular patients . . . and you too, of course—a regular patient, that is."

"You're serious, aren't you?"

"Yep."

"Why Sigmund Freud?"

"Because I think he was a cool guy, and I would want to convince him that God really does exist."

"Wow, that's deep."

"If you say so, Hunter."

"Tess?"

"Yep?"

"Why would you want me to be one of your patients?"

"Because you're such a dork."

"Okay, that's fair enough."

"What's up with all of these questions?"

"I don't know, I guess I'm just feeling curious, that's all." Silence hovered over them for a beat, and then Hunter asked, "Tess, what's *sesquipedalian* mean?"

"Look it up."

"Are you serious?"

"Yep, serious as a heart attack."

"Do you want me to write a three-page essay on the stupid word?"

"Suit yourself . . ." Tessa trailed off for a beat and then asked, "What's your wildest dream?"

To marry you. "My dream isn't near as wild as yours."

"So what, it's your dream. Come on, Hunter, fair is fair. I shared mine with you."

"Okay, if you insist. My wildest dream is to find my happy ever after."

"Are you serious?"

"Yep, as a heart attack."

"Do you mean like, marriage?"

"Yep."

"Come on, Hunter, we all want to get married and live 'happy ever after.' I mean, that's just part of life. At least for most folks. You gotta have a wild dream that you're dying to fulfill . . . right?"

"I've done told you my wild dream."

"Okay, I'll cut you some slack. So what's your biggest fear?"

Hunter concentrated on the big yellow moon for a bit. He was sure Tessa would find him completely humdrum once he expressed his biggest fear. After all, she's more than likely one of the most colorful people he had ever had the privilege of meeting. Sometimes it amazed him that they maintained such a close friendship.

"I guess my biggest fear is that my wildest dream will never come true."

Tessa turned her head so she could get a good look at her best friend. She didn't care for the pensive look masked across his baby face. She decided it was time to lighten up his mood.

"Can I share something with you?"

"Yeah, sure, anything."

"Well, it's a little humiliating."

"Come on, Tess, it's me you're talking to."

"Okay, well, you promise you won't laugh?"

"Nope, I won't make a promise I may not be able to keep."

"Come on, Hunter. Promises are made to be broken."

"Not the promises I make you, Tess."

For a split second, their eyes locked, and Tessa felt her heart skip a beat. She shook her head and dismissed the magical second on the romantic stars that hung so perfectly in the sky.

"Okay, fine. Be that way. I just won't tell you."

"Okay, Tess. I promise not to laugh. There, are you happy?"

"Yep. Well, you know how I've decided Brent is a complete loser and scum of the earth, right?"

"Yes, thank the Lord!"

"Hunter, you don't have to get carried away."

"Sorry, Tess."

"You're good. Anyway, I was in Giants trying to find some good bananas for the homemade banana splits that Mom and I had a craving for. Well, you already know the produce section is by the main entrance. Anyway, I looked up only to see Brent walking into the store. I so wasn't up to talking to him because I had been dodging his phone calls for days. Well, maybe not days. So I noticed a cardboard Chiquita Banana woman manikin, and I decided to stand behind the stupid thing—thinking it was plenty tall and wide enough to keep me safe from Brent, the dragon. Well, just as he was walking by, I sneezed."

"Tess, you're kidding, right?"

"Nope, serious as a heart attack."

"Did he see you?"

"Yep."

"Well, what did you say to the loser?"

"I just laughed, and it felt oh so good to laugh in his face."

"What did he do?"

"He shook his head and told me I was weird and then walked away. The way I see it, my problem is solved. He'll probably never call me again."

Tessa was the first to start laughing, and then Hunter joined in with her. They both laughed until they were out of breath. After a few moments of their outburst, Tessa poked Hunter in the side and teasingly said, "Hunter, I told you promises were made to be broken."

Hunter poked her side and whispered, "You're so wrong. Cuz I had my fingers crossed."

"Whatever, Hunter. We're adults. Finger crossing is for kids."

"Whatever you say. Wait! Look at me!"

Tessa abruptly turned her head to face Hunter. "What? What is it?"

Hunter brushed his thumb under Tessa's nose and whispered, "You had a booger in your nose."

"You're kidding me, right?"

"No, you wanna see it?"

"Hunter, you're so gross!"

"Tess, you know you love me just the way I am . . ."

"Whatever you say, Hunter."

Meanwhile, down in the living room, Jenna and Grant were enjoying each other's company. Grant was in one of his playful moods, and Jenna was eating it up. She came to the conclusion that the man held the key to her heart. Jenna was even contemplating attending church with him in the near future.

The days following Larry's funeral caused Jenna to do some soul searching. She decided she had been unfair to God. After all, it wasn't His fault Scott and Mandy made complete fools of themselves. Jenna was able to get a good look at the two of them while standing at Larry's graveside service. They looked far from being happy.

Jenna realized she could have used the funeral as an excuse for the distance she witnessed between them. The problem was she knew Scott like she knew the back of her hand. The way she saw it, once a snake, always a snake. In Jenna's book, the guy would always be a good-for-nothing snake in the grass.

Grant brought Jenna back to matters at hand by picking her up in the air and twirling her around. "Baby, I love you."

"I love you too, Grant. With all of my heart, I love you."

Grant gently set Jenna down and pulled her in his arms. He kissed her in a way that promised her a lifetime of happiness. He felt her melting in his arms. When he heard a soft moan come from the very depths of her soul, he pulled away so he could look into her cornflower-blue eyes. Oh, how he loved her, and without second-guessing, he asked her what his heart had been longing to ask for weeks. He could sense her heart was softening toward God, and he was sure she was about ready to start attending church with him.

"Marry me, Jenna."

"I would love to marry you, Grant."

"Really?"

"Yes, really."

"Rings . . . I need to buy rings."

"I'm not worried about rings, baby."

"Hey, I have an idea. Let's go to the jewelry store tomorrow and pick some out."

Jenna smiled as she ran her fingers through Grant's thick dark hair. "I think that sounds like a wonderful plan."

"You, Jenna, have made me the happiest man alive."

"You're too sweet. Hey, why don't we plan a special dinner with Tessa, Hunter, Cindy, and Bob so we can tell them about our engagement? I did tell you Cindy and I have been going out to lunch together quite a bit, didn't I?"

"That sounds great! And yes, you told me about your lunch dates with Cindy. I think that's great. I believe she and Bob are good folks."

"You, Grant, have made me the happiest woman alive." Jenna stepped up on her tippy toes and passionately kissed her man.

Later that night, Tessa was awakened by her phone ringing. She sat up in her bed and looked at the clock on her nightstand and saw that it was 2:00 a.m. "Who in the world is calling me at this hour?"

Tessa fumbled around for the phone receiver. "This better be good—"

"Tess, it's me."

"Hunter, what do you want? Do you realize what time it is?"

"Tess, calm down. I have a perfectly good reason for calling."

Silence.

"Well, what is it?"

"I did what you asked me to do."

"Hunter, please forgive me for raising my voice . . . I love you, really, I do. I mean, you're my best friend. But what in the world are you talking about?"

Well, we're making some progress. She just said she loved me. Okay, maybe only as a friend, but that's a start. "I looked up the definition for *sesquipedalian.*"

"Okay, now I'm wide awake, what is it?"

"It is 'given to using long words' and 'a word containing many syllables.'"

"What?"

"Tess, I really think you used your fancy word out of context."

"Whatever, Hunter! It sounded good, didn't it? Oh, never mind—"

"One more thing, Tess—"

"What now?"

"You mean to say you didn't know the definition of *sesquipedalian?*" Hunter asked.

"No. Now you can thank me for the wisdom you gleaned."

"Whatever, Tess."

"Good night, Hunter."

"Good night, Tess."

7

Jenna was running around the house like a chicken with its head cut off. She needed to hurry and finish getting ready because Grant would be picking her up in exactly five minutes. They were making a trip to the mall in Galesburg to look for rings. They planned to go to Peoria if they weren't able to find what they liked in Galesburg. She once saw a set of her dream rings in a jewelry catalog, and she was hoping to find a similar set.

She and Grant spent hours going from one store to another in Macomb, not that they had a lot of stores to choose from because they didn't. Nonetheless, by the end of the day, the only thing they had to show for their quest was sore feet.

"Tessa, have you seen my brown sandals?"

Jenna was beginning to feel anxious. After all, it wasn't everyday a woman went shopping for wedding rings. She was also dying to tell Tessa about her engagement with Grant. They planned a dinner party for tomorrow evening to make their announcement. So she was starting to feel the pressure, and she didn't do well under pressure.

"Which ones? I mean, you only have a hundred pair of brown sandals."

Jenna placed her hands on her hips and rolled her eyes. She was about to respond to Tessa's ridiculous comment just as she saw her walking into the living room with her new brown sandals on.

"The pair that's on your feet."

"Oh, you mean these? I was kind of hoping to borrow them. Hunter and I are going to Argyle."

"No, you may not borrow them. They are brand new, and I plan to be the one breaking them in."

"Okay, whatever you say, Mother. What's up with you, anyway? I mean, here lately you've been acting a little giddy."

"Nothing's up with me . . . I'm fine! Grant and I are going to Galesburg and possibly Peoria."

"Oh, really? Is there something I should know?"

"Yes, I want my sandals back, like now. And don't forget you and Hunter are to be here for dinner tomorrow evening."

"Well, I think you're hiding something from me."

Jenna was about to respond when she heard Grant blow his horn. "Look, kiddo, I wish I had time to chitchat. But Grant's here, so give me my sandals, please."

"Okay, Mom, you win this time."

Later that evening, Jenna and Grant sat at a cozy café in Peoria enjoying a light dinner. She could literally kick herself in the backside for not allowing Tessa to break in her new sandals. After hitting every jewelry store in Galesburg and almost every store in Peoria, she was sure that her feet were covered with blisters.

Just when they were about to give up and make the trip back home without their wedding rings, Grant decided to check out a small jewelry store located downtown Peoria. Needless to say, Jenna's dream rings stood out in the showcase like a couple of rare jewels. Jenna's ring had two small rubies on each side of a beautifully cut diamond along with a white gold wedding band. Grant's band had three small diamond stones set in white gold.

"You know, Grant, I was thinking of maybe going to church with you in the morning."

Grant gave Jenna that crooked smile that she adored. "Really?"

Jenna smiled as she was about to take a sip of her raspberry tea. "Yes, really." She wondered if he realized how cute he looked. Surely he did. After all, she had only told him so a thousand times. She couldn't believe she was about to become his bride. She couldn't wait to share the news with Tessa and the rest of their friends. What few friends they had.

"Well, would you like for me to pick you up? Or would you rather we meet at the church?"

"Well, I would like for you to pick me up, of course."

"Okay, how does the early service sound?"

"How early?"

"Sunday school at eight thirty and morning worship at nine thirty. I guess I could pick you up at, let's say, around eight fifteen."

"That would work out real good. I mean, it would give me plenty of time to get everything ready for our dinner. You know, the house cleaned, cake baked, and spaghetti sauce started." Jenna rubbed the engagement ring on her finger as she whispered, "Or I might want to start the sauce, get the cake baked, and then clean the house." She felt chills run down her spine as she looked into Grant's grey eyes. "Yep . . ." Jenna trailed off when she felt his bare foot rub against her blistered feet. "I think that's the order I'll do everything." *I can't believe he took his loafer off to rub my feet.*

"Does your feet still hurt?"

"Maybe a little, but that feels good—you know, what you're doing." Why was she blushing? This was Grant, for crying out loud. She wasn't a young schoolgirl, but he sure did make her feel like one.

Grant winked at her and whispered, "I'm glad it feels good. I hope you know I plan to help out tomorrow . . . You do know that, right?"

"Yeah, sure, I was planning on it. I don't know why I'm making such a fuss . . . I mean, it's not like we're having a lot of guests . . ." She trailed off as she found herself swimming in his grey eyes. "Yep, Tessa, Hunter, Cindy, and Bob. That's all. But you already know that." *You're blabbering.*

Grant had to smile as he watched Jenna blushing like a schoolgirl. He relished in the fact he had such an effect on her. "Good. Now that we have all of that settled, we need to come up with a date."

"A date?"

"Huh, yes. For our wedding. I'm open to whatever date you would desire." Grant paused for a brief moment and then continued, "As long as you don't plan to have a long engagement."

"Well, I was kind of thinking along the line of a Christmas wedding. How does that sound to you?"

"I think I'm about to receive the best Christmas gift a man could ever ask for."

The next day flew by faster than Jenna could say *snap*. She had to admit, she thoroughly enjoyed the church service. The people at Grant's church seemed friendly enough even if she didn't meet the group of folks Grant worshipped with. Grant must have reminded her a hundred times that most of his friends attended the second service, and it was a little more contemporary. What Jenna liked the most was the peace she felt. It was a peace her soul had been longing for.

Jenna was very pleased with how good her homemade spaghetti sauce turned out. All in all, everything was perfect. The only thing she missed was her engagement ring. She took it off when she got home last night. She didn't want to ruin their surprise by taking the chance of Tessa seeing her ring.

Grant looked over at Jenna and winked as he tenderly spoke, "Well, as usual, dinner was fabulous."

Jenna was about to reply when Tessa perked up. "Okay, guys, let's cut the small talk. What's up?"

Jenna twisted her head to get a good look at Tessa. "What kind of question is that?" She turned her head when she heard her coworker Cindy clear her throat. "What?" Jenna asked Cindy.

"I agree with Tessa, you two are up to something. You know how I hate surprises. So come on, out with it."

Jenna looked over at Grant and smiled as she remarked, "What? We can't have a small gathering without all of you thinking we're up to something?"

Bob chuckled and teasingly interjected, "Hey, don't include me in this little equation. I think dinner was great. You know how you girls are, always jumping the gun—"

Grant interrupted Bob, "Actually, the girls are correct. Jenna and I do have something we would like to share." Grant looked over at Jenna. "Honey, why don't you share the good news with our guests?"

Jenna batted her eyes and spoke with a hint of seduction, "Tessa, Hunter, Cindy, and Bob, Grant and I are getting married."

Tessa grabbed Hunter's hand and pulled him to his feet with her. She let out a load, "Whoa! I knew it! When's the big date?"

Jenna smiled as she looked into Grant's soft grey eyes. "Well, we were kind of thinking about a Christmas wedding. So we decided on December 12."

Cindy whacked her hand on the table and elatedly responded, "Well, by golly, we've got a lot of work to do." She winked at Jenna. "I knew it. You know, the two of you tying the knot. I knew it was bound to happen, sooner or later."

Tessa spoke up, "Oh, I'm so excited! Wow! Cindy is right, we do have a lot of planning to do. Wait! I have an idea. Why don't I get my planner, and we can start jotting down some of our thoughts?"

Grant stood to his feet and playfully said, "Hey, Bob and Hunter, what do you guys say we go watch some TV while the ladies 'plan'?"

Hunter stood to his feet. "I'm with you on that."

Bob laughed. "Hey, what's on the ol' tube tonight?"

Hunter chuckled as he responded, "I really don't know, but I'm sure anything will be better than listening to—"

Tessa looked at Hunter and pointed her finger at him. "Hold on, if I remember right, your dream is to find your—"

Hunter interrupted, "Tess, that's enough."

"Whatever, Hunter."

For the next hour, the girls discussed the wedding. Of course, with the wedding being in December, the theme would be Christmas. Jenna expressed that she wanted an evening wedding with soft candlelight shimmering throughout the church.

Tessa came up with the idea of a big Christmas tree being displayed in the foyer of the church. They all put their heads together and decided to have it decorated with big silver glass balls and white turtledoves. Cindy came up with the idea of asking the guests to place their gifts under the tree and to put the card box next to the tree. Jenna was fond of that idea because she indicated she didn't desire a bridal shower. Finally, Jenna expressed she desired poinsettias placed throughout the fellowship hall.

After all was said and done, they felt certain they were more than able of accomplishing the task of making sure Jenna had the most beautiful December wedding Macomb had ever witnessed. At least that was Tessa's plan. Jenna couldn't decide who was the most excited, her or Tessa. She supposed she was. After all, she was the one marrying the best-looking man in Macomb.

Later that evening, Jenna and Tessa sat in the living room munching on popcorn and enjoying an old Fred Astaire movie, *You'll Never Get Rich*. Suddenly, it occurred to Tessa that soon Grant would be taking all of her mom's time or at least most of it. She wondered where they would live. Would they move? Surely not. At least she hoped not. She felt a lump in her throat as she looked at her mom.

She felt an overwhelming sadness sweep over her. She couldn't bear the thought of losing her friend. Sure, she had Hunter, but her mom was her true friend. They had been together through thick and thin. Tessa felt her mood slide downhill rapidly fast. It amazed her how quickly she went from excited to feeling almost depressed.

Jenna felt her heart fall to the floor when she caught a glimpse of Tessa's demeanor from her peripheral vision. She immediately flipped the television off and turned to face her daughter—her only child.

"Tessa, sweetie, what's troubling you?"

As hard as Tessa tried, she wasn't able to keep her tears at bay. She hugged her pillow tight to her chest in hopes that somehow, it would protect her heart. She didn't want to look up at her mom. Maybe because she was fearful of the answer that was sure to come.

Jenna moved closer to Tessa and placed her arm around her. She tenderly spoke, "Come on, honey. You can talk with me about whatever it is that's bothering you. Is it school?"

Tessa sniffled as she felt herself melt at her mom's touch. "No, it's not school," she sighed, "I wish it was."

"Then, what is it?"

"Are we gonna have to move? You know, once you get married."

"Oh, honey, of course not. Grant and I both agreed to live here. This is our home."

"Mom, will we still be friends?" Tessa hiccupped, "Will I have to move?"

"Of course, we'll still be friends—always and forever. Where did you come up with the notion that you would have to move?"

"I don't know. I guess with you getting married and all. I mean, why would you want me around? I would just be in the way."

"Tessa, listen to me. Grant loves you as his own, and you would not get in the way. Why, we wouldn't expect you to move." Jenna wiped at a few tears that trickled down Tessa's cheeks. "We're all in this together. You and me, buddies for life."

Tessa felt her heart leap with joy and a smile form on her face. She looked into Jenna's eyes and whispered, "Thanks, Mom. I love you."

"I love you too, Tessa."

8

Todd enjoyed the feel of the crisp autumn air as he walked along Riverfront. He was starting to feel a little annoyed about his situation. He thought for sure he would have heard something about a job prospect. His heart was leaning more in the direction of Macomb. Nevertheless, at this point, he would be happy flipping burgers at some greasy hamburger joint. He even thought about applying for a job at Jo's Café in Macomb. Even he could do dishes. He was well trained in the kitchen, so why not?

One thing for sure, if he didn't hear something soon, he would start making some phone calls. For all he knew, his application with Bowers could have been misplaced. After all, people made mistakes like that all the time. Todd was tempted to call the receptionist who received his application and ask her if she remembered him. The only thing he remembered about her was she seemed to be a little bit of a dimwit. This, of course, gave him more reason to believe she misplaced his application.

For the first time, Todd noticed the falling leaves. He supposed he grasped something different in the brown, yellow, and orange leaves. Yes, with each falling leaf, he saw a tale untold. His life. Some would say his mind's eye was playing tricks with his emotions. But not Todd; he knew all too well his life was passing before him like a leaf blowing in the wind.

At that very moment, he knew precisely what he needed to do. He could only hope Maggie would understand.

"What in the world do you mean you're moving to . . . whatever the name of that stupid town is?" Maggie asked with a combination of anger and distress.

"The name of the 'stupid town' is Macomb," Todd said. "Mag, you knew it was coming to this . . . me moving, that is. So just calm down."

"Todd, you need to think about what you're doing here. You haven't got a job and a place to stay. For crying out loud, you're not thinking—yep, that's the problem—your head is in the clouds!"

"Mag, my head is not in the clouds, and I'm aware of all of the facts. No need for you to worry. I have a good chunk of money saved," he assured her. "And remember, I'm not a child," he said with a hint of annoyance.

"Toddy—"

"I asked you not to call me *Toddy*!" he interrupted.

Maggie realized that over the years, Todd had saved a nice sum of money, but that didn't stop her from protesting. Indeed, she planned to be relentless. She knew all too well just how cruel the world could be. She was determined to protect her son even if he did get livid. She looked up at the clock, and she was grateful she had a couple of hours before her first customer.

"Okay, *Todd,* so you have money saved. What are you going to do when it runs out?"

"Maggie, haven't you always taught me to follow my dreams . . ."—he paused for a brief moment to collect his running thoughts—"and to be honest?"

The effect of his words were like a dull knife stabbing away at her already filleted heart. How could she tell him he was wrong when he was right? She did always encourage him to follow his dreams and be honest. Nonetheless, she knew all too well what it was like to see dreams shatter into millions of pieces. Yet there was a small voice whispering in her head, telling her she needed to let him go. All she could think was so much for being relentless.

She felt her heart slam against her ribs as she opened her mouth to speak. "You know, you're right. You're a man. You need to follow your dreams."

Even as she allowed the words to tumble out, Todd felt her pain dripping from the ceiling and seeping from the dingy walls. He was brought back to matters at hand at the sound of the clock ticking away time. Yes, he was reminded that his life was ticking away.

"Okay, when will business start picking up?" he asked.

Maggie didn't want to think about 'business.' She just wanted to sleep and pray when she awoke, this would all be a dream. "Not for a few hours," she whimpered.

He realized he needed to walk softly. However, he planned to be gone before her first customer appeared. He decided to pack as much as he could in his backpack, and in a few days, he would rent a truck for the rest of his stuff. Not that he had a whole lot because he didn't. Nonetheless, he did desire his personal items. "Okay, I'll just go pack a few things, and I'll be back to pack up the rest of my stuff in a few days."

"You mean you're leaving today?" she asked as anguish flooded her soul.

"Yes, I'm leaving today."

I can handle this. It's not like he's moving to another state. "Okay, well, I guess I'll—" her train of thought was broken when she remembered the shoebox of money she kept stashed in her closet. "Wait, I have something for you."

Maggie quickly went to her room to retrieve the money tucked away in the shoebox. She felt her heart swell with pain with each step she slowly took toward her son. Where had time gone? It seemed to her only yesterday she was trying to protect him from the sting of pain this world unmercifully dished out.

Yet here they were about to say goodbye. Maybe not goodbye like she said to his dad, Drake, or to her parents. Nonetheless, it all seemed so heart-wrenching familiar to her. It was almost as if she was destined to loss those who were close to her heart. Yet she was determined to keep her tears at bay. She could only hope he would find his way in life.

She tucked a loose piece of her hair behind her ear and looked into his ice-blue eyes as she tenderly spoke, "Here, this is for you. But promise me you won't open it until you get to that— huh—town."

Todd nodded his head as he tried to speak past the knot that had formed in his throat. He placed his big hand over Maggie's small one and simply replied, "Yeah, sure. What is it?"

Maggie felt a smile form on her face, and a strength she didn't realize she had bubbled up within her inner being. Maybe it was the warmth of her son's touch that caused her to feel stronger than she did just a few short moments ago. Whatever the case, she was grateful she no longer felt like a helpless rag doll.

"You doofus, it's a surprise! Why do you think I asked you to wait to open the box until you reached Macomb?" she teasingly remarked. "Go ahead, take it."

Todd retrieved the shoe box and placed it on the nearby kitchen table. He then did something he hadn't done in years—he pulled Maggie into a big hug. He chided himself for every time he lost his temper with her. He felt tears run down his face as she melted in his arms.

"I love you, Mags."

"I love you too, Toddy."

For whatever reason, at that very moment, Todd loved the sound of *Toddy*. It was like sweet-sounding classical music to his ears. He knew in his heart of hearts he would miss Maggie like crazy. But on the other hand, he knew he was doing the right thing. For the first time in his life, he felt like he was going in the right direction.

He was about to go to his room to pack a few things in his backpack when he picked up the shoe box. He smiled as he thought of all the possibilities that might be in the box. After he shook it a bit, Todd came to the conclusion it was more than likely full of letters Maggie had wrote him over the years. So he decided he would tuck it away in his closet and get it when he came for the rest of his belongings.

Todd was about to walk out the door of the small apartment he called home when he stopped dead in his tracks. The small clock that hung on the wall in the living room seemed to stand out like a sore thumb. He chuckled for a moment as he allowed his mind to replay all of the times the stupid clock annoyed him to no end. Strange, but true enough, he was sure he would miss the ticking sound of that clock. He made a mental note to buy one similar to that very clock once he found his own place.

He turned to look at Maggie and lightheartedly remarked, "Hey, Mags, you might want to think about hanging a few more pictures on the wall. That clock looks a little lonely."

"Yeah, whatever . . . You just be sure to call once you get a room. And call collect if you have to."

"Sure thing. See you soon, Mags."

"Yeah, I'll see you soon, Toddy. Hey, wait, do you have the shoe box?"

It struck Todd kind of strange that she be so persistent about the old shoe box. For a brief second, he thought about going back to his room to retrieve it. But he quickly dismissed the idea because he didn't want to be too loaded down while driving his Harley.

"Nah, I decided to get it when I come back for the rest of my stuff."

Maggie thought about insisting he take it with him, but she remembered he had a good amount of money saved. Also, she thought she could slip a letter in the box. There was a lot on her heart she would love to convey. She only prayed she would be able to put all of her thoughts on paper.

"Yeah, sure, I understand. I don't know what I was thinking, what with you riding your bike and all."

"Okay, well, I'll see you soon Mags." With that said, Todd turned and walked out of the apartment, leaving Maggie alone with her thoughts. Nonetheless, he had the strangest feeling his shadow would forever linger with Maggie.

For the next few moments, Maggie simply stood with her eyes fixed on the clock hanging in the living room. She came to the conclusion that Todd was right; the clock was too small for that much wall space. How many times had he tried to tell her? Yet she was too preoccupied with her own agenda to listen to what he was saying. Suddenly, she came up with an idea. Maggie smiled as the idea began formulating in her mind. She knew exactly what she needed to do.

Within no time, she had called all of her clientele to cancel their scheduled appointments. She liked calling them clients only because it made her feel more professional. Truth be told, she was seriously considering cutting back to only working a few days a week. The way she saw it, she only needed to keep her highly esteemed clients. She could easily let the rest go. Yep, she planned to have a little free time on her hands so she could make some visits to Macomb. She was sure she could persuade Moe into taking her to visit Todd.

Maggie only gave them a vague answer as to why she wouldn't be available for the day. The way she saw it, it was really none of their business. She always tried to keep her personal affairs to herself. Sure, maybe once in a while, she would allow Moe to peep into her private life, but not too often.

Maggie went to her closet and started pulling out boxes full of Todd's school pictures. She had pictures of him from kindergarten to his senior year of high school. After she organized the pictures on her bed just as she desired to position them on the wall, she went to the small pantry to retrieve some of Todd's clear lamination paper. She then set out on her quest of placing lamination on each picture.

Once she completed the task of laminating the pictures, she started hanging each one on the wall. Maggie felt her heart swell with pride as she carefully tacked each picture around the clock. Before she knew it, she was feeling a spark of joy bubble up in her heart. Maybe it was because her house was starting to look like a home. Everything within her believed Todd would come home for regular visits, and she could hardly wait for him to see her brilliant idea.

9

Todd couldn't believe his fate. He had been in Macomb for one week, and he had already landed the job at Bowers and found a cute furnished apartment, and he was on his way to pack up the rest of his belongings. It had been a long time since he felt this good in his spirit. For once in his life, he knew that he was on the right path. He had even been by Jo's Café a time or two. He had to admit, he looked forward to the home-cooked meals and, yes, even Donna.

He was sure his mom and Moe would drop dead in their tracks if they even suspected he was attracted to a woman. He didn't plan to talk to them about Donna, and he didn't plan to pursue any type of relationship with her. He continued to remind himself he was merely experiencing a little boost in his hormones because of the changes in his life. For as long as he could remember, his life was as predictable as the sun coming up in the morning and the moon shining at night. This was all new to him, but he had to confess—even if only to himself—he liked it.

Todd felt his heart turn flips as he allowed his thoughts to linger on Donna. She was a rather peculiar lady. He really couldn't figure her out, and he also couldn't decide if she was a lady. There were times he could see a softness about her that reminded him of the way he pictured a lady being in the recesses of his mind. Nevertheless, there were times she reminded him too much of Maggie. Which, of course, is why he planned to keep his guard up.

Todd felt anxious as he drove through Pekin. In just a short while, he would be home. As hard as it was for him to admit, Peoria would always be home. He was actually excited about seeing Mags. He chided himself for not calling her beforehand. He looked at his watch and saw it was only

8:00 a.m. Surely she wouldn't be entertaining her customers at this hour in the morning. After all, it was Saturday. Didn't she normally sleep in on Saturdays? Todd shook his head as he allowed the notion to play over in his mind. He came to the conclusion that with Maggie Jenkins, it was very possible.

Maggie had just finished taking a hot shower when she heard the knock at her door. She didn't have to second-guess who it might be paying her a visit this early on a Saturday morning because she recognized the knock. Only Tim Blackwell knocked five times and paused for a second before knocking two more times. He was a local business man, and she couldn't remember the last time he had paid her a visit. She knew it had been well over a month. Not that it really mattered because it didn't. What mattered most to Maggie was that he was loaded with cash. Tim always paid well for her service. She glanced at herself in the mirror one final time before answering the door.

As soon as Todd stepped across the threshold, he knew he came at a bad time. But then again, was there ever a good time? It seemed to him Maggie spent more time entertaining men than she did anything else. Yeah, sure, when she learned he was contemplating moving, she slowed down a little. Nevertheless, Todd knew it wouldn't be long before she was back into her crazy lifestyle full force. He shook his head as the smell of stale cigarette smoke filled his lungs. For the life of him, he couldn't figure out why people enjoyed filling their lungs with cigarette smoke.

Todd felt heat rise up the back of his neck as he listened to the muffled sounds coming from Maggie's bedroom. If only he could convince her to move away and start life anew. He could only hope in time she would change her mind, but once again, this is her way of life.

He slipped his keys into his pocket and went to the kitchen to get something cold to drink. He was sure he would be able to complete his task and be long gone before she realized he had been around. He figured he would give her a call later just to let her know he came by.

Todd stopped dead in his tracks when he walked into the living room. He couldn't believe all of the pictures Maggie had hung on the wall around the old clock. Every single one was a picture of him. The place was like a museum. *Todd's Hall of Fame.* Worse yet, a shrine in honor of her long-lost son.

He questioned what she was thinking by doing something so ridiculous. He much more preferred the clock hanging by itself than he did his face plastered all over the dingy wall. He had to resist the urge of ripping every picture off the wall—better yet, knocking on Mags's door and chewing her backside out. Instead, he stomped down the hall and slammed his bedroom door. He wanted Maggie to know that her son was home.

"What the—" Tim blared out as he sat straight up in bed.

"I think Toddy is home." Maggie placed her hand on Tim's chest and purred, "I'll be right back"—she winked at him—"we can pick up where we left off."

"I'll be here." Tim pulled Maggie into his arms and whispered, "Just don't take too long. I need to get to work."

"Oh hush with you, you're the boss. Why, you can come and go as you darn well please."

"Yes, that's right, but remember, I'm trying to set a good example for my employees." Tim winked as he said, "You should know all about being a boss . . . and setting a good example." He then chuckled.

Ouch, Maggie felt the sting of his words penetrate all the way through her heart. Once again, she was reminded of what kind of a poor example she had been for Todd over the years. "Yeah, well, I'll do my best to hurry." With that said, she retrieved her silk robe and made her way out the door.

Todd had just finished packing up another box and was ready to take a load down to the truck. He couldn't get finished fast enough. Even though he had only been away for a week, he missed the solitude of his own place. At least, when he was at his apartment, he didn't have to listen to Maggie entertaining her customers. What irked him to no end was the fact he would continuously be haunted by her lifestyle.

Although he admitted there would not be a day go by when he wouldn't worry about her, it still didn't stop the anger that threatened to choke the life out of him. If only he could convince her to move away from this dive. But he knew that wouldn't happen any time soon. Maybe not ever.

Todd was about to walk out of his bedroom when out of nowhere, Maggie appeared. The look on her face caused his chest to tighten. He immediately felt his defenses rise. Was she okay? Did some jerk do something to hurt her? He knew most of her customers, and they all treated her well.

Nonetheless, he wasn't born yesterday. He was all too aware of how a man's emotions worked. Yep, men could be all lovey-dovey one moment, but if a woman didn't give them what they wanted, they were in for the kill. Todd recognized he was capable of killing any idiot who harmed Mags. She was all he had.

"Mags, what's wrong? Are you okay?"

Maggie looked away from Todd only because he reminded her so much of Drake. She didn't want to think about him, not now, not ever again. It grieved her spirit too much. Mainly because he was a reminder of when her life started going downhill faster than she could say squat. She tugged at her robe as she shuffled from one foot to the other. Why did Todd have to show up without a notice? If she knew he was coming, she would have asked Tim to come back at a later time.

"I'm good. Actually, I was about to ask you the same thing. I mean, with the way you stomped down the hall and slammed your bedroom door."

Why won't she look at me? As bad as Todd wanted to be mad, he couldn't. To him, Maggie looked like a wounded puppy. Not that Todd ever had a puppy because he hadn't. They weren't allowed to have pets in the apartment.

"Sorry for making such a ruckus, Mags. I shouldn't be here long. I was just about ready to pack up the U-Haul and be on my way. You go on about . . . huh, business," Todd felt a prick in his heart as soon as the comment rolled off his tongue. "Hey, Mags, sorry . . . Okay?"

Maggie kept her tears at bay. She knew she needed to get back to Tim, or she would lose a well-paying customer. "No, you're good. Hey, I would love to help, but . . . well, you know."

At that very moment, she wished she could find a hole and crawl in it. Maybe by doing so, she wouldn't constantly be reminded of how big a failure she was. Maybe now that Todd was moving away, she should run off and start life anew. Why not? Isn't that what everyone she loved did? Abandon her. Kick her to the curb. And all of the above.

Maybe her son leaving was a sure sign from God that it was time for her to move on. But she couldn't just yet. She gave most of her savings to Todd. Nevertheless, she would be able to take on more customers now that she didn't have Todd to worry about. With more customers came more money. What was she thinking when she thought about cutting back on her business? She needed out of this web she had been trapped in for more years than she cared to admit. She could do it, she was certain she could. California was starting to sound real good. Suddenly, she felt a spark ignite in her heart.

"Hey, Toddy, how about lunch? I'm sure by the time you finish packing, it'll be about lunchtime."

Todd rubbed his hands over his whiskered face and then rubbed the back of his neck. He knew he should hang around and have lunch with Maggie, but he wasn't in the mood for company. Plus it would be late afternoon by the time Maggie got around to eating lunch. He wanted to stay with his original plan, which was to be back home by early afternoon so he could return the U-Haul truck.

"Nah, I don't think I can this time. But I tell you what, how about a rain check?"

"Yeah, sure, Toddy, we can do a rain check." Maggie took steps toward Todd. "Well, give me a hug." Without second-guessing, Todd opened his arms to Maggie.

At the sound of Tim's voice, she was brought back to matters at hand. Her line of profession, at least that's what she liked calling it. "Hey, Maggie, I haven't got all day."

"I'll be right there, sugar," Maggie replied. "Sorry, Toddy, duty calls."

For Todd, this way of life was as normal as any other way of life. It was what he knew. He looked into Maggie's eyes and whispered, "I understand. I'll be seeing you soon." He really wanted to understand, but he couldn't seem to grasp her way of thinking. No, he didn't like this charade, but he simply went with the flow. He had learned it was easier to pretend than face the truth. Yes, he tried to be honest with Maggie in a direct way. But the way he saw it, the charade was harmless. He was merely keeping peace.

"See you soon, Toddy."

A short time later, Todd was looking through his room to make sure he wasn't leaving anything behind. He noticed the shoe box sitting on the closet shelf. He silently wondered how he could have overlooked it; nevertheless, he was happy he spotted the box. He chuckled at the thought of what kind of silly letters he would more than likely find tucked away in the box. After retrieving the box, he quietly shut his bedroom door. When he walked by Maggie's room, he paused for a brief moment. Without second-guessing, he lightly tapped on her door and mumbled, "Hey, Mags, I'm out of here. I love ya!"

Todd chuckled as he took one last look at all of the pictures of him hanging around the clock. He couldn't believe she took the time to laminate each picture. He decided to leave well enough alone. Heck, it was Maggie's place; if she wanted to look at his mug shot every day, that was her prerogative.

10

Todd fell into a comfortable routine as the days flew by. He was enjoying the sound of Mozart vibrating throughout his apartment when he decided to open the shoe box Maggie had given him. For whatever reason, he was in the mood for a touch of Maggie's soothing words. Maybe he was just a little homesick for her but not homesick enough to move back. Truth be known, he loved Macomb.

He went to the kitchen to pour himself his nightly drink of Jack, and then he ambled into his bedroom to retrieve the box. Todd sat at his desk and took a sip of the dark liquid. He simply eyed the box for a moment before he carefully opened the lid. His heart rate increased a notch or two at the touch of the old box.

He ever so slowly opened the lid and gazed at the cream envelope that lay on top of a blue washcloth. With trembling hands, Todd retrieved the envelope and opened it. He pulled out several sheets of cream-colored paper, and he cautiously unfolded the letter.

My dearest Toddy,

If you are reading this letter, then you have finally opened the shoe box. You can't fool me, I'm sure the box sat somewhere for days or maybe even weeks. But that's okay, God has a perfect timing for everything. Before I go any further, I can only hope you haven't removed the cloth. If you haven't, please do not do so until you have finished reading this letter. Thanks, Toddy.

As you know, I'm not the writer in the family; you are. But I'm going to do my best to pen my running thoughts on paper. You have been gone for less than an hour, yet in many ways, it seems a lifetime. I so miss you, but I realize you're a man. You must do what you feel you must. I suppose if I were to be honest with my heart, I resent our life came to this. However, I know resentment is poison, so I humbly ask God to remove every ounce of selfishness from me. After all, doesn't resentment stem from selfishness? I have probably been one of the most selfish mothers on planet Earth. And for that, I'm very sorry.

I realize I could easily give you one excuse after another for the lifestyle I subjected you to, but I won't. To put it plain and simple, I made the intellectual decision to become a prostitute. Trust me, this is very difficult for me to admit, and I do live with my poor choice every single day of my life. I'm sure this is difficult for you to digest, so if you must stop reading for a moment, I do understand. But don't you dare remove the washcloth. (((((Hugs)))))

With shaking hands, Todd placed the letter on his desk. He looked at the shoebox and contemplated removing the washcloth. What in the world could be in the box? By now, he was certain it wasn't full of letters. Nope, there was something in the box that meant a great deal to Maggie. Maybe it was some of the stories that he wrote her over the years. Maybe it contained some of the missing pieces of his life's puzzle, such as the whereabouts of his dad and grandparents.

He took a gulp of his drink and then another. Before he knew it, he had finished his nightly glass of Jack. He decided to pour himself another drink. What harm could a few extra drinks do? He felt the Jack Daniel's he had stored in his kitchen cupboard drawing him. Without second-guessing, he went to the kitchen to pour himself another drink.

Todd was thankful his stereo held twenty-five CDs, because he had a feeling he was in for a long night. He enjoyed the sound of Mozart as he sat motionless at his desk. He looked at the letter, but for whatever reason, he couldn't seem to pick it up. He was reminded of a time as a child when he looked at hot flames on the stove top, desiring to touch the fire. Yet he had sense enough to know if he touched it, he would get burned.

Todd chuckled as he rubbed his hands over his face. Why was he acting like this? This was Mags, not Donna. Now Donna was a whole other can of worms he would rather not open. One thing he knew for sure was he would get burned if he touched her, which was why he planned to keep his distance from the fire. Todd placed his goblet on the desktop and retrieved the letter.

Okay, if you took a breather, welcome back. Before I go any further, I want you to know that I love you with all of my heart.

Now, where was I? Oh yeah, the choices I have made. Anyway, I think you understand what I'm trying to convey. Let's move on to another subject.

Toddy, I really am concerned about your personal life . . . meaning, your love life. You're a very nice-looking man, and you deserve happiness. Yes, you're young, but still, time stops for no one. I mean, it seems only yesterday I was your age. I want you to promise me you will allow your heart to be opened to love. Okay?

Todd chuckled as he allowed the notion of love to tumble around in his mind. What did Maggie know about love? He once again took a big gulp of his drink and ran his hand through his thick hair. He looked at Mags's letter like it was a hot fire. Why was he feeling so cautious? With shaking hands, he continued to read Mags's letter.

Please don't base all relationships on mine with Moe. We both know I'm not in love with him, and he's most likely not in love with me. However, we do care deeply for one another. I guess I was never destined to experience the kind of love most people have. But that should not stop you from pursuing true happiness. Okay, enough said on this topic.

Okay, so he received his answer; maybe Maggie doesn't know a lot about love. Maybe she simply desires for him to experience something she never had.

Now, about your writing. Please promise me you will follow your dream. I know what you're thinking . . . that you have followed your dream by moving away from Peoria. Maybe you're right. But, Toddy, God has given you a special talent in writing. Please don't allow it to waste away. I challenge you to finish some of those novels you started.

Okay, now I'm going to ask you to stop reading and go ahead and remove the cloth. Well, go ahead . . . What are you waiting for?

Todd chuckled as he reread the last sentence Maggie wrote. "Well, go ahead . . . What are you waiting for?"

"You know me to well, Mags," he whispered to himself.

When he reached for his goblet, he realized it was empty. When did he drink all of his drink? One thing he knew for sure, he wasn't going to look inside the shoe box until he poured himself another good stiff drink.

After scrutinizing the box for what seemed to be hours but was only a few short minutes, Todd picked it up and removed the washcloth. He felt his breath catch in his throat when he caught a glimpse of the money Maggie had tucked away. How much money was there? He picked up a bundle and noticed that this wasn't chump change. Every single bill in the shoe box was fifties and hundreds.

Todd gulped down his drink in one swallow. He felt his hands tremble for another drink. He needed to get out of his bedroom. The walls were closing in. When he stood to his feet, he felt the effect of the alcohol. He steadied himself and then threw the shoe box across the room.

He felt anger surge through his body. He was angry for allowing himself to be so naive to think the box contained letters. He was angry for the life Maggie chose. She could have done better. And yes, he was angry that she would even think he would want or even need her money. After all, he knew how she made the money, and he didn't want any part of it. He didn't need her filthy money. He had a good, respectable job, and he paid taxes, which was something Maggie knew nothing about.

Todd staggered into the kitchen to retrieve the bottle of Jack and went to flip on the TV and turn off the stereo. Surely he could find something to watch to get his mind off life—his life to be exact. After scanning the channels for a bit, he was relieved when he came across a good wrestling match. He sat for hours watching one wrestling match after another. Somehow, it made him feel better as he watched the men throw punches at each other.

The last thing he remembered before drifting off to sleep was the sound of the clock that ticked away on the wall. Strangely enough, he found comfort in that one small clock that hung on the wall above his couch.

Todd awoke late the next morning with a pounding headache. He rubbed his hands over his rough face and attempted to sit up. His neck was sore because he fell asleep with it twisted every which way but the right way. If only he didn't drink so much. He was shocked to see the bottle of Jack nearly empty. Wasn't it almost full when he started? He needed some coffee and aspirins, but first he wanted to brush his teeth.

Todd made his way into the bathroom and freshened up the best he could, and then he ambled into the kitchen to make some coffee. He poured himself a glass of ice-water, and took three pain relievers. Within no time, he drank down his first cup of coffee, and he was pouring a second cup when the events of the night before flashed through his mind like a freight train.

Why did he have to go and get so angry? Wasn't Maggie only trying to look out for him? Man, he really felt like the world's biggest jerk. He decided he would at least finish reading her letter. But first, he was going to take a good hot shower.

After showering, he made himself some bacon and eggs. At least his head was starting to feel somewhat better, but he was hungry as all get out. Looking back on the evening, he realized he didn't eat much for dinner. A turkey sandwich with a few chips wasn't enough to keep a bird's appetite satisfied.

"Okay, enough hee-hawing around. I may as well read the rest of the letter," he said, "and then I'll give Mag's a call."

Okay, Toddy, are you done blowing off steam? I want to assure you I did not give you my entire savings. This is money I have been saving for you since you were a toddler. I wanted to have funds for your college in case you decided to go.

Now, don't think about trying to give it back to me because I won't take it. And you know how stubborn I can be! So please use the money however you see fit. It's yours, Toddy. Okay? The way I see it, this is the very least I can do for you. I mean, I robbed you of your childhood, and for that I'm so sorry. I suppose it would take me two lifetimes to make up for all of my mistakes.

I really have no idea how much money is in the box, but I do know there's enough for you to make a down payment on a house if you would like. And no, I'm not trying to tell you how to spend the money; like I said, it's yours. I simply remember you saying something about a house. Hey, you could buy you a dog! You always wanted a puppy. Or you could just put the money in the bank and allow it to accumulate interest. Like I said, it's yours. I'm not trying to tell you how to spend it or anything like that. You know me, just being a mom. I guess once a mom, always a mom. At least I'm not a bossy mom. Am I?

I only ask that you wait for a few days to call me. Once again, I love you, Toddy, with all of my heart. I have taken enough of your time. Make sure you eat three healthy meals a day, and call soon, but not too soon. Okay, maybe I'm a little bossy.

Love,
Mags (Mom)

11

Todd felt a slight throb of pain in his head and somewhat beyond his twenty-one years of age as he walked down West Jackson Street. He had set out on his quest to purchase a dog. Upon moving into the apartment, his proprietors gave their stamp of approval for pets. When Todd moved into his apartment, he signed a six-month lease. He figured once his lease was about to expire, he would think about purchasing a house.

His next major purchase would be a used but reliable truck. During the cold months ahead, Todd had no intentions of riding his Harley or walking. He looked up at the clear blue sky, thinking today would have been a great day to ride his Harley. But he didn't want to have to contend with a dog on his trip home.

Finally, after what seemed to be hours of walking, Todd approached the small animal shelter. As he approached the building, visions of Maggie bounced around in the corners of his mind. He still couldn't believe the money she had saved for him over the years. He realized he needed to call her, but he planned to take her advice and wait a few days. He still hadn't counted the amount of cash she had stashed in the shoe box, but he knew it wasn't chump change.

Just as Todd placed his hand on the doorknob to open the door, an elderly man flipped the *Open* sign over to *Closed*. The old guy pointed at his watch and then at the business hours posted on the door. They locked up at noon on Saturdays. Todd glanced at his watch and noticed it was exactly one minute past noon. He felt the dull throbbing pain in his head intensify as he shouted loud enough for the man to hear.

"Come on, cut me some slack! It's only one minute past closing time. I walked several blocks to get here."

The old man rolled his eyes and then hastily unlocked the door. He opened the door just a fraction and then peeped his beady eyes from the left and then to the right. He then glared at Todd with looks that could kill. After letting out a loud sigh, he shook his head and muttered, "Oh all right, come on in. But I will only give you a few minutes. After all, I do have a life . . . You know, things to do, and people to see."

Todd was about to ask if the old guy thought he didn't have a life, but he decided it was best to leave well enough alone. "Thanks," he replied.

"What can I do for you?"

"I was hoping to purchase a puppy."

"A puppy?"

"Yeah, sure. A puppy."

"Well, this is an animal shelter. We don't have puppies. We have dogs."

Todd rolled his eyes. "Okay, then. A dog."

"Well, I only have a few," the old man said, "but I'll let you see what I have. They're in the back." He then looked at Todd and barked, "Well, come on. I ain't got all day."

ᙂᙇ

Misfit was the only name Todd could come up with for the new edition to his family. His dog. He thought about naming him Mutt, but somehow, that simply didn't suit. To Todd, the poor little guy stood out like a sore thumb. He had wiry grey and brown hair with one brown eye and the other blue. In a funny sort of way, Todd felt connected with Misfit. Possibly because he also stood out like a sore thumb and was considered a misfit.

"All right, Misfit, I'm going to run to Jo's to grab me a bite to eat. You be a good boy while I'm gone." Todd playfully rubbed Misfits belly and then added, "No messes . . . Understood?"

Todd stepped out of his apartment, leaving the whining sounds of Misfit behind him. He could only hope his new buddy wouldn't keep his neighbors annoyed with his barking. Todd made a mental note to set out on his quest on finding a house. He hoped to find one that would be suitable for Mags.

Todd felt the cool night air across his face as he drove his Harley to Jo's. He could feel that autumn was knocking at summer's door, which meant he soon needed to find a decent truck.

Within no time, Todd found himself sitting at his regular booth. He ordered his regular tenderloin basket along with a piece of Jo's coconut cream pie. Everything seemed to be pretty routine. Heck, his life was fairly predictable, which was exactly the way he liked it. The only thing different about Todd's evening was his waitress. Donna was nowhere to be found. Tonight, Jamie was his waitress.

Todd had just swallowed his last bite of his tenderloin sandwich when Jamie approached his booth. She was a middle-aged woman who looked like she was running on an empty tank. She seemed nice enough, but she wasn't Donna. Todd chided himself for questioning Donna's whereabouts. It was really none of his business. Yet for whatever reason, he couldn't stop his running thoughts from rolling off his tongue like a runaway freight train.

"So Donna's not working tonight?" He felt his heart rate pick up as Jamie looked at him like he had just lost his freaking mind. Maybe he had. When did he start caring so much about snotty Donna?

Why is he blinking his eyes so darn fast? Weirdo, that's what this joker is. A flipping weirdo. "She don't work here anymore."

"When did she quit?"

"Like yesterday, when she moved away."

"Where did she move to?"

"Look, what's it to you? Are you okay?"

"Yeah, sure. I'm okay. Why do you ask?"

"Because your eyes are rapidly blinking. You know, like you got something in them."

Great, it's time for me to hit the road. "They're just a little dry . . . that's all. Hey, I think I'll take my pie to go." Todd paused for a brief moment, thinking he wouldn't be coming back to Jo's anytime soon. "Come to think of it, I'll take whatever you have left . . . to go, that is."

"Yeah, sure. Whatever tickles your fancy."

Later that evening, Todd sat in his living room listening to a piece composed by Edward Elgar titled "Nimrod." After cleaning up toilet paper Misfit had strung all over the apartment, he downed his second glass of Jack Daniel's. He had a feeling tonight was going to be a repeat of the night before. He couldn't believe his reaction to Donna's departure.

He could literally kick himself in the backside. He made a complete idiot out of himself. One thing he knew for certain, he would not be eating any more of his meals at Jo's Café.

Misfit's bark brought Todd back to matters at hand. "What is it, buddy?" Misfit looked at Todd with eyes that convey more love than humans were capable of giving.

"No, we're not going back out. . ." Todd sighed and continued, "Oh, come on. I can use some more fresh air. I guess it's just you and me, partner."

Todd went to retrieve the dog leash, and Misfit whined as if he was in complete objection to wearing the leash. "Sorry, partner. I don't need you running off. Seems that's pretty much the story of my life."

As Todd walked down the road with Misfit eager to run, he couldn't seem to get his mind off Donna. He realized everything worked out for the best. He didn't like how she made his heart feel, but still, her packing up and leaving without a simple goodbye really bothered him. More than he cared to admit even to himself.

He wondered where she moved. He was tempted to probe Jamie a little more, but he thought it best to leave well enough alone. One thing he knew for sure, he was never going to allow his guard to come down again. Not that he allowed his guard down much with Donna. But still, it didn't take much carelessness on his end for her to slip into his stony heart.

When Todd glanced up at the sky, he noticed there weren't many stars beaming down upon planet Earth. He figured the overcast would explain why it was a little cooler than usual. He welcomed the chill. It helped to snuff out the fire of anger that burned deep within his soul. He realized he needed to get a grip on the anger issues that threatened to choke what little life he had left right out of him.

He wondered if there was a place called heaven somewhere beyond the vast dark sky. A place Maggie spoke of when she had her fill of beer or wine. Somehow, it was hard for Todd to believe there was such a place. He found heaven and hell to be just a theory. The way Todd saw it, once a person took their last breath, then it was over.

Todd was feeling his mood go from not-so-good to really bad. It was time to go have a good stiff drink. "Come on, Misfit. It's time to go back inside."

Before Todd realized it, he had downed two glasses of JD on the rocks. He looked over at Misfit curled up by his feet snoozing away without a care in the world. He almost felt envious of his new friend. He made a mental note to buy a bed for him and maybe a few toys. Todd absently glanced at the shoe box that sat on the dinette table. He decided he wasn't going to count how much Maggie-pie had tucked away for him. No, he would simply use it as he needed it until it was all used up.

The soft sound of Mozart playing in the background of his thoughts calmed his nerves. He wondered how long it had been since he called Mags Maggie-pie. More years than he could recall. He set his goblet on the end table and picked up his tablet. Not knowing why, but he felt the need to write.

Sweet Maggie- pie, as I look up at the dark vast sky, for whatever reason, I feel I want to cry.

Please, Maggie-pie, don't ask me why.
Please, Maggie-pie, don't you dare pry.

Sweet Maggie-pie, as I look up at the dark vast sky, for whatever reason, it reminds me your life is such a lie.

Please, Maggie-pie, don't ask me why.
Please, Maggie-pie, don't you dare pry.

Sweet Maggie-pie, as I look up at the dark vast sky, for whatever reason, I wonder what it would be like to develop wings and fly.

Yes, fly away from the cold dark pain. But then I ask myself, what would I really gain? I have come to realize it's the dark pain that's keeping me sane.

Please, Maggie-pie, don't ask me why.
Please, Maggie-pie, don't you dare pry.

Sweet Maggie-pie, as I look up at the dark vast sky, for whatever reason, I wonder if there's light on the other side.

Please Maggie-pie, if you really must ask and continue to pry, then I must be honest, I cannot dare tell you a lie.

Yes, I must now pry. Why, Maggie-pie, did you not try? Sweet Maggie-pie, why did you allow your dreams to die?

So now you know . . . This is why the dark vast sky makes me want to cry.

Todd felt the hot tears running down his cheeks. He reread the poem, if one would call it that, and he felt his chest restrict. The writing was so elementary, yet it described his dark pain to the *T.*

He needed another drink because he was no longer feeling the effect of the alcohol. He went to the kitchen and retrieved the bottle of Jack. He took a big drink of the dark liquor as he dropped some ice cubes into his goblet. He then poured himself a drink. He was about to put the bottle back into the cupboard, but he decided to take it with him. He stepped over Misfit and poured himself one drink after another until finally, he felt his eyelids grow heavy. He drifted off to sleep with one person on his mind—Maggie-pie.

Todd awoke early the next morning with the sun shining through his thin curtains, Misfit licking his face, and a pounding headache. He pushed the dog aside and rubbed the sleep from his eyes. His mouth tasted like something had died in it. He was sure he was about to get sick. He decided what he needed to do was fight fire with fire. He picked up the bottle of Jack and took a healthy drink. He vigorously shook his head from side to side and then downed another swallow of the dark liquor.

His notebook stood out like a sore thumb, and his idiotic thoughts stabbed away at his heart. He ripped the sheet of paper from the pad, wadded it, and chucked it across the room. Misfit started to run for it, thinking Todd was in the mood to play. Todd shot from the coach and picked up the wad of paper like it was fire.

"This is not a toy, Misfit," he said. He then went to the bathroom to freshen up.

He felt somewhat better once he finished freshening up. "Come on, Misfit. Let's go for our morning walk."

12

It was Sunday, and as usual, Jenna had enjoyed the worship service. She still struggled with some of the religious ways of man. But she did enjoy the praise and worship. She learned to appreciate the teaching and preaching of God's Word. By no means did she understand everything Pastor Dawson preached, but she was getting there.

Many of the lessons she learned as a child were coming back to her. In some ways, this troubled her. Mainly because her daddy was such a hard-core walking Bible. Yep, he walked the walk and talked the talk, so to speak. Grant advised her to not compare her dad's walk with God with the pastors, his, and everyone else's, for that matter, but it was hard for her not to.

She never questioned Grant's walk with God because she knew he was a true Christian. The problem was others. She was learning to trust the pastor. However, she found it very difficult to trust the church members. Sure, her first few visits went well. But here lately, she was starting to feel her wall of protection go up a notch or two.

Jenna realized her running emotions had a lot to do with what she had experienced with Scott and Mandy. Jenna was certain she was over him, but still, she had a difficult time trusting the women in the church. She was thankful for Cindy. Over the past several months, the two of them had grown quite close.

Grant assured her he had faith in her, and he was praying. She, on the other hand, assured him she wouldn't give up. She planned to do her best at developing her personal relationship with Jesus. She planned to do her best to not judge others. And in time, she planned to do her best to let her wall down, maybe just a tad.

Cindy and Bob had agreed to have dinner with Jenna and Grant. Jenna made a wonderful shrimp Alfredo pasta dish with salad, and Grant grilled halibut. They were all enjoying one another's company on the beautiful Indian summer day.

"I tell you what I think," Grant says, "I think we should flip a coin to see who does dishes."

"Oh, so you're saying whoever wins gets out of cleaning the kitchen?" Jenna asked.

"Actually, what I'm saying is whoever loses will have to clean the kitchen—"

Jenna interrupted, "Isn't that what I said?"

"No, baby, you said—"

"Grant, forget it! Come on, guys let's do it. Cindy, no worries, we got this."

"Yeah, that's right, girl," Cindy affirmed.

"I don't know—"

"Bob, you hush."

"Okay, baby. You don't have to get huffy. So who's going to flip the coin?"

"I will . . . decide." Jenna went to the windowsill and retrieved a quarter from a mason jar. "Okay, Cindy and Bob, you're our guest. So, Cindy, you flip it. And, Bob, you call it. Okay, ready? Here, you go, Cindy." Jenna tossed the coin to Cindy.

"All right, bud. Heads or tails?" Cindy flipped the coin.

"Tails."

The coin bounced on the kitchen tile floor and spun in a circle for a brief moment. Once it came to a complete stop, they all looked upon the coin as if it was gold. It was Jenna that broke the silence. "Sorry, guys. Looks like you'll be doing dishes. It's heads."

Jenna laughed and then replied, "Have at it, guys. And by the way, you guys did a real good job grilling the fish. Cindy, would you like a glass of wine?"

"Girl, I would love one."

Jenna poured two glasses of wine. "Hey, Bob, help yourself to a beer. You might get a little thirsty while cleaning the kitchen. And, Grant, there's plenty of sweet tea in the fridge."

"Oh, whatever, baby. You and Cindy just go in the other room and leave us men alone."

"Touchy," Jenna chimed.

Grant pulled Jenna in his arms and whispered in her ear, "I can't wait to show you just how touchy I can be." He then planted a big kiss on her lips. He loved the way she responded to his touch. He loved her carefree spirit. He simply loved everything about her.

Bob cleared his throat and remarked, "Okay, enough of the lovey-dovey stuff. We got work to do." They all laughed out loud.

"Hey, Bob darling, make sure you wipe the stove down real good. It looks like Jenna spilled some sauce."

"Just go enjoy your wine. I'll show you a thing or two when we get home, Cindy darling."

"Is that a promise or a threat, Bob darling?" Cindy asked in a coy way.

The two ladies giggled like two schoolgirls as they moseyed into the living room, leaving the guys to the dirty dishes.

Cindy noticed Jenna had a glow she didn't have before. She also noticed she was a little spunkier than she had been for some time. Cindy decided she liked the new Jenna. She took a sip of her wine and then smiled as she thought about the men in the kitchen cleaning. Maybe they acted a bit childish, but she enjoyed watching the guys interact and Jenna clowning around. She came to the conclusion she liked Grant, and he was good for Jenna—real good.

"So, Jenna, are you getting excited about your big day? I mean, it will be here before we know it."

Jenna gave Cindy a dreamy look and replied, "Well, I suppose I'm getting a tiny bit excited." She shrugged her shoulders and continued, "I mean, I am marrying a pretty special guy. He's not only a hunk, but he's charming, loving, caring, in tune with me, and knows how to fulfill my emotional needs. And well, I have no doubt he'll make a good lover."

"I think we got everything pretty much under control. Of course, there's the last-minute stuff to take care of . . . like sending out the wedding invitations and ordering the flowers. Oh, and there's—"

"Cindy, no worries. We got this. I mean, it's a piece of cake. Tessa and Hunter have been keeping close tabs on everything."

"Oh, really? Well, I hope they remember to call about catering . . . I think I'll have a chat with Tess. You know, just to be on the safe side. By the way, where's Tess?"

Jenna took a sip of her wine and then sat her wineglass on the end table. "She and Hunter are studying. Maybe you should have a chat with Tess . . . just to be on the safe side, that is."

"By the way, is Tess still ecstatic about the wedding?"

"I think so. I mean, on the night of our engagement party, she had somewhat of a meltdown. You know, worried about living arrangements and so on. Of course, after I assured her nothing would change other than Grant moving in, she was back to being herself. You know, ecstatic. Of course, there's school and Hunter." Jenna paused for a brief moment. "I tell you, that guy cares a lot for Tess. I just wish she would come to realize just how much he cared."

"I think she will in time. They're young."

"Yeah, you're right."

"So you've been going to church with Grant?"

"Yes, I have."

"How do you like it?"

"I like it, really, I do. I mean, I'm not overly fond of the religious aspects. But I do like the worship and the teaching of the Word of God."

"What do you mean 'religious aspects'?"

"You know, the dos and don'ts that come along with religion . . . like me drinking my wine. I personally see nothing wrong with a little wine every now and then. I mean, as long as I'm not getting filthy drunk or even drunk, for that matter. Grant keeps telling me not to focus on the dos and don'ts. He says to focus on developing a relationship with Jesus. To me, it's all kind of strange. But I just talk to God the best I know how and read my daily devotions."

"Sounds to me like you're coming along pretty good."

"Yeah, maybe."

"Well, I see you and Grant are a match made in heaven."

"Yes, we are. Hey, why don't you and Bob come to church with us sometime?"

Cindy smiled as she took in the glow that reflected from her friend. And Jenna was her friend. They have come a long ways in their friendship. "You know, Jenna, we just might have to do that."

Meanwhile, in the kitchen, the guys were busy chatting. They had finished up the kitchen and was about to join the ladies. Grant could sense Bob wanted some male time. He, for one, enjoyed Bob's company. Grant thought about inviting them to church. It would be good for Jenna and, of course, them too.

"I think the kitchen should pass the girls' inspection. How about you, Bob?"

"I believe so," Bob replied.

"Is there something on your mind, Bob?"

Bob wiped his hands on the front of his jeans as he leaned against the kitchen counter. He pondered on just how much he should share. He felt certain he could trust Grant, but he still had his pride. He let out a sigh and then responded, "Actually, there is. I want to thank you for your friendship. You've been a true friend."

"Hey, not a problem. Jenna and I enjoy you and Cindy. It seems Jenna and Cindy are getting pretty close."

"Yes, they are. Look, things with Cindy and I haven't always been smooth. To be truthful, we contemplated divorce."

Silence.

"I'm sorry to hear that," Grant spoke with a hint of compassion.

"No, don't be. I mean, things are much better. I think Jenna is making a difference. I guess what Cindy needed was a female friend. You know, one she could confide in. And, of course, I believe all of this wedding planning is helping."

Grant chuckled and replied, "Well, I can see a difference in Jenna. I can tell she really likes Cindy. Believe me, Jenna's not one to easily put trust in others." Grant thought about asking Bob if he knew Jenna's story, but he decided it was best to leave well enough alone.

Bob looked off into another world for a bit and then spoke just above a whisper. "I love Cindy. Really, I do."

"Sure you do, Bob."

Silence.

"It's just we grew apart. When we married, we both decided to rule out children. But now, well . . . I think we have come to regret our decision. Like I said, things between us are much better. Look, Grant, I admire the stand you take . . . you know, being a Christian, and all. I can't tell you how many years it's been since we've been to church. Too many. But we both believe in the Lord. I guess what I'm trying to say is thanks for your prayers. I feel the prayers. Really, I do."

"Not a problem, man. Hey, why don't we say a prayer together?"

"You mean, here? Now?"

Grant could sense that Bob felt awkward, but he could also feel the Spirit of God tugging at his heart to pray. "Yeah, sure."

"Okay, sure. Why not." Bob absently looked around the kitchen.

Grant placed his hand on Bob's shoulder and began to pray.

"Heavenly Father, we come to You, giving You thanks for the gift of marriage. Lord, I thank You for the wonderful plan You have for Bob and Cindy. I pray You continue to guide them in the way You would like for them to go. Lord, thank You for restoring their marriage completely. I ask, Lord, that You would continue to strengthen my friend Bob. Lord, You see how transparent he has been, and now I ask You will flood him with Your peace. I pray for Cindy. I ask You, Lord, to draw her to You. Lord, be with her and Jenna's friendship. And, Lord, I thank You for bringing them into our lives. In Jesus's name, I pray. Amen."

Grant pulled Bob into a hug and whispered, "God has this. He's on the job."

Bob felt his chest restrict, and his vision clouded with tears. He managed to choke out, "Yeah, right. God is on the job."

As Grant pulled away from his friend, he felt this overwhelming need to invite Bob to church. He casually asked, "Why don't you and Cindy come to church with us?"

Bob licked his dry lips and nodded his head, and Grant took that as a yes.

13

Tessa and Hunter decided to spend the afternoon hiking at Argyle Lake. They both needed a break from their studies, and what better way to spend a day is there? It was early into October, and nature seemed to have opened up with many vivid colors. The leaves on the trees had turned yellow orange, fire red, and deep purple. The pine trees sent off a fresh evergreen smell. The cattails had gone from being brown, looking much like a velvety cigar, to being full of white fuzzy seeds.

The squirrels were cumbered about getting ready for the long winter months. The birds chirped a lovely autumn melody. There were a few rabbits hopping along the edge of the trails. As Hunter and Tessa hiked deeper into the woods, they noticed traces of deer. There were a few campers that had setup camp for the weekend. The lake looked so clean and put off a fresh scent. The tranquility of nature made everything seem so uncontaminated. It was as if all of God's creation was in complete harmony.

"Hunter, I love this time of the year."

"Me too, Tess."

"I can't believe the earth will be covered with a blanket of snow in just a short while."

"I know. Before you know it, your mom will be tying the knot."

"Yep."

"Are you still cool with it?" Hunter asked.

"Yeah, sure. I mean, Grant is a real cool guy. Of course, you already know that."

"Yeah, he's cool. I think the two of them complement each other. Don't you?"

"Yes, I do. It seems Mom is really getting back into church."

"How do you feel about that?" Hunter asked.

"I think it's great. I mean, the way I see it, she's finally getting back on track. You know, from the way my dad burned her and all." There was a comfortable silence between them for a bit. And then Tessa added, "I missed her going to church. She seems to have her inner peace back, and there's a softness in her spirit that seemed to have drained away when Dad walked out on us."

"Yeah, I think I agree with you."

Hunter breathed in, allowing the fresh clean scent of autumn to fill his lungs. Here lately, he had been so busy with school he forgot what it was like to enjoy time alone with Tessa. He missed her. A lot. Yeah, sure, they spent time on the phone, and they even had an occasional lunch together at Peg's. But somehow, today, there seemed to be more of an intimate feeling between them.

Tessa noticed the temperature was starting to drop considerably. She zipped her jacket and stuffed her hands in the pockets of her jeans. Even though the air was a little nippy, she still enjoyed the sight of God's creation. Here lately, she had been contemplating going to church with her mom. She remembered Grant talking about Campus for Christ and thought it might be a good idea to check it out. At the sound of Hunter's voice, she was brought back to matters at hand.

"Are you cold, Tess?"

"I'm just a little chilly, but I'm good."

"Wanna head back to the car and maybe go grab a bite to eat?"

"Hmmm, I am a little hungry. Why don't we hike just a little further and then go get something to eat."

"So will it be Peg's?"

"Yeah, that sounds good. I'm kinda hungry for one of their famous subs."

"Yeah, an Italian sub does sound good," Hunter stated.

Later that evening, Tessa and Hunter sat in a cozy booth at Peg's enjoying their subs. To Hunter, everything about the day was perfect. He was only saddened that it ended all too soon. He enjoyed watching Tessa fight with keeping the turkey on her loaded sub. Although he didn't like it, he had to admit declaring his love for her would only complicate their friendship. He came to the conclusion that for now, he would much rather maintain a close friendship with Tessa. Occasionally, in the recesses of his mind, his greatest fear of never finding his happy ever after tried to convince him otherwise. But for now, all he could do was hope that one day, Tessa would come to realize they were destined to be together.

Tessa couldn't seem to shake her mom out of her mind. There was no doubt that her mom was starting to show signs of the old Jenna everyone placed trust in. Tessa simply hoped she would continue to march forward. The way she saw it, Grant had become somewhat of a compass to help her mom find her way back to God. Sure, she never lost her faith in the fundamental truths of the Bible, but Tessa definitely noticed her mom had allowed her spiritual foundation to crack.

Perhaps it took her dad running off to bring them to this point. Whatever the case, Tessa felt in her heart of hearts they were on the path of recovering everything that was so brutally taken from them. Yes, their reputation was about to be restored, and people would once again see them as folks who walked in integrity. Not that they had ever stopped living an honest life because they hadn't. But oftentimes, people see things through rose-colored glasses.

Tessa always felt drawn to helping people fix their problems. It didn't surprise her mom when she expressed she desired to become a psychologist. She could recall as a child laying her dolls on her bed and talking to them about make-believe problems. For Tessa, it was therapeutic to help others. Maybe because it helped her not to focus on her own shortcoming of learning to give in to love.

Tessa was no man's fool. She saw the way Hunter looked at her. There was no doubt in her mind he would treat her like a lady. But Tessa also knew how easily love could turn cold. Nope, she wasn't going to ruin what she had with Hunter by giving in to her fleshly desires. Because if she were to be honest with herself, she desired him almost as much as he desired her.

"Hey, Tess, even though you're devouring your sub, you seem to be a million miles away. You okay?"

Tessa looked at Hunter and took a drink of her Coke before attempting to respond to his question. "Sure, I'm good, Hunter. I guess I have a lot of stuff tumbling around in my mind, that's all."

"Wanna talk?" Hunter asked.

Silence.

Tessa brushed some crumbs onto the floor as she considered just how much she should share with Hunter. She finally decided that talking about her mom was safe. She definitely couldn't talk about her fear of falling in love. Especially with Hunter.

"I was just thinking about my mom and Grant. I can't believe in just a few months, they will be tying the knot."

"I know. So how are things coming along with the wedding plans?"

"Great! I think Cindy has about two or three meltdowns a day. You would think she was the one getting married."

Hunter gave Tessa a look of concern and asked, "Why is she having so many meltdowns?"

"Hunter, let's not get serious. You know me, I tend to exaggerate. But she has been having, in my opinion, too many meltdowns. Apparently she's worried we're going to forget some important detail about the big day. I keep assuring her I have been keeping close tabs on our to-do list."

"Aw, she's just doing what any good friend would do."

"Yeah, you're right. I'm just grateful my mom is finally coming face to face with the past. You know, letting bygone be bygone. Yeah, what's done is done, so to speak."

"I don't know, Tess. I think she came face to face with the past long ago. If you ask me, your mom is one special lady. I mean, to me, she has handled herself well while experiencing betrayal. What your dad did was pretty rotten. I could never imagine going through such heartache—"

"Hunter," Tessa interrupted, "you don't get what I'm trying to say."

"Okay, Tess, maybe you can enlighten me on what you're trying to express," Hunter said in a matter-of-fact tone.

"What I meant was she's finally picking up all of the broken pieces of her heart and moving forward. Yes, my dad put her through a lot. Yes, she's a remarkably special lady. Yes, she learned to love again. I mean, she's getting married. But she had shut her heart off to church . . . and to some degree, even God."

Hunter was taken back by Tessa's response. She never ceased to amaze him. She was perfect, at least to him. "I see," he whispered.

"You know, Hunter, I've been thinking about checking out Campus for Christ. Care to join me?"

Hunter smiled and replied, "If you're going, I'm going."

Later that evening, Tessa's mind continued to drift back to pieces of the conversations she and Hunter shared. She couldn't seem to shake the feeling her life was about to change. Kind of like a new chapter. Yes, a fresh clean start for not only her mom but her as well. She felt a little giddy as she pondered on the idea of change. One thing she knew for sure was that she was more than ready for a break.

Suddenly, it dawned on her that maybe there were too many changes transpiring, and most importantly, they were happening too quickly. After all, her mom was about to become Mrs. Grant Williams. It wasn't every day a woman walked down the aisle to pledge her life to another. Tessa was happy for her mom, but she didn't want her to get ahead of the game. To Tessa, life was like a game. You win some. You lose some. But in the end, if you continue marching forward, you come out a champ. One thing Tessa knew for certain was that her mom had come out a champ.

Hunter was right; her mom handled herself well when she was faced with losing out on the game of life. She didn't allow the small-town gossip to keep her from marching forward. While many of the so-called Christians were speculating about why her husband ran off with a younger woman, her mom kept her head up and shoulders squared. She didn't allow the snubs from the snotty churchy folks to stop her from taking the lead and becoming a winner. Because in the end, that's exactly what transpired.

Tessa could remember like it was yesterday when the pastor of the former church they attended came for a pastoral visit. Yep, even though the church board had voted Jenna out of the Sunday school department and asked her to step down from singing in the choir, God humbled them all. Pastor McCall had apologized for the entire church and asked Jenna to come back as a member.

However, Jenna had refused to associate herself with the good old Baptist church. She figured if she wasn't good enough for membership when she was being falsely accused of setting Scott and Mandy up for the temptation, then she wasn't good enough once truth prevailed. Nope, instead, she stood her ground and continued about her daily affairs.

In the end, it was Scott and Mandy who were asked to apologize before the entire church. All it took was one little slipup on Mandy's behalf for the church board members to learn she and Scott had been having an affair for three years before being exposed as the innocent victims that fell into a snare. Yes, she simply made one phone call to one of the elders' wife and spilled the beans. The rest was history. The gossip started spreading like wildfire. They learned what it was like to be on the losing side of life.

Tessa questioned if she could ever have a relationship with her dad. She thought that maybe she could if he would at least show a little incentive on his end. It appeared to Tessa that he was too busy with his new life to have time for her. It didn't really bother Tessa. The way she saw it was, the ups and downs she experienced at the game of life only better equipped her for her future as a psychologist.

One thing Tessa knew was that her mom never stopped believing in the existence of God. She always taught Tessa the importance of good moral values and that Jesus died for the sins of mankind. Tessa had every right to be darn proud of her mom. And she was about to be even more proud as she witnessed her becoming Grant's beautiful bride.

14

Maggie was reclining on the couch working on a word puzzle while waiting for Moe to return from Pizza Hut. Moe volunteered to pick up the pizza, and for that Maggie was grateful. It was Sunday, her day of rest. Not that she knew what it was like to rest. It seemed here lately she was more uptight than ever. She was tired of giving herself wholeheartedly to one man after another, and she missed Todd to death. Literally.

Maggie decided she needed a break from work, people, and her daily routine. She was going to butter Moe up and then ask him to take her to Todd's. Yep, she would make a few phone calls to clear her schedule so she could stay with her son for a few days. She was sure Todd would be willing to give her a lift back home. She realized she couldn't stay gone for long, but she simply needed a few days to regroup. The longer she pondered on the idea, the more excited she felt. She glanced at her telephone and decided to give Todd a call.

Just as she was about to dial Todd's number, Moe came waltzing into the apartment. The smell of supreme pizza tickled her nose.

"Hey, doll, I hope you're hungry. I stopped by the market and picked up some of your favorite ice cream." Moe paused and wiggled his eyebrows as he playfully remarked, "Not that the ice cream will be our desert. If you know what I mean . . ."

Maggie gave him a coy smile and replied, "I know exactly what you mean, Moe, baby."

Later that evening, Maggie decided to ask him about taking her to Todd's. Her head was rested on his chest. She cuddled as close as she possibly could in hopes to get the answer her heart desired. "Moe, you know, I have been thinking—"

"That can be dangerous . . . you know, you thinking," Moe interrupted and chuckled at his wisecrack.

"Moe, cut the smack." *He can be such a jerk!*

"Come on, doll. I'm only pulling your chain," Moe whispered. "You know that, right?"

"Yeah, well, whatever you say, Moe. It's just I'm trying to be serious," Maggie purred as she made slow circles on his chest.

"Okay, doll. What do you want?" *She has something up her sleeve.*

Maggie whispered a short prayer. Even though she didn't attend church and put on the Christian role for society, she was no hypocrite. Maggie had her own way of talking to God. Yes, her relationship with God was more than likely the most unconventional one in the world. Unlike any others. But then again, she hadn't met too many people like her especially of the female gender. She was about as real as they come with Jesus. And quite frankly, she wouldn't have it any other way.

"Moe, baby, I'm really missing Toddy. I mean, it's been weeks since I've seen him. Well, I guess I'm kinda wondering if you would be willing to take me to that silly little town. What's the name of it?"

"The name of the 'silly little town' is Macomb. And no, I won't take ya."

"Aw, come on, Moe. It's not like I ask much from ya—"

Moe once again interrupted, "Sorry, doll, you should have learned to drive a long time ago. Why didn't you ever get your driver's license, anyway?"

"Moe, we've already been through this. You know I wasn't able to finish high school. I had Toddy, and then . . . well, I started my business."

"Look, *Toddy* is no longer a kid. He's a grown man for crying out loud. And you need to let him act like one. He needs his space. Why, I bet he's got the gals hanging all around him."

Maggie didn't like the thought of Todd giving his heart to more than woman. She always had his heart; at least, she believed she did. She knew her son. He wasn't ready for the cruel world. She wished for the umpteenth time she would have been more persistent at keeping him from moving to nowhere land. He was safe with her. She wouldn't allow women with impure motives to break his heart. She would have protected him.

Deep in her heart of hearts, she knew Moe was right. Nonetheless, that didn't change the fact she missed him. She longed to hear the sound of his voice, look into his eyes, and give him a hug. She even missed their silly arguments. Todd gave her a sense of normalcy. In fact, he was the only thing normal about her life. He was her ray of sunshine. She was tired of feeling like she was stuck in a dark room without a light switch.

"Moe, I'm his mother. And that will never change."

"I don't understand why you miss him. I mean, you got pictures of him hanging all over the flipping apartment. And you're right, doll, some things will never change. Like you."

"Come on, Moe, let's not go there."

"Where, Mags? Marriage?"

"You know I don't believe in marriage. And it's my flipping apartment. I can put pictures of my son in every room if I wish."

Moe could feel his blood pressure start to rise. He detested rejection. And that's exactly what Maggie did to him time and time again, and here she was rejecting him again. He was willing to offer her a better way of life. He would even help her to get her education and teach her how to drive. But no. Not Maggie Jenkins. She liked giving herself to every Tom, Dick, and Harry who came along.

Moe jumped out of bed to retrieve his jeans. He was going to walk out of her life and, this time, not look back. He could do better than her. He was ready for a wife. What was he thinking? Maggie was a prostitute. She'd never change. He was brought back to reality at the sound of her voice.

"Where are you going?" Maggie hissed.

Moe abruptly turned to face her. In many ways, she looked like a child. But in more ways than he cared to admit, she looked like the harlot she was. "I'm leaving . . . for good. We're through. Do you hear me? We. Are. Through. Not that we ever really had anything."

Maggie felt the hot tears sting the back of her eyes, but she learned long ago how to dry them up. She only cried in front of one person. Todd. His words were cutting, but her heart was too callused for them to penetrate into her soul.

Maggie squared her shoulders and tilted her chin as she sneered, "Hey, Moe, on your way out, don't let the door hit you on the backside."

Moe hastily threw fifty bucks on the bed and then spoke through clenched teeth, "This should cover our evening!"

He then walked out, leaving Maggie alone with her thoughts.

Maggie finished off the last of her wine. She had been saving the bottle of Chateau Petrus for a special occasion. She figured being free from the hassle of Moe constantly annoying her about Todd, marriage, and her failures qualified as a special occasion.

She was happy to have Moe out of her life. Really, she was. She didn't need him. He was a thorn to her flesh. She would be fine without him coming around. Why, to her, he only thought of himself. Sure, he treated her all right. But it was the way he constantly badgered Todd that made her mad. Moe simply didn't understand the relationship she had with her son. Todd was the only family she had. And she longed for him like crazy.

Maggie felt sure once Todd found out Moe was out of the picture, he would come to visit her. She was hurt that he hadn't been to visit once since he moved other than to pack up the rest of his belongings. But that wasn't really like a visit. She was tied up with a well-paying customer. She thought for sure he would at least come around every other Sunday. Todd knew she always rested on Sundays.

Maybe Moe was right. Todd more than likely had a few girlfriends. But still, he should at least come to see her every now and then or give her a call. It's like he was becoming her ghost. Just like his dad, Drake.

Maggie felt her chest tighten as she allowed her eyes to scan each and every picture she carefully arranged on the wall around the small clock. She attempted to stand but felt the effect of the wine, so she sat back down. She rested her head on the back of the love seat and allowed her eyes to drink in the sight of her flesh and blood. Her Toddy.

Maggie couldn't get over how much he looked like his dad, Drake. He was such a nice-looking young man. Yet in many ways, he was very much like a child. Once again, she had to admit Moe was right. Even though she hated it, she was forced to admit to the truth that she never allowed Todd to become a man. She always treated him like a child. And for that she was sorry because she couldn't seem to shake the feeling she had hindered him from becoming the productive adult God intended for him to be.

By now, Maggie wasn't feeling the effect of the wine. No, instead she felt an overwhelming sadness sweep over her. She absently wiped the hot tears that trickled down her cheeks. She knew what she needed to do. She figured if she couldn't see her son, then she at least needed to hear his voice. How had she allowed so many weeks to slip by without giving him a call? After all, she was just as guilty as Todd. Once again, she put men, money, and her personal life before her son.

Maggie slowly stood to her feet and walked to the kitchen to pour herself a glass of ice water. With shaking hands, she opened a container of pain relievers and swallowed two of the small pills. After she drank her ice water, she started herself a cup of hot tea. By now, she was feeling completely sober. It was as if she hadn't drunk a drop of wine. Once her tea finished steeping, she ambled into her bedroom to get nice and comfy so she could enjoy her conversation with Todd.

Todd was deep into his novel, *A Time to Kill* by John Grisham, and listening to some Mozart when the sound of his telephone caused him to jump. He contemplated answering the phone as he took a sip of his Jack Daniel's on the rocks. He decided to allow the answering machine to take the call. He wasn't in the mood to talk, especially not to Mags. He knew it had to be her. Who else would be calling him at this time of the night—or anytime, for that matter? He had the phone installed for emergencies and his job.

"It's Todd. At the sound of the peep, leave a message."

Todd heard the peep and the sniffles. "Oh, great, she's crying. Something must have happened with her and Moe. I'm not in the mood for drama," he said to himself.

"Toddy, it's me, Mags. You there? If you are, please pick up. I just need to talk to ya for a minute or two. I miss you like crazy. When are ya coming to see me? Come on, Toddy, pick up the phone. I know you're there. Maybe Moe is right. You might be out on the town. I really didn't want to tell you this over an answering machine, but I—" Maggie's voice was cut off.

Todd sat motionless staring at the one picture he had framed of Maggie. She was standing in the kitchen stirring some of her homemade spaghetti sauce when Todd snapped the picture. He supposed the reason it was his favorite picture was because she looked so carefree. He rubbed his hand over her face and then abruptly placed the picture back on the end table.

Todd knew he should call her back. But he simply couldn't. He had been drinking a little more than he should have, and he wasn't in the mood for her questions. He took another drink of his Jack and then another. Before he knew it, he was ready to pour himself another stiff drink on the rocks.

After pouring his drink, he tried to get back into his novel, but he was interrupted by Misfit. He was thankful for his dog, but he sure wasn't in the mood for a late-night walk. He had no one but himself to blame for Misfit growing accustomed to going on walks way into the night hours. Most of the time, he enjoyed walking Misfit while the rest of the world was sound asleep. But tonight was different. Tonight, he would much rather be left alone with his thoughts. Somehow, denying Misfit his walk just didn't feel fair.

Todd rubbed Misfit behind the ears as he asked, "What is it? Huh? You want to go for a walk?" Misfit wagged his tail and barked. "Okay, let me get your leash."

Todd set his drink on the end table but only long enough to place the leash on Misfit. He retrieved his keys and then picked up his drink. He figured he would sip on it while he walked Misfit. He chuckled as he replayed Maggie's words in his mind.

"Yeah, right. Out on the town. I don't think so, Mag. The only girl I came close to liking skipped town," Todd mumbled to himself.

15

Jenna's Wedding

Jenna stood in her living room looking out the oversized picture window. The snowflakes were falling steady but not too heavy. It was December 12, her wedding day. She was grateful for the time alone. It was hard for her to believe she was about to pledge her heart to the man of her dreams. God had been good to her. There were times she felt so undeserving, but she simply received God's grace with a thankful heart.

Julia, Grant's first wife, was walking around somewhere in this world. Jenna realized it was very possible she may still be carrying Grant's last name, at least by law. But Jenna was about to take his name by law and in the eyes of God. Not only would she have his name, but most importantly, she would also have his heart. And he had hers. Yes, in just a few short hours, she would become Mrs. Grant Williams.

Jenna relished in God's peace. Never had she been so sure about her future than she was at that very moment. She felt certain her heart was going to explode with overwhelming joy. She wondered what Grant was doing at that very moment. Knowing him the way she did, he was more than likely praying for their special day. He was such a true man of God. She only wished she could be just half of the Christian as him. As hard as she tried, she found it difficult not comparing her walk with God to his.

Grant had assured her she was coming along fine. She supposed she needed to give herself credit where credit was due because she was growing spiritually. She had to admit she still had a hard time with organized religion, but at least she had no problem receiving the fundamental truths of sound doctrine.

Her theory about God being too busy for her was starting to completely crumble at her feet. She found herself praying at the oddest times. Fact is, here lately, she had been talking to God pretty regularly. She loved that she could share her deepest secrets and fears with the Creator of the universe. Grant insisted they pray and have devotional every evening, and she loved it.

And there was Tessa. Jenna could sense a positive change in her daughter. Not that she was a bad kid because by all means, she wasn't. She just seemed more confident. Jenna was pleased that she and Hunter were becoming actively involved with Campus for Christ. She had to chuckle as she thought of Hunter. Jenna was sure there wasn't a thing in this world he wouldn't do for Tessa.

In Jenna's heart, she believed Hunter would be her future son-in-law. She had absolutely no qualms with the two of them becoming seriously involved. The way she saw it, it would all work out in God's perfect timing.

Jenna glanced at her watch and decided she needed to start getting ready for her wedding. She was thankful they agreed on having an evening wedding. She highly doubted the whole gang would have everything in place for their first-class Christmas wedding if they decided on a morning or afternoon wedding. At least with the wedding scheduled for seven, there should be no problems whatsoever.

CB ∞

CheeeeeeeeeeCheeeeeeKeeeeeKeeeee . . .

"Hunter, for crying out loud, turn your stupid walkie-talkie off! I told you we only need to use them if we are separated."

"Okay, okay, Tessa, you don't have to be so irritable. I mean, I thought my idea of using the walkie-talkies was a pretty good one."

"You, Hunter, don't have to be so sensitive. Yes, your idea about the walkie-talkies is great. Yes, I have every right to be irritable. My mom is getting married in just a few short hours, and we still have at least three hours of work . . . and I still need to get ready . . . and the list just goes on and on. And for crying out loud, where's Cindy and Bob?"

"They're picking up the poinsettias. They only have one hundred poinsettia plants to load in the bed of Bob's truck. That's all."

"Well, Hunter, we need those plants for the fellowship hall, where we're having the reception. Which is when we'll use your cute little walkie-talkies. You know, while you're arranging the plants on the tables, and I'm here in the sanctuary taking care of last-minute details. I'm so glad Cindy and I came to decorate the sanctuary last night. Don't you think it looks great?"

"Roger."

"Hunter, you're such a dork."

"Ten-four, good buddy . . ." Cheeeekkchheeeeeekkcheeee. "Oops, sorry. I thought I turned mine off. I must have turned it up."

Tessa stomped her right foot and spoke a little louder than she intended, "Good buddy, I'm going to throw these stupid walkie-talkies out the door!"

Hunter placed his hand on Tessa's shoulder and calmly stated, "Tess, it's not healthy for you to have a meltdown on your mom's wedding day."

Tessa gave Hunter a blank look, and then they both started laughing out loud. "You're right, Hunter. And I'm sorry for being so short with you. I guess I'm acting a little childish."

"You know, Tessa, I have a lot of history with these walkie-talkies," Hunter remarked in a matter-of-fact tone.

"Is that right?" Tessa replied.

"Yup."

"You care to enlighten me?" Tessa asked.

"Well, when I was eight, I received these for Christmas from my granny. That year, they just happened to be my favorite gift. And then when I was nine, my dad and I went hiking at Argle. Of course, I made sure we had my walkie-talkies. Well, I somehow strayed away from my dad, and I have you to know it was these walkie-talkies that helped my dad to find me."

Tessa gave Hunter one of her mischievous looks and spoke with a hint of playfulness. "Well, Hunter, I think after today, you should place your walkie-talkies in a special showcase."

"Whatever, Tess—"

Hunter was interrupted by Bob, "We need some help unloading these poinsettias."

"Oh, thank goodness you're here! I was getting worried. Where's Cindy?"

"No reason for you to worry, Tess. We got this," Cindy remarked as she stepped around Bob. "Hey, the tree looks great. You guys did a remarkable job decorating it."

"Thanks," Tessa and Hunter spoke in unison.

Bob cleared his throat and then said, "Okay, we have a little over two hours to wrap everything up. So how about you gals take care of whatever it is you need to do here in the sanctuary, and we guys will take care of the fellowship hall." Bob paused as he looked at Hunter and then continued, "Come on, Hunter, we have one hundred poinsettias to unload."

"Sounds like a plan," Cindy chimed.

"Hunter, don't forget to radio me if you have any questions."

"Ten-four, Tessa."

Bob and Cindy looked at each other and shrugged their shoulders. "I think we're missing something," Cindy said.

Hunter was about to go into detail, but Tessa quickly pronounced. "Don't worry, I'll fill you in, and Hunter can fill Bob in."

Cindy shook her head and simply replied, "Okie dokie."

Bob rubbed his hands together and said, "Oh, I already placed the pinecones in the fellowship hall. I figured you girls can come and arrange them when you finish up in here."

"That sounds great. We shouldn't be much longer," replied Cindy.

"Okay. Come on, Hunter, let's get this show on the road," said Bob.

"Ten-four."

"Hunter, you're acting like a kid. We're adults . . . tone it down, good buddy."

As Hunter was on his way out the door, he commented to Tessa, "Tess, make sure you have your walkie-talkie on."

"Sure thing, Hunter."

ငဒ ၆ာ

Grant stood in his studio apartment listening to the clock tick away. It seemed to him that the day was dragging by. He still had a few of his personal belonging to pack up, but he had most of his packing completed. He was ready to begin his new life with Jenna and Tessa. He could hardly believe this day had finally arrived. Grant wasn't one for fairy-tale love stories, but he was sure he was about to step straight into his happy ever after.

Grant decided since he still had a few hours to kill, he would spend some time reading the Good Book and praying. The Lord had directed him to the Book of Ephesians. Within no time, he was reading Ephesians 5:25–33.

"Husbands, love your wives, even as Christ also loved the church, and gave himself for it, that he might sanctify and cleanse it with the washing of water by the word, that he might present it to himself a glorious church, not having spot, or wrinkle, or any such thing, but that it should be holy and without blemish. So ought men to love their wives as their own bodies. He that loveth his wife loveth himself. For no man ever yet hated his own flesh, but nourisheth and cherisheth it, even as the Lord the church, for we are members of his body, of his flesh, and of his bones. For this cause shall a man leave his father and mother, and shall be joined unto his wife, and they two shall be one flesh. This is a great mystery, but I speak concerning Christ and the church. Nevertheless, let every one of you in particular so love his wife even as himself, and the wife see that she reverence her husband."

The Word of God penetrated straight to the core of Grant's heart. He had no doubt he loved Jenna, but he felt this overwhelming need to pray he would love her as the Bible instructs.

"Farther, I come boldly before Your throne of grace thanking You for this wonderful day. I simply can't believe I'm about to marry the love of my heart. I know You have promised if I delight myself in You, in return, You would give me the desires of my heart. Father, it's my deepest desire that You would help me to love Jenna even as You love the church. Please strengthen me where I may be weak. I pray You will grant me the wisdom to be the husband and stepfather you would want me to be. I ask You would correct me in your loving kindness if I should get outside of the boundaries of Your Word. I love You, Lord. I pray this in Jesus's name, amen." Grant felt nothing but God's peace, and with peace came assurance that he would make Jenna a fine husband.

ᏣᎦᏎᎧ

They had everything ready for the ceremony, and it all looked breathtaking. Cindy simply stood in awe of God. With each passing day, she was learning to trust Him more and more. It was God who kept all of them from falling apart while they were trying to take care of the last-minute details.

Tessa and Hunter did a magnificent job decorating the Christmas tree. They placed big silver and blue glass balls, white doves, and clear flashing lights on the tree. And there appeared to be a lot of gifts from family and friends placed neatly under the tree.

Cindy had to admit, Tessa's decorating skills were pretty impressive. She had lined the center aisle with blue oversized vases and stunning silver silk poinsettias in each vase. She intertwined white silk material between each vase. There were soft blue Christmas lights weaved around the four pillars at the front of the sanctuary. There was just a small amount of soft white icicle Christmas lights coming from the ceiling.

The fellowship hall was decorated simply but stunningly. They placed green linen table clothes on each table, and the beautiful red poinsettias, along with pinecones neatly placed around them as a centerpiece. They placed a stocking stuffed with Hershey's Kisses at each dinner setting. The bride and bridegroom's table had a bouquet of red roses with white baby's breaths. And Hunter came up with the brilliant idea of hanging mistletoes directly above their seats.

Now, Cindy could breathe because it was almost time to start the ceremony. She found the perfect place for her and Bob to sit at the very back of the sanctuary, where she could have a clear view. She was pleased to see that guests were quickly filling the sanctuary.

She had to smile as she took in the sight of Grant. He looked handsome in his black tux. He didn't seem to be at all nervous. Strangely enough, it was Hunter who looked a little uptight. He always seemed so cool, calm, and collected.

Jenna expressed she wanted to keep the ceremony simple. She asked Tessa to be her bridesmaid and Hunter to be the best man. Pastor Dawson's daughter, Bella, would be the flower girl. An elder from the church would be walking Jenna down the aisle to give her away. After the ceremony, they would be off to Chicago for their honeymoon.

The pianist started playing the processional, and everyone stood on their feet as Bella came in, tossing red rose petals with each step she took. Tessa looked beautiful in her pale-blue vintage tea gown. Finally, Jenna made her grand entrance. She looked gorgeous in her white chapel train satin tulle wedding dress with lace, and her hair flowed with soft curls. She had a bouquet of blue roses with white baby's breaths.

Cindy was sure Grant was going to pass out at the sight of his beautiful bride. She also noticed the look on Hunter's face when Tessa gracefully walked through the double doors. There was no doubt he had it pretty bad for Tess. But my, how Grant loved Jenna. The chemistry between the two of them was out of this world.

Cindy's heart felt full as she listened to the heartfelt vows Jenna and Grant wrote. Her heart skipped a beat when her husband placed his hand on her knee. She felt a spark of love igniting between them, and she once again stood in awe of God.

Bob whispered just loud enough for her to hear, "I love you, baby."

"I love you too," Cindy whispered back.

Before everyone knew it, they were enjoying the reception. Tessa spotted Hunter from across the room, and they made eye contact. She playfully held up one of the walkie-talkies she had retrieved from the kitchen. Hunter nodded his head and went to the kitchen for the other walkie-talkie.

"Hunter, do you have yours on?"

"Ten-four."

"You're such a dork, but you look pretty sharp in that tux."

"Tess, are you flirting with me?"

"Whatever, Hunter . . ."

PART TWO

1993

16

The cold winter months gave way to springtime, and spring gave way to the hot blazing summer. It was hard for Grant to believe he had been married to Jenna for six glorious months. He was sure by now they would have had their first disagreement, but they hadn't, and he considered himself one blessed man.

It was unusually hot for July. Grant had drank so much water that he felt certain he would float out of Bowers. He was grateful to be on break. At least the employees' break room was nice and cool. He had just finished eating some trail mix and downed another bottle of spring water when he spotted the young man who caught his eye on more than one occasion. Grant was curious about the man. Grant had noticed the guy rarely spoke, and when he wasn't working, he always had his nose buried in a book.

Grant glanced at his watch and took note there was ten minutes left before he had to get back out on the floor. He decided he was going to try and strike up a conversation with the guy. Without second-guessing, Grant moseyed over to the young man. He stood directly in front of him and cleared his throat in hopes of pulling him away from the novel he was deeply involved in.

"Hey, sorry to interrupt. Do you have a minute?" Grant asked.

Silence.

Okay, so it wasn't going the way Grant had hoped. In fact, he wasn't getting anywhere with the guy. It was as if Grant was a ghost. The guy simply continued reading like Grant didn't even ask him a question. Strange. Real strange. Well, Grant wasn't one to easily give up. He decided on another approach. He sat across from the guy, and he once again cleared his throat.

"That must be some story. I like to read, so I can identify with you. You know, being deeply engrossed in a book."

Todd sighed as he looked at Grant over the top of his novel. His eyes implied he wasn't in the mood for company, and then they started rapidly blinking. He spoke in a matter-of-fact tone. "Do you mind? I only have a few minutes left before I go back to work, and I would really like to finish this chapter."

Grant tried to appear calm as he replied, "So you have a voice. What about a name? My name is Grant, by the way."

Todd didn't say a word. He simply shut his book, stood on his feet, and walked out of the break room, leaving Grant completely muddled with his own thoughts. One thing he knew for certain was that he planned to get to know the mysterious young man. He looked around the break room to find that it was cleared out. Even though he still had a few minutes of break time left, he decided to get back to work. Grant planned to place the guy on his prayer list, and before leaving, he was going to ask around to see what he could find out.

CB BO

Jenna could tell something was troubling Grant. She couldn't recall ever seeing him so complex. All evening, he said every bit of five words, and she had to pull those out of him. Granted, Tessa talked enough for all of them. She was excited about fall semester kicking in, and she planned to jump in full force. She expressed she was ready to get Spoon River behind so she could start attending WIU.

Tessa and Hunter were busy taking summer classes, and they both seemed to have a made-up mind to speed things up a bit. Jenna had to admit she was proud of her daughter. She seemed to be adapting to JR College quite well. And Jenna had no doubts she would adapt to the fast-paced life that would come along with attending a university.

Jenna was thankful that Tessa chose WIU. She could continue living at home, which would save a lot of money. Most importantly, Jenna wouldn't have the worries of her daughter moving away to some strange city. No doubt Jenna would spend most of her time worrying about Tessa's safety and if she was taking appropriate care of herself. Of course, her worrying would cause her relationship with Grant to undergo stress. So all in all, life was good.

This would be the first summer in years that Jenna was able to relax. She had worked every summer since she had started working at Spoon River, but Grant had requested she take summers off. To her surprise, the school dean had no problem finding a substitute for the hot summer months. However, in just a few short weeks, she would be back to teaching fulltime.

"Mom, why don't you let me clean the kitchen."

"Are you sure?" Jenna asked.

"Yes, I'm thinking you and Grant could use a little time alone. I mean, he seems to be a little distant."

Jenna was shocked that Tessa actually took note that something was troubling Grant. Maybe she wasn't lost in her all-about-me world after all. But then again, she shouldn't be surprised. Tessa had always been astute. Whatever the case, she was grateful Tessa was sensitive to Grant's disturbed disposition.

"Are you sure? I mean, I know you have your studies."

"I'm absolutely sure. Now, go on. Out of the kitchen."

"Okay, if you insist. But you don't have to be so bossy," Jenna teasingly remarked.

"I get the bossiness honest from you."

"Is that right? Well, make sure you cover the casserole dish before placing it in the fridge. I wouldn't want—"

"Bacteria to grow—" Tessa interrupted.

"And we all get food poisoning," Jenna finished.

"Mom, I'm soon to be nineteen. I'm in college. I can handle cleaning the kitchen."

"Okay. Okay. Good night, Tess. I love you."

"Good night, Mom. I love you too. Now go take care of your hubby."

Jenna looked at her only child and silently wondered when she became a woman. "When did you grow up?" she asked in a hushed tone.

"I haven't. I just know how to act like a grown-up. At least, once in a while."

With that said, Jenna ambled into the den to find her husband lost in his thoughts. She spoke just above a whisper. "Grant, baby, let's go upstairs. You know, so we can have some alone time."

Grant shook his head a few times as if he was trying to shake the disturbing thoughts out of his mind. He painted on a smile and replied, "That sounds great. The night is still young . . ."

Once they were both nice and comfy in bed, Jenna placed her soft hand over Grant's hardworking hand. Before she dared to speak, she allowed the silence to hover over them for a beat. This new side of Grant was one she wasn't accustomed to. She wanted to tread softly in this new territory.

"Baby, what's troubling you?"

Silence.

"You know you can talk to me, right? Did I do something to upset you?"

Grant sighed and then replied, "Yes, I do know I can talk with you, and no, you didn't do something to upset me."

"Then what is it? I don't like seeing you like this."

Grant made small circles on her hand with his thumb and then asked, "Have you ever met somebody that made you feel lost for words?"

"Of course, I have. I mean, you do remember I teach the adult education class at Spoon River?"

"Yes, of course. You're right. Maybe I should just start from the beginning."

"Yes, that would be good."

"By the way, are you ready to go back to work? I mean, in just a few short weeks, your summer vacation will be over."

Jenna shrugged her shoulders as she answered, "Yes and no. I mean, I immensely enjoy my job. But on the other hand, I have enjoyed my time off. After all, it has been years since I was able to be free for the summer. At first, I almost didn't know what to do with myself, but I quickly found things to occupy my time. Actually, I think by the time fall semester rolls around, I'll be ready."

"Good. You know, I wouldn't mind you staying home full-time. But I don't desire to interfere with your career."

"I thank you for that." Jenna smiled and then gave him a kiss on the cheek. "Now, back to you. What has you so disturbed? Or should I say, who has you so disturbed?"

Grant sighed and remained silent for a beat. When he finally spoke, his words came out in a hushed tone. "It's a young man at my job."

Complete silence.

Jenna was the one who broke the silence. "Well?"

"That's just it, I don't know what to think."

Grant allowed his encounter with Todd to play over in his mind. The young man really had him puzzled. For whatever reason, he felt compelled to get to know him. He would never forget the look on the young guy's face as he tried to converse with him. There was no doubt in Grant's mind the guy lacked social skills.

"The thing is," Grant said, "I feel this overwhelming need to know him. Maybe I'm mistaken, but it's like he's completely lost . . . if that makes sense."

"Yeah, sure, it make sense," Jenna whispered.

"I have seen him around the plant on serval occasions, but I never really thought too much about him. Well, today, in the break room, I tried to strike up a conversation with him but to no avail. I mean, it's like the guy showed no humanly emotions at all. I don't know, baby . . . I'm simply trying to find some sort of logic in all of this."

Jenna allowed Grant's words to play over in her mind before she dared to speak. "Well, baby, I think you're allowing your intellect to get in the way of God's wisdom. I mean, to me, the logic is very simple. God has allowed your path to cross his for a reason. And I believe that a good-looking man has taught me we need to take all things before the Lord in prayer. After all, God is not the author of confession."

Grant twisted his head around to get a better view of his wife. He was amazed by her spiritual growth. Yes, she still drank an occasional glass of wine, but he could see she had cut back. He was utterly proud of her.

"Tell me, Mrs. Williams, when did you become so spiritually prudent?"

"Well, Mr. Williams, I believe some of your prudence has rubbed off on me."

"I love you, baby."

"I love you too. Why don't we pray for this young man? And maybe later, you can invite him over for dinner."

"Well, I agree he needs our prayers. But only time will tell if I should invite him over for dinner."

"Why don't you lead us in prayer?" Jenna asked.

"I can do that."

Grant draped his arm around Jenna and began talking to their Maker.

"Father, we come boldly before Your throne of grace on behalf of the young man I tried speaking with today. Lord, You know him by name, and we ask that You will lead us in our prayers as we pray for him. Lord, it seems I have developed a burden for him. I ask You will open a door of opportunity for me to speak with him and that You give me the words to speak. I pray You shower him with Your peace and I prayer for his soul. In Jesus's name, amen."

"Lord Jesus, I may not say long prayers, but I know You hear my prayers. I pray for this young man's state of mind. I pray that You use my husband to help him find his way to You. In Jesus's name, amen."

Grant pulled Jenna closer to him and whispered in her ear, "Now, about the night still being young. What do you say you and I have a little fun?"

"I'm game . . ." Jenna purred.

CRBO

Todd sat at his desk trying to get involved in reading *Pet Sematary* by Stephen King. Every now and then, he would glance at Misfit and feel chills runs down his spine. He sipped on his Jack as his mind continued to drift away from the novel. Truth be known, he couldn't seem to get Grant off his mind.

Todd had to admit he was intrigued by the guy. The guy possessed a peace Todd had never witnessed before. Todd decided if Grant came back around to talk to him, he would give him a chance. Yep, it was time he got to know some folks.

He placed his book on the desk and called out to Misfit. "Come on, boy, let's go for a walk."

17

Tessa enjoyed relaxing under a willow tree after running two laps around the park. It was early Saturday morning, and she planned to enjoy her day alone. Tessa loved coming to the park when the weather would permit to run and read. She was sitting nice and comfy beneath the swaying branches of the tree enjoying the cool breeze that came along with the early morning hours. She took a sip of her Gatorade and then placed the cap back on the bottle. She planned to start reading one of her favorite books titled *I'M OK, YOU'RE OK* by Dr. Thomas A. Harris.

This was her third time reading the book, and she had to admit, she agreed with Dr. Thomas A. Harris's theory. A person's childhood played a tremendous role on their adult behavioral disposition. Tessa was thankful her mom so quickly bounced back after her divorce. Over all, Tessa felt she turned out to be a decent adult, and she had her mom to thank. Sure, she still had a lot to learn about the highs and lows of life, but what college-aged student didn't? She was grateful she didn't crave the wild side of life like many of her peers. Tessa realized she had her mom to thank for the good moral values that was instilled in her from the time she was a child.

Tessa wasn't ignorant that her mom faced some bumpy roads after her divorce, but she still admired her bravery. She was downright proud to be Jenna's daughter. There had been times she questioned how her life would have turned out if her mom and dad would never have divorced. Strangely enough, she couldn't imagine being raised by her biological dad. She much more preferred having Grant as her stepdad.

Grant was a cool guy. He had the patience of Job, and the love of Jesus radiated from his heart. Tessa was no fool; she knew God had used him to bring a ray of sunshine into her mom's once-dark life. Yep, he brought a lot of good changes into all of their lives. One thing for sure was that her mom loved the daylights out of him, and he put his entire heart into loving both of them. Tessa could sense his love toward her. It was as if he had become the epitome of *dad*. Yep, he was the dad she had always dreamed of having.

Tessa allowed her thoughts to go back to over a thousand yesterdays. She could remember her dad being away on long business trips and her mom stepping up to the plate to play the role of both parents. She couldn't recall her dad attending one parent-teacher conference or going to one of her Christmas plays. It was always her mom who stood by her side and encouraged her to take that extra mile to better her grades. It was her mom who had faith in her when Tessa couldn't seem to have faith in herself.

On the rare occasion her dad would spend time with her, all he did was criticize her to no end. Tessa could still hear his taunting words in the recesses of her mind. *"Tess, you can do better. Remember, you have your dad's genes. Why didn't you think before you answered me?"* The criticizing never ended, and he did the same with Mom. The only difference between her and Mom was Mom wouldn't give in to his spitefulness. Mom always had a comeback, and that infuriated her dad.

He was a control freak, and he detested anyone who would challenge his authority. Tessa could easily see now he was a very weak-minded individual, which was why he would throw cheap, spiteful words at people. One thing for certain was that Mom wouldn't allow him to control her. She could remember her mom jumping on to him for the way he spoke to her.

In Tessa's heart, she knew all things had turned out for the best. She really had no idea if her dad was happy. She could recall when she spoke to him briefly at her grandpa's funeral. To Tessa, he seemed to be coldhearted. Mandy, on the other hand, seemed to be happy. Who knows, maybe she needed someone to tell her when or not to speak. But then again, Tessa noticed Mandy was a little reserved. Maybe Mandy wasn't so happy, after all.

There were a few times Tessa thought about paying her dad a visit. But she dismissed the thoughts just as quickly as they came. She honestly didn't think she harbored bitterness in her heart toward him. However, she had to be honest, he wasn't exactly at the top of her friend list. Truth be told, he wasn't on her friend list at all. Tessa questioned if that was healthy on her behalf. No, she didn't hate him, but she didn't like him either. She was sure she loved him simply because he was her dad.

On more than one occasion, Tessa had thought about asking Hunter to go with her to visit her dad. But she didn't think that would be fair to Hunter. She valued their friendship too much to put him through such a treacherous visit. In her heart, she realized she would be deceiving herself and her friend if she tried to paste a fake smile on her face for the few short hours she spent visiting her dad.

Tessa often wondered what Hunter's parents were like. He said he had an okay relationship with them, but they were quite a bit older. He claims he was a menopause baby. She had a few brief encounters with them. She was able to tell they were up there in age. Hunter seemed to be okay with it, but he did spend a lot of time away from home. Tessa decided she was going to ask Hunter if she could get more acquainted his folks.

Of course, Hunter was a whole other can of worms Tessa didn't care to open. Literally. Yes, she liked him a lot. Truthfully, maybe it was just a tad bit more than friendship level. Yes, he had become her best friend. Tessa was sure she could share her happiest moments and her saddest moments with Hunter. She felt completely uninhibited around him. However, there was still some hidden secrets she had tucked away in her heart. She loved that they were both completely footloose and fancy-free.

Nevertheless, she was able to discern his heart was completely smitten by her. Yes, he tried to hold his feelings at bay. No, he didn't do a very good job at it. The thing was she didn't want to take advantage of him. Really, she didn't. Yet she could never imagine her life without him. To her, it was as if they made a silent pact with one another not to cross the line of giving into falling in love. She was sure she loved him, but she wasn't in love with him. But she realized that Hunter crossed the line. She supposed she was secretly flattered by his unspoken love he tucked away in his heart for only her.

Tessa didn't have her heart completely closed to one day falling in love with Hunter. She simply wasn't ready for that type of relationship. To her, what they had was genuine, and if she allowed her heart to fall in love with him, it would make things too complicated. Even though there were a few times Hunter tried to make his feeling for her unquestionably known, he had agreed to Tessa's terms for their relationship.

Tessa had to admit she always looked forward to spending time with him. He made her laugh. He laughed with her and not at her. He wholeheartedly listened to her. When they were together, it was just her. Hunter never made her feel unimportant. He always made her feel special without making her feel uncomfortable. To put it plain and simple, Hunter was about as authentic as they came. And that was just one of the many qualities she liked about him.

Tessa looked up at the clear blue sky and whispered, "Even if Hunter is somewhat of a dork, he has a heart of gold. And he's not a bad-looking guy. So maybe . . . I should just read my book."

൙൱

Todd was running at a study pace when Misfit took off running after a squirrel. He had been coming to do his morning run at Glenn Wood Park for several weeks. He liked it. After a good run, he would relax at a picnic table and read while Misfit rested.

"Misfit, get back here!" Todd yelled as he took off running in the direction of his runaway dog. "Come back here, boy."

Todd continued to run until he saw a beautiful young woman call for Misfit. He slowed down to a brisk walk. He was amazed Misfit responded so obediently to the soft voice of the woman. But then again, why should he be so shocked? The woman had some beautiful long legs and curves in all the right places. What amazed Todd the most was the simple fact she caught his eye.

"Hey, what an adorable dog," Tessa remarked.

Todd came to a complete stop just a few short feet from Tessa. As hard as he tried, he wasn't able to avoid eye contact with her. She had the most beautiful blue eyes he had ever seen and a smile that was out of this world. Suddenly, he felt awkward. He shifted from one foot to the other and then replied, "Thanks."

"You're welcome. What's his name?"

"Misfit," Todd could feel heat start to rise up the back of his neck. He could tell by the expression on her face she was a little taken by Misfit's name. After all, how often do people name their pet Misfit? Only weirdos, like him, which is exactly why he didn't need to be wasting this nice lady's time.

"Did you say *Misfit*?"

"Yes." Todd felt his eyes start to rapidly blink. He hated it, but he couldn't seem to stop them from blinking faster than he could run. And that was pretty fast.

Tessa took a good look at Misfit and smiled as she stated, "I get why you named him Misfit. I mean, with him having one brown eye and one blue. Actually, I kind of like it." She paused for a moment as she rubbed behind Misfit's ears. "Hey there, Misfit. You're a good boy. Aren't ya?" Misfit barked in agreement.

Todd could feel the hot sweat run down his back, and he was sure he smelled pretty raunchy. He hoped she wasn't able to smell the Jack that gushed out his pores. He glanced away for a brief second and then looked back at the woman he couldn't seem to pull away from. Her book caught his eyes. *I'M OK, YOU'RE OK. Yeah, right . . .* was all that came to his mind. He was far from being okay.

It was as if Tessa was reading his mind when she casually asked, "Have you ever read this book?"

Todd tried to keep from looking shocked by her question as he replied, "No, I can't say I have."

"Do you like to read?"

"Yes."

"Well, this is only my third time reading this book. It's really good. Very informative."

"I'll have to check it out. I'm sure I can probably get a copy from the library."

"Probably so. Hey, you're not from around here, are you?"

"No."

"What brings you to the big town of Macomb?" Tessa tried not to notice his T-shirt was clinging to his broad chest. He was definitely one good-looking guy, but he seemed to be extremely shy.

"My job."

"Boy, you're real talkative. Where do you work?"

"Bowers."

"Really? My stepdad works there. He has for years. So you like it?" By now, Misfit was stretched out at Tessa's feet licking on his paw.

Why am I still standing here I should take my dog and hightail it home. "I do."

"Yeah, folks around here say it's a pretty cool place to work. By the way, my name is Tessa, but most people call me Tess." Tessa paused for a moment, hoping the strange man standing in front of her would offer her his name. After a few moments, she decided to just come out and ask him. "And your name is?"

"Todd."

Tessa looked into Todd's ice-blue eyes and smiled as she whispered, "Todd. That's a nice name."

"Thanks."

"You're welcome. Looks like Misfit is comfy. You're more than welcome to hang out with me. I mean, I already did my two laps. I'm sure I look a mess." Tessa absently pulled at her ponytail.

Todd once again felt heat rise up the back of his neck, and his eyes rapidly blinked. He looked away from Tessa as he replied, "I need to go."

"Okay, nice meeting you, Todd. Maybe I'll see you around. I mean, Macomb is a small town."

"Maybe. Come on, Misfit, let's go." Misfit's ears perked up, and then he took off running with Todd behind him.

18

Hunter listened as Tessa relayed to him her encounter with the guy from the park. He had to admit, he felt a little uneasy. He could see the handwriting on the wall, so to speak. Tessa, being the kindhearted girl she was, would want to find out more about this guy and fix his problems. Hunter supposed it only came natural for Tess to want to dig into people's minds and solve all of their problems. After all, she was studying to become a psychologist. Hunter would be shocked if she didn't try to find the hidden key that would release this guy to freedom.

The passion she puts into helping others was just one of the many qualities he loved about her. She was so genuine. It seemed to Hunter that every person who crossed her path walked away a winner simply because her carefree personality would be like a ripple effect and would flow into their lives. How could it not? Hunter was fully persuaded that's what happened to him, and he was grateful it did.

Before he became friends with Tessa, he was a fairly predictable guy. He didn't have much of a life other than school. But now, he had Tess and school. Hunter wouldn't change a thing about his life. He was happy with his career choice. Sure, some would say majoring in agricultural business would be a boring vocation. But not Hunter, and most importantly, Tess thought he's making a wise choice.

Once Hunter graduated with his master's, he planned to get hired at the pioneer plant working in the lab testing corn or maybe in the human resource department. What Tess didn't know was he also planned to make her his bride. Sure, there were many hurdles they needed to jump and tons of obstacles they would need to overcome, but Hunter new in his heart she was his soul mate. He was sure there wasn't a thing he wouldn't do to prove to her they were destined to be together.

They were relaxing in the family room at Tessa's place, enjoying a cold glass of Coke, and soft tunes were playing in the background. Tessa's folks went to Peoria for the day. Jenna said she planned to shop until she dropped, and Grant indicated he planned to catch her when she dropped. Hunter thought they had the ideal marriage. He wished his parents had just half of the fire in their marriage Tessa's folks had. It was pretty obvious to all who rubbed shoulders with Jenna and Grant that they were madly in love.

"I don't know why I can't seem to shake this guy out of my spirit, Hunter."

"Well, be careful. I mean, we live in a crazy world."

"I know. But I really believe he's harmless. I'm kinda thinking God has a divine plan. I mean, the Bible does say it's God that orders our steps."

"This is true," Hunter responded.

"Why are you looking at me like that?" Tessa asked.

"Like what?"

"I don't know . . ." Tess trailed off for a beat and then continued, "you just have that I-don't-like-it look."

"Hey, you're my best friend. I just care about your well-being. Like I said, we live in a crazy world." *You have no idea how uncomfortable I'm feeling about this character, Tess.*

"Hunter, I'm a big girl. I can take care of myself." *Stop thinking with your heart, Hunter.*

I'm very much aware that you're a big girl. But one day, I plan to take care of you. "Okay. Just promise me you'll not try to be a hero and put his life back together. Can you do that much for me?"

"No. But I promise if he tries to get out of hand, you'll be the first to know. Deal?"

"Deal."

There was a comfortable silence between the two of them for a beat until Tessa broke the silence with an off-the-wall question. "Did I mention his dog, Misfit, has one brown eye and one blue?"

Hunter painted on a serious look and spoke in a matter-of-fact tone, "No. But I've heard enough. I think if some fat chance you should see this Todd character again, you need to brush him off."

"What are you talking about, Hunter?"

"Think about it, Tess. Who names their pet Misfit? I would say a real misfit would give their pet such a name. And there's the fact the dog has one brown and one blue eye. Plus didn't you say something about Todd rapidly blinking his eyes?"

"Yes, I did. But Hunter, you're judging. I believe I heard Pastor Jones say we should never judge a book by its cover."

Hunter winked at Tess and chuckled as he stated, "Okay, you got me. I tell you what, we'll just stick with our deal. If he should ever get out of line, you'll let me know. Not that I think you'll ever see him again because I highly doubt you will."

Tessa gave Hunter that heart-melting smile of hers and asked, "Would you rock him, sock him for me, Hunter?"

Hunter didn't have to second-guess. His answer rolled off his tongue faster than his brain had time to think. "Yes, Tess. I would do that for you."

It became so silent that one could hear a pin drop. Tessa allowed her eyes to linger on Hunter's buff body much longer than she intended. *When did he start filling his shirt out so well?* She silently wondered. Finally, after what seemed to be hours but was just mere seconds, Tessa cleared her throat and asked, "So you up to a game of Zelda or X-Men?"

"Both."

"Oh, so you're feeling lucky?"

"Whatever, Tess."

Before they realized it, two hours had slipped by. While playing the games, they both laughed and carried on like two school-aged children. Tessa was no fool; she knew all too well that Hunter allowed her to win. But Hunter was just like that, always placing her before him. Suddenly she remembered she desired to learn more about her best friend's home life.

"You know, Hunter, it has occurred to me that I know very little about your parents. I mean, I've only seen them from a distance a few times. And for whatever reason, you never invite me over to your place." Tessa sat patiently waiting for Hunter's response. She was about to open her mouth to speak when Hunter sighed.

"There's not much to tell. I mean, compared to yours, my family is fairly bland."

"Hunter, I realize it's difficult to measure up to my family, but I didn't ask for a comparison. I simply want to know a little more about you. After all, we are best pals," Tessa teasingly remarked.

"Well, since you put it that way, I guess I have no choice but to comply. As you know, my folks had me a little later in life. Mom says I was a menopause baby. Anyway, they tried for years, with no success, to have children. When my mom turned forty-six and my dad forty-eight, I was conceived. Of course, the doctors were concerned that I would be born with Down syndrome, but as you see, I'm perfectly healthy. Actually, they're pretty cool. I mean, they pretty much leave me alone to do my own thing. Don't get me wrong, they know how to lay down the law. I have learned the hard way not to disrespect them in any way, shape, or form."

Hunter paused for a moment as he contemplated asking Tessa over to his place. He decided it was best she simply meet them for herself. "I tell you what, it's early, so why don't you come over to my place?"

"Are you sure?"

"I'm sure. It's Saturday night, which means they're up acting like a couple of party animals watching *Hee Haw* reruns."

"Really, Hunter? *Hee Haw*?"

"Yep. You game?"

"Sure, let's go," Tessa replied.

Oh my goodness was all Tessa could think as she stepped back in time. A time before she was even thought of. She would guess the year to be 1955 or somewhere around there. In the kitchen, all of the appliances were pink. Yes, that's right, a pink stove top, pink refrigerator, pink countertops, and pink wallpaper. Absolutely crazy. Hunter simply shrugged his shoulders as he expressed that his mom loved pink.

Then came what Tessa assumed to be the formal dining room. The carpet was puke yellow, and the dinette table was dark brown with six yellow vinyl chairs around it. The walls were covered with dark wood paneling. Talk about depressing. No wonder Hunter preferred hanging out at her house. Sure enough, she heard *Hee Haw* blaring from the television. She silently wondered if the TV was a black-and-white set. Tessa had to stifle a laugh as she noticed the pictures of Hunter neatly hanging in chronological order.

"Hunter, I never realized you wore glasses. And oh my, look at this one with your headgear! Let me see your teeth, Hunter. Come on, give me a big smile."

Hunter couldn't help but blush. *Is she flirting with me? Surely not.* He smiled and replied, "Now you know why my teeth are so nice."

Tessa got oh so close to his face. Yes, so close he could feel the warmth of her breath as she whispered, "You do have nice teeth, Hunter."

Hunter tapped her nose and whispered back, "Thanks. Now, are you ready to meet my parents?"

"You betcha."

"Tess, promise you'll be nice."

"Come on, Hunter, you know I'm always nice."

"Whatever, Tess."

"Hunter, promise me your parents have a colored TV."

"Hahaha, Tess."

Tessa looked at Hunter very seriously and asked, "Hunter, does it have those cute little bunny ears? You know, antennas—"

"It's colored and no bunny ears. Now come on," Hunter interrupted.

"Hunter, let's not get touchy." Tessa started tickling his side. "Come on, big boy, lighten up."

"Tess, payback will come. And when it does—"

"Hunter, is that you? Did you bring a friend home?"

"Yes, Mom, it's me. And yes, I brought a friend."

"Well, get in here so your dad and I can meet her."

Oh how sweet was all Tessa could think when she laid eyes on Hunter's folks. They were the perfect picture of ancient love. There was his mother sitting in her recliner donning a pink house robe and big pink rollers in her hair. Pop sat in his recliner next to her with a bowl of popcorn in his hand.

"Mom, Dad, this is Tess."

Mom's eyes lit up. "Well, it's so nice to finally meet you. Hunter has said a lot of sweet things about you."

"Mom . . . that's enough," Hunter managed to choke out.

"Oh really?" Tess asked, "And your name is?"

"Oh yes. My name is Beverly, but you can call me Bev. And this is Hank."

Hank held his popcorn bowl toward Tessa and asked, "Would you like some popcorn?"

Hunter quickly stated, "No, Dad, it's okay. We're not staying. I only came by to get my wallet, yeah, that's it. So we can go get something to eat. I was thinking maybe Jo's Café. Does that sound good to you, Tess?"

"Actually, Hunter—"

"You would rather go to Peg's. Not a problem."

Tess decided to play along with Hunter rather than put him on the spot. Like he did her. "Yeah, Peg's sounds great."

"Hunter, I can't believe you haven't eaten yet. Why, it's going on seven. Why don't you let me warm you and Tessa some tuna casserole? How does that sound?"

Hank piped up and said, "Bev, dear. Let the two of them go out on their date. For crying out loud, they're young whippersnappers. Why, the night is still young."

Hmmm, date? Sounds good to me. A lot better than the tuna casserole. "Mom, it's okay. Dad's right. The night is still young. Let me just go get my wallet, and we'll be on our way."

Hunter glared at Tessa. "What, Hunter?"

"You ready?"

"Oh, I thought I would just wait here for you."

"Hunter, I think that's a good idea. I would like to get to know this pretty young lady a little more," Beverly remarked.

"Not this time, Mom. Remember, it's getting late. I'll bring Tess back another time. You know, so the two of you can chat."

"Well, I suppose you're right."

"Of course, he's right, Bev. Have a good time on your date, son. Hey, by the way, she's a cutie," Hank stated.

Hunter was sure his face turned every shade of red available for the art world. And he was sure Tess was about to burst into laughter. He placed his hand at the small of her back and nudged her to move forward.

"Okay, Mom, Dad, we'll see ya later."

"Yeah, see ya later, Bev and Hank. We need to get out on the town . . . you know, our hot date."

Once they made it out of the house, Tessa burst out into uncontrollable laughter.

"Tess, not so loud. They will hear you."

"No, they won't. They're too engrossed in *Hee Haw*. Come on, let's go out on the town."

Hunter chuckled and replied, "Okay, cutie."

"Watch it, whippersnapper, or I'll show just how much of a 'cutie' I can be. By the way, Hunter, I've decided when I open my private practice, you'll be entitled to a family plan."

"Whatever, Tess."

"Hunter, have you forgotten that I'm driving? So I get to pick where we eat."

"Okay, fair enough."

"I'm kinda hungry for Chinese."

"Sounds good, Tess."

19

Grant was determined to learn more about the mysterious man who kept him up late into the night hours praying. It was incredible what God had revealed to him as he prayed for the young man. He learned by the Spirit of God that the man was holding on to a lot of pain. The way Grant saw it, God had allowed their paths to cross for one reason. God wanted to save the young man and bring deliverance to his soul.

As soon as Grant arrived at his job, he planned to speak with his foreman about the guy. Surely he would at least know his name. He was just getting out of the shower when he heard the sound of Jenna's sweet voice. He learned she loved to sing in the morning, and he had to admit she had a nice voice. Apparently, she sang in the choir for many years. He planned to have a talk with her about getting back on the wagon. Their church could use a voice like hers.

The smell of bacon and eggs wafted in the bathroom. He had just finished wiping the steam from the mirror and had splashed some aftershave on his face when he heard her call for him. Grant smiled as he patted the aftershave on his face, and then he sprayed on some deodorant.

"I'll be down is a sec, baby. I'm just finishing up." Within no time, Grant was dressed and was making his way into the kitchen. He slowly walked up behind Jenna and wrapped his muscular arms around her as he whispered in her ear, "Have I told you lately just how beautiful you are?"

Jenna turned and slipped her arms around his neck and whispered, "Yes, but I never get tired of hearing you say it." She nuzzled her nose in his neck as she ran her fingers through his hair. The smell of his aftershave tickled her nose and caused her womanly senses to scream. "Mmmm, you smell good." She felt her heart skip a beat as she looked deep into his soft grey eyes. "And you're one good-looking dude."

Grant chuckled and replied, "Is that right?"

"Yes, and your eggs are getting cold."

"Aw, come on, baby, you're no fun."

"And you have exactly twenty minutes to eat and get out the door for work. Which means I have forty-five minutes to eat, dress, and head to the school," Jenna said.

"Okay. But when I come home tonight, we will pick up where we're leaving off."

"Sounds good but only not in the kitchen," Jenna purred.

"Baby, I kinda like the kitchen."

"Grant, you're pushing it."

"Okay, let's eat."

ᘓᘔ

Grant had just arrived at work. He still had fifteen minutes before he had to clock in, so he thought he would speak with Nick, his foreman. Nick was fairly predictable; he always spent time in the break room drinking coffee and shooting the breeze with the guys before clocking in.

Within no time, Grant noticed Nick, and fortunately for him, Nick was sitting alone. He ambled over to the vending machine and purchased a granola bar to snack on later, and then he went over to the coffee pot and poured himself a cup of coffee. He blew on the hot beverage and took of sip of the dark liquid. It was just like he liked it. Good and strong with no sugar or cream. He had always liked his coffee black. He then went over to sit with Nick.

Grant had known Nick for years. He liked him. He was a man of integrity, and he had a good standing reputation in the plant. One of the things Grant liked about him the most is the relationship he had with God. There was no questioning his faith. Nick made it known to everyone who crossed his path that he was a child of God.

Nick was not ashamed to declare what the good Lord had done for him. Fact was he would use his personal testimony as a way to witness to a lot of the young men. From what Grant had gathered, Nick used to live on the wild side. He was addicted to drugs and alcohol, and he was a real womanizer. But then, he met Debbie, and she pretty much gave him one choice. If he wanted a relationship with her, he would have to first come to know Jesus. To hear Nick tell it, she wouldn't bend or bow to him until she knew for sure he had Jesus living in his heart. That was well over thirty years ago, and Nick had been living strong for the Lord since.

Grant always admired the relationship Nick had with his wife. It was plain as day he loved the daylights out of her. Every time the two of them were together, their love would spill out unto others around them. Nick's face lit up every time he took in the sight of his wife. Grant had to admit, it was their marriage that caused his heart to burn for a wife. And for the first time in his life, he completely understood how Nick felt.

Nick looked up from the rim of his coffee cup and was happy to see that Grant took a seat next to him. "Hey, how's married life?"

Grant's mind went back to the passionate kiss his wife gave him earlier and the way she had prayed for him before he left for work. He smiled and spoke with sparks shooting out of his eyes. "I'm one blessed man, Nick."

Nick chuckled as he spoke with a hint of pride, "God is good."

"Yes, He's good all the time, Nick."

They both sat in a comfortable silence for a bit until finally, Nick asked, "What's on your mind?"

Grant took a sip of his coffee and then started drumming his fingers on the table in a staccato fashion. He contemplated how he should approach Nick about the young man. He absently glanced around the break room to see if he would catch a glimpse of the guy. Grant secretly hoped he wasn't yet in the premises. From what Grant had observed, the guy normally came in to work with just a few minutes to spare.

"It's one of the employees. The young man you hired a while back ago. I think he works on the line with Johnston. He's pretty much a loner. He's always reading books . . ."

Nick lifted his eyebrows and asked, "Is there something I need to be concerned about?"

"No, I don't believe so. I was hoping you could give me his name. I mean, the Lord has given me a burden for the young man."

"Oh, that's easy enough. His name is Todd Jenkins. He's a good worker but about as quiet as a mouse. I've tried striking up a conversation with him but to no avail."

"Yeah, me too. He seems rather odd. Don't you think?"

Nick wasn't quick to answer, but when he did, his words were seasoned with grace. "I guess it's a matter of perspective. I mean, maybe he thinks we're a little odd. After all, Jesus seemed a little odd to a lot of folks. The way I see it, the guy does his job well and leaves folks alone."

"You're right, Nick."

Nick looked at his watch and tapped his hand on the table as he stated, "It's about time for him to come in. He normally gets here with just a few minutes to spare. I do know this, if God has placed him on your heart, then God has something up His sleeve for not just him but you too." With that said, Nick stood to his feet and added, "I think I'll use the restroom before getting to work."

Grant pondered on his conversation with Nick. He came to the conclusion that Nick was right. God had something up His sleeve for him and Todd. Grant smiled as he thought about the guy's name. He closed his eyes and silently prayed. *Thank You, Lord, for giving me his name. Now, I ask You give me wisdom to complete the mission You have placed me on. I pray for Todd's heart to be softened to You. In Jesus's name, amen.*

When Grant opened his eyes from praying, he was surprised to see Todd glancing his way.

A few hours later, Todd was sitting in the break room trying to read his novel. But for whatever reason, he couldn't get Grant out of his mind. The look in Grant's eyes would forever be etched in Todd's heart. There was such a light shining from his eyes, one Todd had never seen before. It almost gave him an eerie feeling. It was as if Grant was able to read his heart. Which, of course, was outrageous. Those kind of things only happened in his novels. But then again, when he was a child, Maggie was pretty good at reading him.

Todd decided he was going to do the right thing. When Grant came into the break room, which should be in about fifteen minutes, he was going to apologize for his rude behavior. After all, Grant was only trying to be friendly. But being friendly with people was something Todd was not accustomed to. He was use to defending himself or Maggie from the slurs of others. But this wasn't Peoria, and he was no longer living in the small apartment above the pool hall. This was the cozy town of Macomb where folks were friendly. Yeah, sure, he had a little run-in with the guy at the pet store when he purchased Misfit. But hey, everybody is entitled to having a bad day every now and then.

Todd's mind slipped back to a few days ago at the park. It seemed his mind did that a lot, and he couldn't decide if he liked it. He had to admit, he saw something special about Tessa. She was unlike any woman he had ever encountered. Not that he had encountered many because he hadn't. He came to the conclusion the reason he felt attracted to Donna was because she reminded him of Maggie. How stupid of him. He was trying to start life anew.

Tessa, she was the complete opposite from Maggie. She was a breath of fresh air, a priceless work of art, and her beauty was pure. What Todd admired the most was she appeared to be easy-going. He could tell it would be easy to strike up a conversation with Tessa. She didn't seem to be judgmental, but rather, she was free-spirited. Tessa was the kind of woman he could easily give his heart to. Which is why he needed to stop thinking about her.

First of all, he knew the chances were slim they would ever again cross paths. But if by some fat chance they did, he knew what he would have to do. He would have to hightail it and run from her. She was too good for him, and he needed to remember that. Nevertheless, he would never forget her beauty. How could he? Her beauty would forever haunt him, just like Grant's grey eyes. Speaking of, Grant was walking straight toward Todd. How could he have not noticed him coming into the break room? He knew how. His mind was preoccupied with Tessa.

With each step Grant took toward Todd, he felt God's peace. With God's peace came the assurance he needed. He knew without a doubt God was up to something big. As he approached Todd, he whispered another prayer, asking God for wisdom.

Todd stood to his feet when Grant made it to his table. He felt his heart rate speed up a bit, but he refused to back down from doing the right thing. He put his hand out and said, "Hello, I'm Todd Jenkins."

20

Maggie was getting ready for her next customer. She had been pulling four or even five tricks a day whereas before, the most she pulled was three. All she did was work, if one would call it work. She had let down a bit on her standard. She was entertaining men from all different walks of life. Most were married businessmen looking for something they couldn't find at home.

She glanced at the small clock she kept on the vanity. She saw she still had forty-five minutes before her customer from Chicago paid his monthly visit. He indicated he had a friend he wanted Maggie to meet, a man who was confused and who needed a good woman to make him feel like a real man. She simply replied she was willing to meet him, but it would cost him. She decided she would charge her regulars the same, but she was doubling up on her new customers.

Supposedly, the guy lived in East Peoria and was a friend of a friend. Tonight, she planned to find out more about the joker. Maggie had no qualms with changing her mind if she felt any bad vibes. She had been doing this line of work long enough to know when to back off. Where there was smoke, there was fire. Sure, she lived in the heat, but she had learned how to endure the heat without getting burned. Yes, she let down on her standard, but she was no fool, and she wasn't desperate. She still had some scruples about her. At least, she wanted to believe she did.

For the past few weeks, Maggie had been mulling over the conversation she had with Moe. As much as she hated to admit it, Moe was right. Years ago, she should have walked away from this lifestyle. She had ruined her life, but even worse, she ruined Todd's. She had tried calling Moe only to learn he had changed his number.

As hard as it was for Maggie to admit, she missed Moe. She regretted she allowed him to so easily walk out of her life. He treated her well, and he would make some lucky lady a fine husband. Just not her. She allowed yet another good opportunity to slip through her fingers. She refused to spend the money he threw at her as he walked out of her life. She still held on to hopes he would one day return. When he did, she would welcome him back with open arms.

A small photo of Todd caught Maggie's eye as she was applying her final touch of makeup. She slowly picked up the picture and held it close to her heart. She tried to hold back the tears that stung the back of her eyelids. She wasn't in the mood to reapply her makeup. But as hard as she tried, she couldn't seem to keep the tears at bay. She allowed them to freely trickle down her cheeks.

Maggie felt her breath catch in her throat as she allowed her sons name to roll off her tongue. "Toddy, I miss you. Why won't you take my calls or come and visit me? Am I that bad of a person? Do you hate me that much? Even if you do hate me, I love you."

Maggie hastily placed the picture back on the vanity and started wiping the tears from her eyes and cheeks. She looked at her reflection in the mirror and was taken by the dark circles under her eyes. Even she could see she was aging. How many good years did she have left? Five, tops ten? She applied some concealer under her eyes and powder on her face, and she sprayed a dab of perfume behind her ears. Before she knew it, there was a knock at her door.

A few hours later that evening, Maggie was waiting for her new customer, Trent. Shane, her client from the windy city of Chicago had asked her to take the man in for the evening. He even paid for the guy's evening, and he paid Maggie rather well.

Maggie sat for one solid hour listening to Trent talk about his military career. She was shocked at the life he lived, that's if he was being truthful. Maggie felt in her heart he was. She doubted very much Trent had such a vivid imagination. Although she knew it was possible because Todd always had a very active imagination. However, Todd never expressed his verbally. He always penned his thoughts on paper. Mainly because he wasn't very articulate. She silently wondered if Todd was still writing.

Maggie had learned Trent fought in four wars, which was something that was almost unheard of. He was a part of Operation Bright Star that took place in 1980, the war in Honduras in 1983, Operation Praying

Mantis that took place in 1988 in the Persian Gulf, and he was medically discharged while fighting in the Gulf War in 1991. He didn't share why he was medically discharged, and she didn't ask. She simply listened.

Maggie found him to be rather interesting to say the least. She also found him to be sweet on the eye. When it came to her customers, she never allowed her eyes to soak in their masculine ways. But she couldn't seem to keep from soaking in Trent. His masculine body only took up half of her living room. Well, maybe not half but a large portion. He had a nice smile. His hair was sandy blonde, and his eyes were chocolate brown. Maggie noticed that his eyes appeared to be much older than his forty-three years of age. Her heart ached to find out why there was such a depth of sadness that went deep into his soul.

Maggie was brought back to the moment when Trent asked her a simple yet complex question.

"So tell me, Maggie, have you ever been in love? Or is this life . . . huh . . . all you're accustomed to?"

She sat across from him in her wingback chair and tried her best to look confident as she answered, "Yes, in fact, I have been in love. No, this life is not all I'm 'accustomed to.' Although I must be frank, I have been living this life since before you started fighting in wars." She picked up her wineglass and took a sip as she allowed her eyes to linger on his broad chest. She decided it was best to change the subject. Mainly because Maggie would almost bet she had fought more wars than Trent. Maybe not in the same sense, but she had to fight for survival. "Cheers. Here's to you. Thanks for serving our great land," she casually remarked.

He retrieved his wineglass from the coffee table, and when he spoke, his voice was husky and just above a whisper, "Cheers."

"This is very good wine. You know your wine . . . you shouldn't have brought it. Thanks." Maggie was starting to feel the effect of the wine. She knew wine, and this was not cheap wine.

"It's the least I could do. After all, you didn't have to agree to entertain me. I suppose I should apologize for talking so much."

Maggie waved her hand and replied, "No apology necessary. I have enjoyed listening to you. I find you to be a rather interesting man."

"You know, Maggie, I find the man who broke your heart to be a complete fool. I can sense we are both still in combat. There's a war still raging in our minds because of our hearts being ripped out and stomped on." The silence weaved a web around them. "I have been trying to develop a strategy that would help me to gain the victory over this war, but I can't seem to come up with one. Maybe you can be of some help, Maggie. Can you?"

Maggie couldn't believe the audacity of this man; yet as hard as she tried, she wasn't able to stop herself from being completely mesmerized. It was as if he had read her thoughts. She blinked her eyes a few times and then responded in a way that shocked even her. "Yes, indeed, I have. It's called prayer."

"To which god do you whisper your prayers to, Maggie?"

"Trent, I pray to the only true living God, Jesus."

"Tell me this, has He answered your prayers, Maggie?"

Maggie wasn't quick to answer because she wanted to answer truthfully. How can she explain to the man who had seen more death than most people do in a lifetime and had experienced so much pain that God had not answered many of her prayers? Fact was most of the time, God seemed millions of miles away from her. But she realized God had not taken one step away from her. She's the one who took many steps away from God.

Maggie tilted her head to one side and simply answered, "No, He hasn't."

"I see . . ." Trent allowed time for his simple words to penetrate through the barrier that was thrown between them. "Maggie, now I know why I find comfort in sharing my heart with you. You're a very honest woman. I was expecting you to give me a common answer that would appease my curiosity, such as just because God hasn't given me what I asked doesn't mean He hasn't answered my prayers. Or God knows what's best. Although all of these answers are legitimate, but they are also a way to elude. At least, that's the way I see it, Maggie."

This man had Maggie's mind completely baffled, but she was determined to turn the tables on him. "I promise you, Trent, I'm not the type of woman that would evade a situation."

Silence.

"Would you like for me to give you a grand tour of my palace, Trent?"

"That would be nice, Maggie."

"Shall we start with my favorite room?"

"And where might that be?"

"The kitchen. I see we're in need of more wine. And then I'll take you to what I think will be your favorite room."

Later that evening, Maggie lay peacefully in the arms of Trent. She had not felt such contentment in years. Moe most certainly did not make her feel like she had reached heaven. Maggie realized she needed to keep her guard up. Yet somehow, she felt it was too late. Yes, Maggie was sure she had already let it down.

Trent loved the feeling of Maggie in his arms. He loved the feel of her soft skin, the smell of her hair, and the sound of her voice. How long had it been since he felt that place of oasis? He felt completely free from the memories of Melody. Memories that threatened to snuff out the small amount of life that still remained in his soul. He knew he should get up, get dressed, walk away, and not look back. Trent needed to get this night behind him because if he didn't, he was sure to get burned. Yet he couldn't seem to move. His heart refused to be controlled by his mind.

Trent's mind reverted back to God. He used to be a strong believer in God, at least until Mel dumped him for his buddy Kent. How could he put his trust in a God who took his baby girl from him? After many sleepless nights with his heart ripping out of his chest, he turned into a stone. He became fearless and careless, which was why he ended up discharged out of the military. He needed to stop thinking about his past because with thoughts of his past came anger. He decided to ask Maggie another question about her God.

"So tell me, Maggie, if your prayers are left unanswered, why do you continue to pray?"

Maggie stretched and then cuddled a little closer to Trent. The warmth of his body felt good on her soft skin. She made small circles on his chest and simply replied, "I suppose I stand room for correction. God has answered one of my prayers."

"Oh really. Would you care to enlighten me?" Trent asked with a hint of challenge.

"He gave me the strength to parent an awesome son."

At that moment, more questions than Trent was capable of keeping up with bombarded his mind. But somehow, he only had the courage to ask Maggie one question. "Maggie, Shane did pay for the entire night, didn't he?"

"No, he didn't. But don't worry. I'm kinda thinking the bottle of wine covered the night."

"Thanks, Maggie. That's very generous of you."

"I'm feeling rather generous. By the way, I don't work on Sundays, so you're welcome to hang out in the morning."

"Wow! You're sweet."

"Thanks."

Silence.

"Good night, Trent."

"Good night, Maggie."

The next morning, Maggie awoke with the smell of bacon wafting in her room. She smiled as she pictured Trent in her small kitchen cooking. Yet somehow, it all felt right.

21

Over the next few weeks, Maggie and Trent fell into a routine that felt natural for both of them. For Maggie, Trent was an answered prayer. He gave her hope at a time in her life when she felt completely hopeless. Todd had pretty much written her off. He refused to return her calls, and Moe had walked out of her life. So yes, she felt completely alone. But now, she had her Sundays to look forward to.

Like clockwork, Trent showed at her place at precisely 10:00 a.m. every Sunday. Today, they planned to go on a picnic, which was something Maggie had not done for years. All week, she had looked forward to their day. That's what they called Sunday, *their* day. In between her customers, she found herself daydreaming about their times together. With each passing day, she felt herself falling more and more for Trent. And she could sense he was falling for her. Yet they never once talked about love or a future. They simply went with the flow and enjoyed the time they spent together.

Surprisingly enough, they have yet to have one argument. If they did not agree, they were adult enough to simply agree not to agree. Neither one of them have talked a lot about their previous relationships. Maggie was waiting for the right time to learn more about Trent's ex-wife. She had high hopes that today, she could approach the subject. She found it rather odd that he didn't ask a lot of questions about Todd. Every time she tried to bring up her son, Trent would change the subject. She could discern he had questions but wasn't yet ready to tackle them. What bothered Maggie the most was the darkness that was tucked away in Trent's heart. She was starting to feel a little concerned about the secrets he kept about his last tour overseas.

Maggie had read that men and women who served combat time rarely spoke of their experiences. But she wanted to know everything there was to know about Trent. So she would be patient. After all, isn't love patient? Besides, she still had some dark secrets tucked away in her heart. She hoped to start sharing some of her dark demons with him.

The one thing Trent was very adamant about was she was not, under no circumstances, to discuss her customers with him. It was almost as if he was in denial that she was a prostitute. She complied with his request. When they were together, she took on a complete different personality. She was no longer only giving herself away for several, but she was giving herself wholeheartedly away for love. For Maggie, at least one day out of the week her life seemed normal. She only prayed they not run into any one she may know. It wasn't often Maggie intermingled with the outside world, so she was a little apprehensive, especially for Trent.

How would he react if they should run into one of her customers? If they should run into someone who knew her as Mags the *prostitute*, how was she to respond? Oh, to have a normal life was all that tumbled around in her mind. Maggie decided to take her sweet grandmother's advice, God rest her soul. Worry was interest on trouble before it happens. Today, she planned to have fun and live a normal life.

"Now, what to wear?" Maggie whispered to herself, "Think *park*. Darn, I'm not used to going on a real outing."

In the end, she decided to wear a pair of her comfy blue jeans and a coral-colored cotton blouse. She applied a small amount of makeup and pulled her hair up into a simple twist. She sprayed a dab of perfume behind her ears and then slipped on her beige sandals.

Within no time, she heard a knock at her door. She was still trying to get used to Trent knocking. Moe always helped himself in, but then again, Moe did have a key to her apartment. She was grateful he left his key when he walked out on her because it would have been a pain to change her locks. And there's the fact that Todd still had a key. After all, it was still his home. She wanted him to know he was always welcome back home. She would have hated it if he would have tried to come home only to find the lock had been changed. No doubt he would have felt like she was rejecting him. And that was the last thing in the world she wanted him to feel.

Everything within Maggie wanted to tuck this day away in her heart. For years to come, she was sure she would treasure every single moment of this day. They enjoyed a simple lunch of bread, cheese, fruit, and ice tea.

They relished in the smell of the flowers and the sounds of nature as they walked around the park hand in hand. Trent was the perfect gentleman, and he treated her like a queen. He was everything she ever dreamed of having in a relationship and more.

They were sitting in a small coffee shop enjoying an ice coffee when Trent cleared his throat and spoke in a hush tone. "Maggie. . ." He trailed off for a bit and then continued, "You're beautiful."

Maggie blinked her hazel eyes trying to clear her running thoughts. She wasn't used to being told she was beautiful. Especially with such emotion intertwined in the heart of a man. Sure, from time to time, her customers would whisper sweet nothings in her ear. However, there would be no emotions involved in the words. But with Trent, Maggie could hear his heart in the words he spoke. Was this love? She really had no idea. She thought she loved Drake, but now, after today, she wasn't so sure.

Maggie absently looked around and silently thanked God for sparing her the pain of having a run-in with one of her customers. She also reminded herself that Trent was not a customer, but he had become someone whom she valued and admired in more ways than one. As Maggie looked into Trent's chocolate-brown eyes, she managed to forget there was still much to learn about him. She reasoned in her heart that in time, they would come to know each other quite well.

She continued to look into his eyes over the rim of her cup as she took a sip of her coffee. Before she dared to speak, she needed to moisten her dry mouth. She sat her cup down on the saucer with a clang and shyly replied, "Thank you . . . That's very kind of you."

"You're welcome. What do you say we go back to my place?"

Maggie arched her neatly shaped eyebrow and responded with a hint of surprise. He had never invited her to his place. She supposed it was because of her line of work. "Really? Your place?"

"Yes, really. Honestly, Maggie, you don't have to sound so shocked."

A short time later, Maggie found herself sitting on an overstuffed couch in Trent's cozy man's cave. At least, that's what he called it; however, she preferred to call it a living room. She was rather impressed with his ability to decorate. The room had a hint of a masculine touch, but it was not too overbearing. She was curious as to how he may have decorated the rest of his home. Maggie was sure in time, her curiosity would be appeased.

"Can I get you a glass of wine?"

"Yes, that would be nice."

"Okay, just make yourself at home." He paused for a moment and then added, "Maybe later I'll show you the rest of the house."

Maggie questioned if he read her thoughts. "That would be nice . . . I would really like that."

Trent winked and replied, "Be back in a few."

As Maggie took in every detail of her surroundings, she noticed a picture of a little girl sitting on the fireplace mantel. She ambled over to the fireplace and retrieved the picture. She would guess the girl to be five or six years of age. She was beautiful. She had Trent's chocolate brown eyes.

Trent cleared his throat as he walked over to the fireplace. He handed Maggie her glass of wine and then whispered, "To a great day."

Maggie clicked his wineglass and replied, "To a great day." They both took a sip of their wine, and then she asked, "Who is this little angel?"

"Her name is Tyleen. I called her Ty for short. She's my daughter."

Maggie noticed how he spoke with such reverence. "She's beautiful."

"Yes, she was."

Maggie was a little taken aback by the way Trent spoke in past tense about his daughter. She racked her brain trying to come up with something to say, but she was at a loss for words. So she simply placed the picture back on the mantel and took another sip of her wine.

"Why don't we have a seat? There are a few things I would like to discuss with you."

"Yeah, sure."

Maggie went back to the comfy sofa, and Trent sat close to her, but he was careful to leave a small amount of distance between them. He laid his head on the back of the couch and looked off into the distance for a beat. Maggie's own thoughts were bouncing around in the chambers of her mind. Where was all of this leading? Was she ready to hear what he had to say? Of course, she was. Suddenly, it occurred to her that God was answering one of her prayers. She had prayed earnestly that God would open Trent's heart to trusting her. She made a mental note to tell him God had indeed heard her prayer.

Trent twisted his head so he could have a clear view of Maggie. He wanted to look in her hazel eyes and swim in the depths of her pure soul. Yes, her line of work was about as adulterated as they came, but

Maggie Jenkins's soul was not contaminated. She was simply a victim of circumstances. That's all.

"Is Maggie your birth name or nickname?"

"Maggie is my birth name."

"Is that right?"

"Yep."

"What's your full name?"

"Oh, it's nothing fancy. It's actually pretty plan. My mom simply named me Maggie Sue."

"Jenkins?"

"Yes." Maggie retrieved her wineglass from the coffee table and took another sip. She counted to ten before looking back at Trent and asking the obvious. "Why?"

"Just curious, that's all. I think it suits you."

"Thanks. So if you don't mind me asking, what's your full name?"

Trent chuckled and then answered, "Trent Wesley Anderson III."

Maggie whistled as she sat her glass of wine back on the coffee table. She calmly stated, "Now, that's a pretty classy name. I'm surprised a classy guy like yourself would give a girl like myself the time of day."

Complete silence.

Trent didn't like the way Maggie belittled herself. He especially didn't like that her self-esteem was so low she would think so poorly about herself. She was a vibrant, benevolent, soft spoken, clever, and very attractive woman. Sure, her line of work wasn't exactly something to be proud of, but he planned to change that. At least, he hoped to. He was a little wary about approaching her with what was on his heart, but he did want to address the issue of her self-worth.

"Maggie, what do you mean by 'girl like myself'?"

"Need you ask? Trent, where are we going with all of this small talk?"

Trent stood to his feet and asked, "Would you like some more wine?"

Maggie retrieved her glass of wine and finished what was left. "Yes, that would be nice. Thanks."

"You're most welcome."

Within no time, Trent was back with the remaining bottle of wine in an ice-bucket. "I thought I would just bring the bottle on ice."

"That's very clever. And a cute little ice bucket, I might add," Maggie chimed.

"You like this, huh? I purchased it while stationed in Germany."

"Wow, Germany! I've never left this city, much less the state."

"You know, Maggie, I was thinking we can spend the entire evening, or night, just getting to know each other a little better. Does that sound okay?"

"Yes, of course . . . I mean, what better way to spend our evening . . . or night."

22

Yes, God had heard Maggie's prayer, and yes, she was as nervous as a sinner walking into His holy sanctuary for the first time. Was she really ready for this? Sure she was. After all, this is what she longed for. She wanted to get to know the man who had captured her heart, and in return, she wanted him to know her. All of her. But now the moment she had been praying for had arrived, she silently questioned how much she should share. Suddenly, like lightning, her own advice flashed across her mind. She needed to be completely honest and unreserved. Isn't that what she taught her son? Yes, she was ready to allow Trent into the dark rooms of her heart. But first, she desired to take a peek into his heart.

Trent felt his heart pounding in his chest like a jackhammer. Was he really ready for this? He supposed he would need to open the closed doors in his heart if he wanted to learn more about Maggie. Where should he begin? The idea of sharing his military experience tumbled around in his mind, but he realized he had already shared much of his military career with her, just not the worst part. So in the end, he decided to start with his marriage to Melody.

"So I guess I can go first," Trent stated.

"Yes, I think that would be appropriate. After all, this is your idea."

"You know, Maggie, I could take the easy way out by saying ladies first."

Maggie felt her heart skip a beat. When was the last time she was called a lady? She really had no idea, but she liked the sound of it, and she knew for certain she could get used to it. Especially by Trent. "I suppose you could, but I allow you the wonderful privilege of sharing your story with me first." She smiled and then took a sip of her wine.

"Okay, well, since you put it that way, I guess I have no choice."

Trent loved the way she made him feel so completely unreserved. As much as he hated to admit it, he had fallen in love with her. He only hoped she would trust him with her heart. At least a small portion of it. If everything went as he planned, he was sure he could easily win her entire heart.

"Let me start with Melody. . ." He trailed off for a heartbeat. "I suppose I can sum my relationship up with her in one word—*deception*. Okay, maybe I'm being a little harsh. We fell in love the summer of 1975 and was married by the summer of 1977. I joined the army, and within no time, I was accepted for ranger school. We were stationed at Hunter Army Air Field in Savannah, Georgia. We loved it there, and before we knew it, she was pregnant with our little angel, Tyleen. By 1983, I was sent to Honduras. I sent the family back home to Peoria. It was hard to leave them. But duty called. After my short tour in Honduras, I sent for my family. We moved into a small trailer just a few miles from post. We were still stationed at Hunter Army Air Field. I was gone a lot on training, and Mel—she suffered with depression."

Maggie could sense that Trent was about to share a piece of his heart that was difficult, even for him to reflect upon. She felt empathy for him. After all, she understood all too well how hard it was to reflect back on painful memories. But she realized there was a time and place that certain topics needed to be addressed, and this was the time and place.

Without second-guessing, she placed her hand in his. She loved the feel of his callused hands, and the warmth of his touch caused her heart to flutter. It occurred to Maggie that she didn't even know where he was employed. She figured by the feel of his hands, he worked hard labor. He definitely wasn't office material. Nevertheless, to Maggie, he was perfect. Yes, of course, he had flaws. But who didn't?

Maggie couldn't dismiss the notion that maybe she was nothing more than therapy for Trent. If she had a dollar for every time one of her customers had paid her to simply pour their heart out, she would have a good savings. After all, she was safe territory. There would be no worries of a commitment because she was a lady of the evening. Somehow, the thought made her want to release his hand. She was beginning to feel her mood slip into the shadows. Maggie was tired of being a puppet on a string. And at times, that's precisely how she felt.

Trent loved the way her soft hand felt in his. He felt a strength surge through his human spirit. She was willing him to continue, he could feel it.

He absently glanced over at the picture of Tyleen on the fireplace mantel. She was his pride and joy. He had never shared his feelings with another human about her. Not even his mom, God rest her soul. He most certainly refused to talk to God. To Trent, it was God who stripped him of everyone dear to his heart. And now, here he was once again, allowing his heart to be vulnerable. But he couldn't seem to stop himself from giving in to love.

Maybe it was because he sensed Maggie had a truck full of baggage. Surely she would be able to identify with him. Whatever the case, he felt completely at ease with her. Just the simple fact that she was willing to allow her guard down a notch or two was enough to make him feel comfortable. She didn't have to trust him, yet she did. Nonetheless, he was thankful she trusted him.

Trent felt Maggie trying to pull her hand away, so he tightened his grip just a tad. But not too much. He didn't want her to think he was trying to be overbearing or rough. He was sure she had experienced men treating her poorly. But he wanted to change all of that. He saw the beautiful china doll that was locked away in the heart of Maggie, and he didn't want to mar her.

He made small circles on her hand as he allowed his mind to travel down memory lane. Trent cleared his throat and then continued. "Tyleen was my pride and joy. She brought a ray of sunshine into my life. But then one day, while I was on field duty, I received orders from my platoon sergeant to pack up my belonging. The company commander wanted to see me right away. He neglected to inform me of the nightmare that awaiting me on the home front. As soon as I arrived at my commander's office, I was confronted with news that permanently changed my outlook on life."

Trent closed his eyes as images of his baby girl flashed across the screen of his mind. She was a rare jewel that sparkled for the world to see. But this God that Maggie trusted, the same God he use to trust, snatched her from him. And for the life of Trent, he couldn't seem to imagine why a loving God would allow his baby to drown. At the sound of Maggie's sweet voice, Trent was brought back to matters at hand.

"You know, baby, we don't have to do this." She moved closer to him and whispered in his ear, "I could think of other things we could be doing." She started nibbling on his ear, and then she made butterfly kisses across his cheeks until she finally captured his lips. Her kiss was deep and full of raw passion. She was about to move onto his lap when he pulled away.

He loved the way she felt against his body. He loved the way she called him baby. He loved the idea of taking her to his bedroom and showing her what real love was like. But he knew he couldn't allow the doors to his heart to shut. He couldn't allow another day go by without opening his heart completely to her because if he did, he might lock his heart and throw away the key.

"No, baby . . . I can't stop. Tonight, I want us to really get to know each other."

Maggie puckered her lips and then purred, "If you say so, big guy."

"You have no idea how bad I would love to take you up on your offer. But I can't."

"Okay."

"Well, I think you know where I'm going with this, so I'll try and be concise. My baby girl drowned in our pool. Melody was taking an afternoon nap when Tyleen decided to jump into the pool. About an hour later, Mel found her floating in the water."

Maggie felt her chest tighten and the air leave her lungs. She tried to imagine the pain Trent must have been carrying for all of these years. She could never imagine losing her Toddy. Yes, they had gone through a lot of tough times, and yes, Todd had drifted into the shadows for a while. But in the end, they also bounced back to be stronger and wiser. At least that was Maggie's perception.

When she spoke, her voice was shaky, "I'm so sorry that you had to go through such a difficult . . ." As hard as she tried, she wasn't able to keep her tears at bay. "I can't even imagine the heartache . . . the pain that you must carry . . ."

Trent ever so tenderly wiped the tears from Maggie's eyes. "Shhh, I'm okay. I have you. Yes, the pain will always be tucked away in my heart, but at least you brought sunshine back into my life."

"Aw, you're sweet."

"Thanks."

Complete silence for a beat.

Trent wrapped his arm around Maggie and then continued, "Needless to say, my marriage went to pot. We both started drinking heavy. I realized I needed to get myself together, or I would lose my career in the military. So I quit drinking as much, but with each passing day, she drank more. Until one day, I came home from a hard day of training in the field to find my wife in bed, wrapped in the arms of one of my buddies. My immediate thought was to kill both of them. But instead, I walked out and went to the closest bar, and I got stinking drunk. She left me for Kent . . . that's the guy's name that I fought with in Honduras. Yep, I covered his back a few times."

There was a blanket of silence for a beat, and then Trent continued.

"We divorced, and last I heard, they were living somewhere out west. Anyway, I put my entire heart into the military. I made sure I was assigned to every war that involved the army. But then my last tour, the Gulf War, while on a night raid, I got careless. I allowed my partner to get shot. I should have had his back covered, but I allowed my mind to be distracted by a young child. A little girl that reminded me of my Tyleen was coiled up in a ball in the corner of a dark room. When my partner Clark was shot, I was busy consoling the child. I laid on the child and was shot twice—once in my leg and another time in my shoulder."

Trent pinched the bridge of his nose and looked off into the distance. Maggie held his hand close to her heart and was about to speak when Trent continued.

"It was a young boy that shot us. I would say that he was about thirteen or fourteen. I can still see the expression in his eyes as he was getting ready to fire his gun to kill me. There was fear written all over his face. It was as if he was shocked that he had fired the gun, and he was about to kill me, so he thought. After he fired his weapon twice, he took off running. The last thing I remember was the hushed sounds of the little girl's cry."

Trent paused as his mind reflected back on that dark eerie night. He raked his free hand through his hair and then whispered, "So you see, Maggie, this is why I have a difficult time believing in God."

23

Maggie sat motionless for a heartbeat. She wanted so terribly bad to erase the pain etched across Trent's masculine countenance. But she, of all people, knew that wasn't at all possible. All she could do was pray for God's guidance. Everything within her knew it was God who caused their paths to connect. They both understood heartache, shame, and failing. Yes, they had both been dealt a bad hand of cards. But now, all of that is about to change. They now had each other. Even if their relationship never developed into anything more than friends and lovers, they at least understood each other and could have empathy for one another.

"I'm so sorry you went through such pain and experienced such loss," she managed to choke out.

Trent looked at Maggie through slanted eyes and asked, "Why should you be sorry, Maggie? It's not your fault. It's your God's fault. He's to blame."

Maggie quickly interjected, "No, you got this all wrong. Can't you see, it's God that caused our paths to cross? And He has answered my prayer. . ." She trailed off for a bit and then continued, "Yep, He sure has. I prayed for this night, you know—you and me, opening up to one another."

Trent gently brushed a strand of her light-brown hair from her face and looked into her hazel eyes as he tenderly whispered, "If you say so, Maggie. So now I'm all ears. I'm ready to hear your story. Thanks, by the way, for being such a good listener."

Maggie was able to discern Trent wasn't up to hearing about God. And that was okay. She was patient. Her "story" had taught her to be patient. She took another sip of her wine only to discover it had gotten warm. She was so engrossed in listening to Trent share his heart-wrenching story that she forgot about her wine. It was as if Trent had read her mind because he retrieved the cool bottle of wine and was about to top her wineglass off with some fresh wine. Maggie placed her hand over her glass. She had had enough wine. She needed to be able to think with clarity while she shared her past with Trent.

"Thank you. But I think I've had enough wine."

"I hear ya. I'm kind of in the mood for some coffee. How about you?"

"Actually, coffee sounds great."

Within no time, Trent was back with a carafe full of coffee and a tray with two cups, cream, sugar, and cookies. "I thought we could use something sweet with our coffee. I hope you like chocolate chip cookies."

"Aw, a man after my heart."

"Maggie, I'm trying. To win your heart, that is."

Maggie looked into Trent's eyes and found herself swimming in a sea of chocolate. What was it that she saw in those big puppy dog eyes? Love? Maybe, maybe not. One thing she knew for certain, he had her heart in the palm of his callused hands. "Well, I believe you're off to a good start."

"Would you like cream and sugar in your coffee?"

"I can do that—"

"No, I won't hear of it. Tonight, Maggie, you're my guest."

For a heartbeat, Maggie felt a little awkward. She wasn't accustomed to being treated with such respect. She licked her dry lips and shook away the awkwardness. "I'll have a little of both."

Trent poured her coffee into a cup and then added some cream and sugar. He placed the cup on a saucer along with two cookies. "Here you are, my dear." Trent poured himself a cup of coffee while Maggie nibbled on her cookie.

"Mmmm, this is really good. Did you make these yourself?"

"Aw, a woman after my heart. That you would dare to think I'm capable of whipping up such a masterpiece. I bought them at the bakery, just a few blocks from here."

Maggie was starting to slip back into her comfort zone. She spoke with a hint of flirtation, "Why, Trent, I honestly believe your hands are capable of creating all types of masterpieces. As a matter of fact, even now, at this very moment, I can feel them fashioning my heart."

"Baby, enjoy your cookie and tell me your story. Who knows, maybe later, I'll show you just how much your hands have fashioned my heart."

After indulging in two cookies and starting her second cup of coffee, Maggie decided she was ready to open every door to her heart. Doors she kept shut to the outside world most, if not all of her life. Somehow, in comparison to Trent's, her life seemed like a piece of cake. Nevertheless, she had her share of hard knocks, and she was ready for some love, peace, and joy.

"You know, Trent, as we both know, life is full of challenges and problems. I mean, we never know what awaits us. Why, our worst nightmare could be lurking just around the corner, anxiously waiting to plow us down. As I said, I could never imagine the pain you must have felt after the death of your beautiful daughter. Yet, somehow, you pulled through. Wow! You're quiet a man. You of all people know life is not a bed of roses, but one must work real hard at it. I guess what I'm trying to say is, I admire you more now than I did yesterday. Or even a few short hours ago, for that matter. And I'm sure in just a short time, I will admire you more than today. Tyleen, she was so beautiful, and a piece of her will always remain alive within you."

Complete silence for a heartbeat.

"I thank you, Maggie. There's something I would like to say. Something for you to tuck away in your heart and ponder on when you're alone in the midnight hour."

Silence.

"Well, are you going to share with me or not?" Maggie asked.

"Maggie, a rose must remain with the sun and the rain, or its lovely promises will never come true."

"Wow, thanks for sharing that profound piece of revelation. I will tuck it away in my heart. Actually, you just gave a great analogy of my story. You see, I allowed all of my promises to die. But I will remain optimistic. I believe in miracles. I believe dreams really can come true. I believe God has something mighty big up His sleeve. But for now, I'll simply share with you what I have allowed to die."

Maggie adjusted herself a little and laid her head on Trent's broad shoulder. Next to him, she felt safe. It all felt right. She breathed in his clean scent and then shut her eyes as she allowed her mind to drift back to a time when she knew what it was like to have a family.

"My daddy was a truck driver. He drove trucks for as long as I could remember. He was a good man, and he loved my mom with all of his heart. He worked long hard hours on the road making deliveries, but every time he came home, he always had a gift for Mom and me. I can remember running into his strong arms as soon as he walked through the doors of our small two-bedroom bungalow. We didn't have a whole lot of material riches, but there was a lot of love. My mom was a faithful member of the First Baptist Church, and she made sure we were at church every time the doors were opened. Daddy, he went with us when he was home. Yep, my childhood was perfect. My mom use to always tell me that one day, I would do a mighty work for the Lord. I used to dream of becoming a Sunday school teacher or maybe go off overseas and become a missionary."

Maggie sat quiet for what seemed to be eternity.

"But then one hot summer day, I met Drake. Man, I fell hard for him. I mean, he swept me off my feet. Sheesh, I was only fourteen when I met the joker, so it wasn't hard for him to take my breath away. Well, to make a long story short, I got pregnant with Todd and had him at the age of fifteen. My folks had a fit, and that's putting it mildly. Daddy pointed his finger at me and demanded I pack my belongings and leave. My mom simply turned her back on me as Daddy continued to scream Bible verses at me while he helped me pack my few belongings."

Maggie felt the hot tears trickle down her cheeks as she allowed her dad's cold words to replay in her mind. It was as if she was reliving that day all over again. Yet in a strange sort of way, for her, it seemed therapeutic.

"I could remember thinking, what happened to my loving parents? I mean, I was carrying their grandchild. Well, I walked away and didn't dare go back. That was the last time I saw them. I was told through the grapevine they have both passed. So I asked where they were laid to rest, and I went to visit them at their graveside. You're the only living soul I have ever shared this with. Funny how I feel so comfortable opening up to you."

"Maggie, look at me." She ever so slowly lifted her head and looked into his chocolate-brown eyes. "I feel so honored that you feel comfortable sharing with me." He kissed the tip of her nose and then captured her lips. He started to deepen the kiss but knew he needed to pull back. Later, they would have time for the physical. Now, however, they needed to clear out all of the cobwebs in their hearts. Lord help him, he loved this woman. "Now, go on and tell me the rest."

"Well, I walked to a pay phone and called Drake. He picked me up at a nearby gas station. Of course, I didn't dare tell him I was pregnant with his child. But I was sure he would have been thrilled. We spent endless days and nights basking in each other's love. At least, I thought he loved me. Well, once he figured out that I was 'knocked up,' as he so romantically stated, he left me high and dry. To make a long story short, I met Teri.

She was a prostitute, and well, she took me under her wings. I guess one could say she taught me how to become a professional lady of the evening. We became friends and agreed to share an apartment. But once I had my Toddy, she kicked me out. By this time, I had some money saved. I moved into my apartment, and well, you pretty much know the rest of my story."

Trent could tell Maggie was feeling shame. Shame was the last thing he wanted her to feel. In his eyes, she was one of bravest women he had ever met. He would love to get his hands on this Drake character. How could a man walk away from such a beautiful woman and his child? Maggie deserved happiness, and he planned to make her happy.

"Can you tell me about Todd? I guess in a funny sort of way, I feel I know him. I mean, walking into your apartment pretty much reminds me of Todd's Hall of Fame."

Maggie moved away from Trent and playfully poked at his ribs as she teasingly spoke. "Watch it there, big guy. I worked hard laminating those pictures. If you ask me, I think I was being pretty crafty and conservative too, I might add."

Trent gently grabbed Maggie's hand and pulled her closer to him. He pulled her oh so close that he could smell her minty breath and feel the warmth of her body. He whispered, "I have no doubt you were being crafty and conservative too, I might add. I guess when I walked into your apartment for the first time, I saw your true heart was splashed all over the wall. Yep, a true momma. One that loved her son with her entire heart."

For a fraction of a second, Trent thought about kissing her, but he decided they needed to continue their conversation. "Okay, I guess I need to confess to you my reason for avoiding talking with you about your son is because of Tyleen. I guess, until now, I wasn't ready to tackle the topic. But now you know about my baby girl, I would like to know more about Toddy."

Maggie breathed in and then ever so slowly exhaled. Where was she to begin? She decided to keep her thoughts about Todd short and simple. "Well, I guess your opinion about my décor says a lot. I do love my son with my entire heart. He's my world, my sunshine, and my pride and joy. He's a very intelligent young man and very creative. He loves to write, and he's very good at it. He is somewhat of a loner, and I guess that causes me some concern."

Maggie paused for a moment. She rubbed her hands together and then picked at her thumbnail. She closed her eyes as she bit her bottom lip.

This was more difficult than she thought it would be. In many ways, she watched her son die a slow death. Why in the world did she supply him with Jack Daniel's? What will Trent think of her? More than likely that she was of no account. Will he still want to continue to see her once he learned the truth? If only she could turn back time. But she of all people realized that wasn't at all possible. She made her bed, literally, and now she'll have to live with the choices she had made.

Without second-guessing, she simply blurted out the war that raged within her mind. "Truth be told, I failed miserably as a mother. I'm the reason Toddy stayed locked away in his room, drinking Jack Daniel's. I even supplied him with the Jack. My lifestyle pushed him completely out of my life. He won't even return my calls. I have no idea what's going on in his life . . . and I have no way of going to visit him. I miss him so much!"

And then she fell into Trent's opened arms and allowed her hot tears to fall.

24

For a heartbeat, Maggie sat motionless as the dark shadows of yesterday threatened to torment her mind. Her raw emotions caused her to feel exhausted, yet she also felt relieved that she had finally shared her tainted past with Trent. He deserved to know the truth, no matter how painful it was for her to relive. She did what was right. She didn't candy coat her dark past, but she allowed her heart to be completely unreserved. Yes, she spelled it out clear for Trent to read. There would be no reading between the lines. To put it plain and simple, she was a class-A failure.

Maggie pulled away from the warmth of his touch and squared her shoulders. Undoubtedly, he would show her the way out. Why would he want her to stay? Who wants sloppy leftovers? Why did she ever think they could have a future? Absolute nonsense. She was destined to give herself to one man after another. Maggie Jenkins would leave this life with a tale left untold.

Trent felt such a strong connection with Maggie. He couldn't describe what it was, but he knew it felt right. He planned to persuade her to make some permanent changes in her life. Yes, there was a lot they would need to work through, but he was up for the challenge. He was ready for this. He wanted to meet her son, he wanted to go to sleep with her in his arms, he wanted to wake up with her in his arms, and he wanted to shower her with the love she deserved.

He patted the sofa and whispered, "Baby, come back here."

She edged her way back into his arms and relished in his touch. Oh, how she wanted to declare her love for him. But instead, she simply laid her head on his shoulder and allowed him to drape his masculine arm around her.

"You know, Maggie, as I said, a rose must remain with the sun and the rain, or its lovely promises will never come true. I do believe you have weathered out many rainstorms and remained in the hot sun for long enough. Yes, I would say it's high time some of your promises start coming true. Because believe it or not, even I believe your God gave you some pretty awesome promises."

Maggie wasn't sure what to think. What was Trent trying to say? Her emotions were all over the map. She wanted to ask him where he was going with his little analogy, but she couldn't seem to open her mouth. It was as if her lips were sealed shut with super glue. With each passing second, she felt her heart racing faster. She couldn't help but feel a surge of hope. Maybe, just maybe, God was about to make some positive changes in her life.

"Maggie, baby, look at me."

She ever so slowly lifted her head and allowed her eyes to lock with his chocolate-brown eyes. She loved his eyes, his perfect nose, his full lips, and his chiseled facial features. She felt her breath catch in her throat as she managed to squeak out, "Yes?"

"You're the most beautiful woman I have ever laid eyes on."

"Really?" was all she could choke out.

"Yes, really."

Maggie wanted to pinch herself to make sure she wasn't dreaming. She couldn't believe he actually thought her to be beautiful. Yes, many men have told her she was a hottie, but she was rarely called beautiful. She tried to recall if Moe called her beautiful, but she couldn't seem to remember. If he did, surely she would remember. She recalled him calling her doll on more than one occasion. Whatever the case, did it really matter? All that mattered was Trent thought she was more than just a tumble in the sack.

Trent gently wrapped a strand of her soft hair around his index finger. He let out a low whistle and then commented. "You, baby, take my breath away, and you have my heart in the palm of your soft hand. I love you, Maggie," his voice was smoother than butter.

Could she trust him? Yes, she loved him, but could she really trust him? The one syllable word, *trust*, continued to tumble around in her mind which was already all over the map. She needed to give in to what her heart was screaming. *Trust him!* Maggie decided she was ready to take a leap of faith and plunge into this human emotion called love.

"I love you, too." She kissed his cheek, his nose, and then his luscious lips. After a few moments of their hearts soaring to the heavens, she pulled back and whispered, "And I think you're pretty hot."

Trent couldn't help but chuckle at the way she called him hot. She had no idea what she did to him. It was the little things she did that caused his knees to go weak and his world to spin. She was just Maggie. She never tried to be someone she wasn't, but she was just herself. He wouldn't want it any other way.

He realized she could have kept her dark mistakes from him, but she chose to share every hidden secret that was locked away in her heart. And that only made him love her that much more. He was feeling a little giddy, almost like a young teenager, as he looked into her hazel eyes. He longed to pull her into his arms and kiss away all of the pain and heartache. But he of all people knew that was not at all possible. So he decided to rib her a little for calling him hot.

"You know, Maggie, you really shouldn't use such flattery. I mean, really, I can't recall being called hot by such a beautiful lady." He paused for a bit and then continued, "Don't get me wrong, I like it. Especially coming from you."

Maggie moistened her lips, winked, and then mustered up her most seductive voice. "Baby, you're not just hot, you're sizzling hot." She crinkled her cute little nose and added, "And you're also the jack of all trades."

"Oh boy, flattery, will get you . . . somewhere with me, baby. There's a few minor details about us, I would like to talk to you about. Do you mind?"

"No, not all. I have all night."

Trent gently traced her lips with his index finger. He allowed his thumb to rest under her chin. They both sat in complete silence as they looked into each other's eyes. Maggie was trying to appear confident, but he saw vulnerability etched on her flawless face. He could only hope she would agree to his request, or he would be the one donning the vulnerability mask.

"You know, Maggie, here lately I have been thinking a lot about us. It's pretty clear we both share mutual feeling toward one another."

Trent paused as he contemplated how to broach the subject of marriage. He was sure his heart was leading him down the path of happily ever after. The shadow of darkness had finally passed, and he was walking into his sunshine. They have yet to have dissention against one another. They were like a hand in a glove, at least, that was his perception. But what if he was wrong? What if she still held on to dreams of yesterday? Was she really over Drake? Trent came to the conclusion that the only thing he could do was trust his heart.

He sighed and then softly placed both of his hands over her cheeks. His heart was racing faster than his mind could think. He hoped his eyes would convey what his heart so desperately longed to speak, but he couldn't seem to open his mouth. His tongue felt thick and his mouth dry. It was Maggie that caused a boldness to surge through him as she placed her soft hands over his. Her eyes spoke volumes. Yes, he saw a pure love and raw attraction projecting from her hazel eyes.

"Maggie, I love you. I want to help you. I want you to help me. Heck, you have already helped me. You brought sunshine on my cloudy days. I would like to make a proposition . . . if you don't mind." *Boy, I'm blowing this! I just sounded as if I wanted to make some sort of business deal.* "I'm not doing very well, am I?"

Maggie smiled as she tucked her chin. "Well, I suppose that depends."

"Oh? Depends on what?"

"On the proposition, of course."

"Yes, of course. Will you excuse me for just a moment?"

"Sure."

Trent was about to step across the threshold when he turned and said, "I'll only be a minute."

"Okay . . . One thousand one, one thousand two . . ."

"Right, I'll be back in a flash."

"One thousand ten."

"Maggie, you can slow it down just a tad."

Trent made his way back to Maggie within no time. She was flipping through one of his military magazines when he walked into the room. She looked up and immediately went back to counting. "One thousand and ninety-nine. Impeccable timing."

"Yes, impeccable timing," he slowly walked over to her and dropped to one knee, "but then again, I guess it's all part of being a former ranger for the United States Army."

"I guess so. Look, Trent, what are you up too?"

Trent presented her a beautiful antique ring with a ruby setting. "Maggie Jenkins, will you do this soldier the honor of becoming his bride?"

Maggie felt her world start to spin and her breath catch in her lungs. Isn't this what she longed for? She longed for Trent to want her not for just a few fleeting months but for forever. But she had been down this path before. Only to have her heart trampled on. Drake made so many false promises. It was all just an illusion on her behalf. She had waited and prayed for Drake's return for more years than even she cared to admit. Drake? What about him? What if he returned? Surely she was over him. She had given her heart to Trent. But was Maggie capable of giving her entire heart to another? This was too much. She felt drained. She felt as if she needed to get back to her own apartment. At the sound of Trent's voice, she was brought back to reality.

"Baby, it would be nice if you said something . . . anything." Trent felt his emotions take a nosedive. He was no man's fool. He saw the fear and uncertainty in Maggie's eyes. She was almost as white as a sheet. Why, it was as if she had seen a ghost. Maybe she had. Maybe memories of yesterday were tormenting her mind. She simply needed space. Yes, that's it, he was moving too fast, in all honesty, maybe even for himself.

Maggie quickly collected her running thoughts and tried to appear calm. This was Trent, the man she had fallen in love with. She could do this. There was absolutely nothing to fear or be ashamed of. He's a caring, loving, and genteel gentleman. He was so unlike any other man she had spent time with and was only the second man she had dared to allow into her heart. Yes, she shared the haunted memories of her past with him, but he didn't really know her likes and dislikes. Yes, that's it. She needed to make it clear to him that they needed to learn each other's likes and dislikes.

No, that wasn't the answer. She simply needed her space. She needed to go back to doing what she did best. Todd was right. One can lead a horse to water, but one can't make her drink. She had been drinking from polluted waters for so many years that the taste of freshwaters was bittersweet to her senses. Why did he have to go and ruin things? Why couldn't he have just left well enough alone? Yes, she wanted to take their relationship to another level. But marriage? Honestly?

Maggie placed her hand over Trent's, and she spoke just above a whisper, "I'm ready to go home. I have a busy day planned tomorrow."

Trent was barely able to speak past the lump that instantly formed in his throat. "Look, Maggie, I understand if you need your space." His grandmother's wedding ring fell to the floor when he pulled away to rake his hands through his hair.

Maggie reached down to retrieve the ring. She placed it in the palm of her hand and then looked at Trent. She could hardly see him through the tears in her eyes. "Baby, I do love you." She wrapped her dainty fingers around the ring and then continued, "I just need time. That's all. I mean, things are going too fast."

Trent felt a flicker of hope surge through his heart. She loved him. Of course, she did. What they shared was real. However, he couldn't bear the thought of her giving herself away to countless men. She was too good of a woman for that. She had a good soul. She was a child of God. Yes, maybe he had problems believing in her God, but she still believed, and he planned to remind her of that.

"Baby, I agree. Maybe I was rushing things along. It's just that I love you so much."

"I know you do."

"Maggie, going back to the proposition."

"Yes."

"I propose that tomorrow, you spend your day contacting all of your clients to inform them that you have retired from your profession as lady of the evening. I, in return, will cover all of your bills and make sure money is kept in your account. Now, before you say no, I realize I'm asking a lot—"

"Okay."

"Okay?" he asked.

"Yes, okay."

"Well, I wasn't done with my proposition."

"Don't push it, buddy."

"I was only going to ask in return, you schedule me for every day of the week. Except for Sundays, of course. I would like to get to know you a little better. Oh, and Sundays are to remain our day. Free of charge, of course."

Maggie couldn't believe what her ears were hearing. It was as if Trent had read her very thoughts. She gave him her heartwarming smile and then spoke in a coy way, "Baby, you have yourself a deal." She then opened her hand to relinquish the ring, but to her surprise, Trent placed his callused hand over hers.

"I would very much like for you to keep the ring." When she tried to protest, he held his hand up in protest. "I'm not asking you to wear it on your hand. I'm only asking you to look at the ring if you should feel doubt about us. The ring was my dear grandmother's. It's very sentimental to me."

Maggie was lost for words. Trent's words were sweeter than honey. She could literally see the love in his eyes. He was definitely a keeper. She would be a fool to walk away from him. Yep, she was about to prove her son wrong. She was not only going to drink from the cool waters, but she was also going to allow the freshwaters to cleanse her soul.

Maggie ever so slowly placed the ring on her right finger and then tenderly replied, "If you don't mind, I would like to wear it. Besides, I have you scheduled for every day of the week, so I don't believe doubt will be able to easily take up residence in my heart."

"Okay, if you insist," Trent teasingly remarked.

25

Todd replayed the message Maggie left on the answering machine a few times. He wanted to be certain he had heard her correctly. According to her, she had met her soul mate, and she had fallen in love. What really threw Todd for a loop was the mere fact she contemplated marriage. As hard as he tried, he simply couldn't imagine Maggie settling down and tying the knot, so to speak.

He eyed the small answering machine as he sipped on his drink. He had slowed down on his drinking, but for some reason, the sound of Maggie's voice caused him to crave the dark liquor. Todd questioned why he once again felt the need to hear the sound of Maggie's voice. He slowly sat his goblet on the end table and then pushed the Play button on the machine. He then heard the sound of his own voice.

"It's Todd, leave a message at the sound of the beep."

And then Maggie's sweet voice chimed. In an odd sort of way, it was like sweet music to his ears.

"Toddy, it's Mags. Why are you ignoring me? I have only called umpteen times. First things first, I love and miss you like crazy. Okay, I know I only have a minute, so I have to get straight to my reason for calling. Toddy, I've fallen in love, and I believe I'm going to get married. His name is Trent, and he's wonderful. I just know you would like him and he you. He already asked me to marry him, but I haven't exactly given my answer. Anyway, like I said, I really think I'm going to do it. Can you believe it Toddy? I finally found my soul mate. Hey, Toddy, I'm finally getting my life together. You know, I quit the job . . . I'm no longer, well, you know what I'm trying to say. Look, call me, my number is the same. Have you met any friends? Do you have a girlfriend? Have you started writing that novel? Okay, hugs and kisses. Remember, I love you!"

Todd downed his drink and was about to pour himself another when the sound of Misfit's bark deterred him. He looked around to find his dog standing by the door. Todd felt a little bit of a rush as he stood to his feet. Maybe he was feeling the effect of the Jack Daniel's, or maybe it was the sound of Maggie's voice that got him all hyped up, or maybe it was a combination of both. Whatever the case, he knew he needed to pull himself together because he had his job to think about. Todd had become a bit cautious after showing up on his job with a hangover a time or two. And then there was Grant. There was something about him that made Todd want to do better for himself.

Todd walked over to Misfit and playfully rubbed behind his ears. "What is it, boy? Huh? Are you wanting to go for a walk?" Misfit wagged his tail and barked a few times. "I guess that's a yes. Well, I tell you what, I think I'm in the mood for the park."

CB EO

Tessa had just finished placing her dish in the sink when she heard her mom call for her. "I'm in the kitchen, Mom."

Jenna came waltzing into the kitchen with sparks flying from her eyes. There was no questioning the love she and Grant shared for one another. Tessa was happy for her. For both of them, really. "There you are. What's up?"

"What's up?" Tessa asked.

"Yes."

Tessa giggled and then spoke a tad bit chipper than she intended, "What's up? I just enjoyed a bowl of chicken noodle soup along with some yummy buttered whole-wheat bread. That's what's up."

Jenna placed her hands on her hips and then replied, "Oh, I was about to ask if you wanted to join us for lunch at Peg's. But since you already ate . . . I tell you what, why don't you come along and have a salad?"

"I would love to, but I'm supposed to be at the park with Hunter. We're going to do some studying together. As a matter of fact, he's probably already there, wondering where I'm at."

"Okay, but we'll do it another time. Grant wanted some family time with his two favorite girls."

"Yes, I'll definitely take a raincheck. You and Grant go have fun. But hey, if you really love me, bring me back an Italian sub. I'll have it later."

"Okay, we can do that."

"I gotta go. Love you, Mom."

"Love you too, Tess."

Within no time, Tessa was turning into Glenn Wood Park. She loved her little Toyota Tercel her mom surprised her with. It was easy to drive and got good gas mileage. She chuckled at the sight of Hunter sitting at their favorite place under a weeping willow tree. It was their favorite spot because it was far enough from the public pool that they wouldn't hear the sounds of screaming kids. She put her car in park, grabbed her oversized handbag, and then exited. She looked up to see Hunter coming her way.

"Hey, you. I was beginning to think you forgot."

"Nope, not at all. I just got a little tied up with Mom."

"Is everything okay?" Hunter asked.

"Yeah, she invited me to Peg's for lunch with her and Grant, and we got caught up in conversation."

Hunter placed his hand over his chest and teasingly remarked, "And you declined on my account? I'm so touched. I mean, you just made my day. You made me feel so special."

"Whatever, Hunter. You don't have to get carried away." Tessa playfully nudged his shoulder with hers and then continued, "Besides, I could really use your help with my studies."

"Oh, I get it. You're planning to use my intelligentsia and then throw me to the curb."

"*Intelligentsia?* Really, Hunter? Boy, you just used that word out of context. I'm not so sure I made the right choice. Maybe I should have went to lunch with my folks."

By now they were making themselves comfortable under the willow tree. "Oh, really. How so? The word, that is. And yes, you made the right choice. By spending your afternoon with me, that is."

"Hunter, intelligentsia is reference to a group or class of people. Yes, I desired to tap into your intellectual ability of thinking. However, now I believe the logical thing for me to do is simply dig a little deeper into my thinker." She paused for a moment and took a deep breath. "*Comprendes?*"

"Oh, I understand quiet well. Are you sure it shouldn't be *entiendes?*" They both busted out in laughter.

CR&

Todd stood in the shadows, not desiring to been seen by Tessa. He knew it was her. He would recognize her laugh from anywhere. He didn't want to be seen by her, but he wanted to soak in her beauty. As hard as he tried, he couldn't seem to shake her out of his mind. She had literally kept him awake at nights. He questioned why she continued to haunt his memories like an unwanted plague haunted its victim. He supposed it was her raw beauty and purity.

Whatever the case, he realized she was way out of his league. Sure, she was polite when he experienced his brief encounter with her right here at the park. But she was more than likely just being friendly because of Misfit. Todd knew all too well that girls like her never fell for guys like him. He was raised in a dysfunctional home, whereas she was more than likely raised in the all-American home. If there was such a thing.

Todd knew he needed to leave because he had Misfit tied in the bed of his truck. He was sure that Misfit was fine. He had parked under shade and made sure Misfit's bowl was filled with cool water. They ran a few laps around the park, so Misfit was pretty tuckered out. Todd raked his hands through his hair and was about to walk to his truck when he noticed the guy sitting next to Tessa poking at her. They appeared to be enjoying each other's company. Why did this make him feel jealous?

Todd longed to be the man sitting next to her. Was this guy even a man? He appeared to be young. Too young for Tessa, at least that was Todd's opinion. No doubt he was her little yuppie boyfriend. He looked like one of the college guys who attended the university, which would explain why she was attracted to the character. Todd leaned against the picnic table and allowed his mind to get lost in the thoughts that flooded his heart.

In the eyes of Todd's heart, he was the man sitting under the willow tree with Tessa. They were laughing and enjoying the afternoon sunshine while drinking some cool spring water. She was sharing her likes and dislikes. He made sure she had his full attention while she chatted away.

And then, he noticed a lock of her hair fall over her blue eyes, so he casually tucked it behind her ear. He could easily swim in her eyes because they are as blue as the ocean. In the eyes of Todd's mind, he was about to kiss her, when he heard Misfit's bark. He shook his head and chided himself for thinking such foolish thoughts.

CRBO

"Hunter."

"Yes, Tess."

"Did I ever tell you why I love the weeping willow tree?"

"No, I don't believe so. But I would love to know why."

"It's really kind of silly," Tessa replied.

"Probably not near as silly as my reason."

"Okay, when I was I child, I use to pretend the weeping willow was my house. . ." Tessa trailed off for a beat as she allowed her mind to go back in time. She continued, "Yep, I would place all of my dolls under the tree and mother them for hours. I must admit, back then, I made a pretty good mom. However, now I'm not so sure I'll make a good mother."

"Aw, come on, Tess. You'll make a great mom. So who was the daddy?"

"Promise you won't laugh?" Tessa asked."

"I promise I will try not to laugh."

"Okay, good enough. My husband—the father of my baby tender loves—was Ken."

As hard as Hunter tried, he wasn't able to contain his laughter. Tessa threw her pencil at him and shrilled, "Hey, I loved Ken and Barbie. I thought Ken was a pretty cool guy, and I found Barbie to be the most beautiful doll ever."

"Absolutely crazy," Hunter said, "but then again, I guess now I know why you want to be a psychiatrist."

"Hey, watch it."

"Okay, okay, so you had an infatuation about Ken. I mean, it's not that big of a deal. At least you outgrew the dude. Let me ask you this, did you have one of those Ken dolls? And did you pretend to be Barbie?"

"Duh, of course I did. Okay, enough about my reason for loving the tree. Now, tell me yours."

"Well, I guess fair is fair. My buddies and I use to pretend to live in the Wild West, of course, we were wild and crazy cowboys. Anyway, we used the willow tree as a jail."

"Hunter, that's so cute. So did you ever end up in jail?"

Hunter shrugged his shoulders and replied, "Maybe a few times."

"Okay, so did you figure out how easy it would be to escape?"

"We were kids, pretending. You know, kinda like you never figured out that your husband was a complete moron."

"Hey, back off, Hunter. That's the father of my babies you're talking about." They both laughed out loud.

"Well, I have to admit, Tessa, your reason for loving the tree is a little sillier than mine."

"That's a matter of perception, Hunter."

Hunter tapped Tessa on the nose and whispered, "I suppose you're right."

Tessa felt her heart skip a beat and then whispered, "I know I'm right. Hunter, it's been a while since we lay under the stars at the tracks. Why don't we meet there tonight at around nine o'clock?"

"Sounds good to me, Tess."

26

Trent wanted to pinch himself to make sure he wasn't dreaming. His life was almost perfect. Once Maggie became his bride, his life would be perfect. They were at the local supermarket to purchase some steaks for dinner. He was about to ask her if she wanted New York strip or rib eye when the thundering sound of a male's voice interrupted his train of thoughts.

"Hey, doll, is that really you?"

Maggie wished the ground would open from under her feet and swallow her. Was her ears playing tricks on her? Was that really the sound of Moe's voice that hovered over her like an unwanted rain cloud? Surely her eyes and her ears were not playing tricks on her because as sure as she was Maggie Jenkins, Moe was standing just a few feet away. Her sunshiny day was about to be rained on. He was so close she could smell his cheap aftershave and alcohol on his breath. He had picked up a few pounds around the waist, but other than that, he hadn't changed much.

Trent couldn't believe Moe knew his Maggie. Trent worked with the guy at Caterpillar. Moe hadn't been working there for long, but Trent knew trouble when he saw trouble. There was no questioning Moe was trouble. He was short-tempered, and not many of the guys at work cared much for his attitude. On more than one occasion, Trent smelt sour whiskey on Moe's breath.

Moe staggered over to Maggie and pointed his index finger at her as he slurred out, "It is you? Doll, what are you doing here? Shouldn't you be working? It's not Sunday, is it?" Moe looked at Maggie in a condescending way and then hissed, "Why do you have to be so beautiful?"

Trent had to literally hold his right hand down with his left hand to keep from punching Moe square in the nose. Who did he think he was? He had no right talking to his woman that way. Trent took a step toward Moe and was about to speak his mind, but Moe glared at him and asked, "Are you with her? Wait. I know you. You work at Caterpillar. Where I used to work."

"Moe, she's my fiancée, and I don't particularly care for the way you're talking to her. Yes, I work at Cat. What do you mean by where you used to work?"

"That sorry foreman fired me today for no reason." Moe glanced back at Maggie and then back at Trent. He shook his head and remarked, "Did you say you're engaged to be married to that low, down, no good for nothing—"

"Why, you sorry drunk—"

Maggie jumped in front of Trent, and she looked at him with pleading eyes. She managed to keep her voice calm as she tenderly spoke. "Come on, baby, let's just go. Please?"

Trent wanted to take her in his arms and protect her from the accusations Moe threw her way. But he knew all too well Moe's harsh words were words his Maggie was accustomed to hearing. He knew one day this would happen. Yep, sooner or later, they were bound to run into someone from Maggie's tainted past. He should have been prepared for it, but he wasn't. Hearing someone speak so poorly about the woman you loved was something a guy is never fully prepared for.

She was right. They needed to leave. He wanted to learn more about his soon-to-be wife. And he planned to start by finding out just what kind of relationship she had with Moe.

"You're right, baby. Come on, let's go."

Maggie sighed with relief, but she knew she had some explaining to do when they got back to Trent's place.

Moe stood flabbergasted for a few moments. After his brief encounter with Maggie and Trent, he found himself completely sober. He couldn't believe after all of these months, he finally saw Maggie. She looked beautiful. He was shocked that a guy like Trent would marry a girl like her. He was even more shocked she refused to become his bride. Wasn't he good enough? What did Trent have that he didn't have? Only one thought came to his mind: a job.

Moe raked his hands through his hair and then down his whiskered face. Reality set in like an unwanted flu virus. He was jobless, and if he didn't get his act together, he would soon be homeless. Moe absently looked around the store, and once he realized there were no spectators, he made his way out the door. He felt so very alone, and for the first time in his life, he felt completely helpless. Maggie's son, Todd, flashed across his mind like lighting. He felt a chill run down his spine as he thought of the taunting remarks he slurred at the young guy.

Moe drove in the darkness as he allowed his mind to drift back to years ago. When he was a young boy, he remembered a church bus picking him up every Sunday for Sunday school and morning worship. For the few short hours he spent in church, he remembered feeling such a strong peace. A peace he had not felt for years. His mom and dad never went to church with him. His dad claimed church was for weak-minded folks. His mom simply claimed she served the good Lord her own way at home. His folks weren't bad people. They always treated others the way they would want to be treated. They simply never advocated going to church.

Moe could recall his best friend making a pact with him when they were about eight years of age. His friend promised if Moe went to Sunday school with him, he would in return walk with Moe to school and teach him how to throw a ball. Moe never liked walking to school by himself mainly because his peers made fun of him. He could hear the acidic words like it was only yesterday. *Hey, goofball, are you gonna try out for baseball again this year?*

Moe was never good at playing sports. His dad always told him he was born with two left hands. And then there was his birth given name, Hermon. For the entire twelve years he attended school, his classmates ribbed him about his name. He gave himself the nickname Moe once he graduated high school. He thought Moe sounded much more macho. Yeah, right, who was he trying to fool? He was about as macho as a clown in a circus. At the moment, he felt like a big clown.

There was one particular song Moe remembered the church choir singing during the morning worship called "Amazing Grace." The first stanza seemed to play over and over in his mind. Before he knew it, he was singing from the very depths of his heart.

"Amazing grace! How sweet the sound
That saved a wretch like me!
I once was lost but now am found,
Was blind but now I see."

Moe felt hot tears roll down his whiskered face. How long had it been since he cried? Too many years. As he sang, he felt the peace his soul had been longing for. Suddenly, it occurred to Moe he was feeling the same peace he felt when he was a young boy in church. He realized exactly where he longed to be. Church. And he knew of the perfect inner city church just down the road from Maggie's.

CӠ ᘓ

Trent drove in complete silence. It seemed he had been driving for miles, but he had only gone a few miles. His heart bled for the woman he loved. He wanted to shield her from her past, but he knew all too well that wasn't possible. Even if they packed up and moved, a piece of her past would always follow her. Yes, the chances would be slim for them to have another encounter like they endured tonight, but the dark shadows of yesterday would always lurk in the recess of their mind.

He loved her with all of his heart mind and soul. He was willing to walk with her through every dark hour and protect her reputation. She was his soul mate, and he refused to allow her to be battered, mistreated, or harmed in any way. He would defend her to the very end. Why? Because that's what love does. He had his own demons that threatened to torment him, so who was he to judge? Even if he had the perfect life, he wouldn't judge her. Come to think of it, Maggie made his life perfect. In his eyes, everything about her was perfect.

Trent didn't like seeing her looking so vulnerable. He wished they would have stayed home and ordered some pizza or Chinese food. It was his lame idea to go out and buy steaks. What was he thinking? He could sense she needed her space, but oh, how he wanted to pull her in close to him. His consolation was knowing she was strong. She would come around, and when she did, she would act as if nothing happened. He decided he didn't want to know how she came to know Moe or what kind of relationship they had. He simply wanted to put this night behind them. If that was at all possible.

In spite of everything, Maggie felt Trent's love. She felt absolutely no negative vibes projecting from the man who captured her blackened heart. She twisted the engagement ring on her finger and silently thanked

God for a second chance at love. Heck, to Maggie, she was also receiving a second chance at life. She was no longer the woman Moe knew, but she was Trent's fiancée. She was not going to allow one bad episode to ruin a perfectly good evening. It was pretty obvious Moe had drank one too many shots of whiskey.

Maggie supposed in a funny sort of way, she felt sad for Moe. Yes, he was a little rough around the edges, but deep in his heart, he was a good guy. She hated to hear he lost his job. She had no idea he worked at Caterpillar with Trent. Maggie was sure she would experience more encounters such as tonight. After all, Peoria wasn't that big of a city. At least they would be living in East Peoria. Somehow that made Maggie feel a little more at ease about pursuing a future with Trent in this area. She only prayed Trent was up for the challenge. From what she witnessed tonight, she would say that he was.

She also wished Todd would return her calls. She would love for him to meet Trent. If only she had done things differently. Todd deserved better. But she knew all too well she couldn't turn back time. All she could do was pray and wait for her son to come back around. She knew in her heart of hearts he would. She would be patient.

Maggie wondered what he might be doing. It killed her that their relationship drifted so far apart. Why in the world did he have to go and move to Macomb? What troubled Maggie the most was his drinking. She could only pray he wasn't sitting alone in some dark apartment, drinking his life away. She felt chills run down her spine at the very thought of him being alone in this cold world. Surely by now he had adapted and had friends. Who was she trying to fool? This was Todd she was worried about. He was more than likely the biggest introvert on planet earth.

Maybe she should ask Trent to take her to Macomb. She was sure he would be more than willing to comply. He had mentioned he would like to teach her how to drive. Maggie had made up in her mind that she would take him up on his offer. It was time she learned how to venture out into unfamiliar territory.

27

Maggie had finished up her last bite of Caesar salad, and she was about to ask Trent if he would like a refill on his tea when he rested his hand on hers. She allowed herself to get lost in his chocolate brown eyes. He had the most beautiful almond-shaped eyes and had eyelashes that most women would give anything for. After the lifestyle she led, how could she be so blessed? There was no questioning his love for her. She saw it written all over his face and radiating from his eyes. She wondered if when he looked into her eyes, he was able to see the depths of her love for him. She certainly hoped so.

"Baby, the salad was great," Trent commented.

"Thanks. I actually think I enjoyed it much more than I would have steaks," Maggie replied. At the mention of steaks, she was brought back to the situation at hand. She realized she had some explaining to do. It was time for her to tell him about Moe.

"I couldn't agree more," Trent tenderly remarked. "Baby, what do you say we just forget about what happened at the store? I would much rather focus on our future and getting to know more about you."

Maggie bit the bottom of her lip as she considered what Trent suggested. She would love to simply put her past behind, but she knew that would not be possible. There would always be a piece of her dark past lurking around the corner threatening to haunt her and even Trent. As a child, she would dream of falling in love, and now her dream had finally come true. Maggie refused to take a chance of losing Trent. She had to keep the door of communication open. Even she knew all it took was just one time of trying to sweep her dark past under the rug, and the door would slowly start to shut.

"Trent, I agree with you. We do need to get to know each other better, and I love focusing on our future. Now that I have you, I couldn't imagine life without you." She paused for a heartbeat and then continued, "So I think I'll start with Moe. I want you to know about him. I desire to keep every door open in my life for you to freely peep in. Even those doors I would much rather slam shut. I especially desire to keep the door of communication open."

Trent felt his heart swell with love. He didn't think it was possible he could love Maggie any more than he already had, but he did. He loved that she wanted to be completely unreserved with him. He could sense she had allowed her heart to be an open book for him and him alone to read. He planned to enjoy every chapter. Even the dark chapters she would much rather forget.

"Maggie, I love you. Thank you for longing to share every chapter of your life with me. I promise to never judge, but my love will simply grow stronger. To me, Maggie, you're a flawless jewel."

Maggie allowed his soothing words of love to seek into her heart. He was more than she could have ever dreamed of having. To her, he was perfect. She smiled at him and then proceeded to tell him about Moe.

"Thank you for loving me and seeing it my way. I can only pray as time slips by, you will continue to love me."

"Oh, no worries, I will."

"Well, I think I can simplify my relationship with Moe. Convenience . . . Moe was simply a convenient relationship. He was safe for me. I knew he would make my life seem somewhat normal, and there was no danger in me falling in love with him. I really can't say how long we continued to see each other. He simply came around on Sundays, and after a few years, I allowed him to have a key to my apartment. I guess my reasoning for giving him a key was so if something should have happened, he would be able to get into my apartment. He did leave the key when he broke off our relationship."

Maggie paused long enough to refill both of their glasses of ice tea. She took a sip of her tea and then continued, "You see, everything was going great. So I thought until Moe fooled around and fell in love with me. On more than one occasion, he asked me to marry him. The first few times, I was able to blow him off. But he became more and more serious, and eventually, I wasn't able to change the subject. So to simplify everything, he stormed out of my life about as mad as a wildcat. Needless to say, it seems he has not cooled down much."

She felt her mouth going dry, so she took another sip of her tea. "I guess in some ways, I missed having him around. It was as if he fell off the planet. Moe is not really a bad sort of guy. Fact is he treated me very well. I can't say I like the way he spoke to Toddy, but I was able to put him in his place. It was just that my Sundays seemed empty without Toddy and Moe. I refused to work on Sundays until loneliness set in. Anyway, that was then, and this is now. Hey, I was a little shocked to learn the two of you worked together."

Trent chuckled and then replied, "Well, we didn't work together as alongside each other. I saw him around a few times." Trent thought about mentioning that he was trouble, but he decided to leave well enough alone. "And you're 100 percent correct. That was then, and this is now."

Trent brought her hand to his lips and tenderly placed a kiss on the palm. She relished at the feel of his lips. He then winked and whispered, "I would like to learn more about you. You know, your likes, and you can throw in your dislikes, if you desire."

Maggie managed to say, "Okay." He had a way of tilting her world. She finally whispered, "Did I ever tell you that my favorite flowers are daisies?"

No, but I'm thankful for that tidbit of information. I will tuck it away in my heart."

"What about you? What's your favorite flower?" Maggie asked.

"Dandelions," Trent replied.

"Really? Why?" Maggie asked.

"Because they grow wild, and they are full of wishes."

"Well, we have yet another thing in common."

"Oh?"

"Yep, daisies grow wild too."

"Maggie, I believe we have many things in common."

Maggie smiled as she looked off into the distance. She felt her heart fill with joy as she allowed her mind to travel down memory lane. A time when she was close to her mom. "Mom loved to dance. Often times, after Dad left for work, she would play some of her old records and teach me how to move and grove to the songs. She taught me everything from slow dancing to doing the twist. She loved Elvis. We danced together for hours. I can remember her picking me up and twirling me around. Yep, those were some good times." She looked up at him and asked, "Can you dance?"

Trent laughed and remarked, "Baby, I have two left feet. I would love for you to teach me a few moves."

"I can do that. Did I mention my favorite song?"

"Nope, I don't believe you have. Please, tell me."

"It's 'Somewhere over the Rainbow.' I use to listen to it for hours at a time."

"Has your dreams finally come true, Maggie?"

"Yes, I finally found my way over the rainbow."

"I'm glad," he said.

"What about you? What's your favorite song?"

Trent felt a little ornery as he allowed his answer to roll off his tongue. "'Wild Thing,' I think I love you."

"So, your favorite song is 'Wild Thing'?" Trent started laughing, and Maggie joined him. "Well, is it?"

"It used to be."

"So enlighten me. Who wrote the song?"

"Chip Taylor wrote the song." Trent smiled and started singing, "Wild thing, you make my heart sing." He then stood to his feet and asked Maggie to dance with him while he sang to her.

"Oh, so now you're ready to learn how to dance?" she teasingly asked.

For the next few moments, they swayed to each other's heartbeat. It was Trent who broke the silence. "Remember the little country church you fell in love with just outside of Pekin?"

"Yes, I do. If my memory serves me correctly, I suggested we get married there."

"Yes, you did. I just thought you would like to know I took the liberty to speak with the pastor."

Maggie arched her eyebrows and looked at Trent in a rather coy way. "And?"

"Well, he indicated it was better for man to marry than to burn. Of course, I wholeheartedly agreed with him."

Maggie rubbed the nape of his neck and purred, "And?"

"Well, I kinda took the liberty to set up a date for him to marry us."

"I see," Maggie chimed.

"I see? Is that all you have to say?"

"Have I told you I enjoy eating popcorn in bed?"

Trent held back his laughter. "No, I don't believe so. But I don't have a problem with that as long as it's covered with lots of butter."

"Yes, I like lots and lots of butter. Did I mention to you I really want a toy Yorkie?"

Trent brushed her lips with a kiss and whispered, "No, but tomorrow, I'll go buy you one."

"Really?" she asked.

"Yes, really. What shall we name him?"

"I was thinking we could name her Yorkie."

"Sounds wonderful. Shall we invite Yorkie to our wedding?"

"But of course." She captured his lips and kissed him with a passion that told him what he desired to hear. Come next week, she would be his bride.

"Exactly what day did you have set aside for our wedding?"

"Friday."

"I'm kinda thinking it would be nice to invite Todd."

"I think that's a great idea. Do you think he will come?"

"I don't know, but it won't hurt to give him a call."

"Baby, I totally agree with you," Trent replied.

Later that evening, Maggie sat in her tiny apartment. She had been busy packing up her belongings. By this time next week, she would be living where her heart was. With Trent. They say home is where your heart is, and hers was where ever Trent was. After spending some time in prayer about calling Todd, she felt the peace she longed for. Trent gave her the exact address to the church, so Todd shouldn't have a problem finding the place. She took a few deep breaths and then picked up the phone to call her son.

Todd had just come in from taking Misfit for his evening walk and was about to jump in the shower when the phone rang. Without second-guessing, he picked up the receiver and answered, "Yeah."

"Toddy, it's me, Mags."

Silence.

Todd didn't know what to say. Her voice sounded so sweet to his ears. He had forgotten just how soft-spoken she was. At that moment, he realized just how much he had missed her. Why hadn't he called her before now? He could kick himself in the backside for ignoring her for so long. She did the best she could. He had no right giving her the cold shoulder.

"Maggie-pie?" Her nickname came out like a question. He felt the walls around his heart begin to crumble.

Maggie felt her heart skip a beat at the sound of her son's voice. How many years had it been since he called her Maggie-pie? She wished she could reach through the phone and touch him. She longed to hold him. She longed to tell him how much she loved and missed him. She longed to look into his ice-blue eyes and smell the scent of aftershave. But she realized she couldn't, so she simply replied, "Toddy, it's about time you take my call. I miss you like crazy."

"I've been pretty busy. I miss you too."

Maggie heard the sound of a dog bark in the background. She asked, "Is that a dog I hear?"

"Yes."

"Well, what's your dog's name?"

"Misfit," Todd answered.

Silence.

There were so many questions Maggie longed to ask, but she held her tongue. She knew her son all too well. He would close up on her if she started asking too many questions. So she went straight to the point. "Toddy, this Friday I'm getting married. I would very much like for you to come."

Todd felt his eyes blur with tears. He managed to choke out, "Okay."

Maggie couldn't believe it. Her son had just agreed to attend her wedding. She was so excited that she couldn't help but let out a little shout. "Really? You'll come?"

Todd held the phone receiver out and shook his head as he listened to Maggie shout with joy. He cleared his throat and asked, "Are you going to tell me where you're getting married?"

28

Todd was at Peg's sitting in a cozy booth across from Grant. It was Wednesday, and they agreed to have dinner together. He had been spending more and more time with Grant, and he discovered he really liked the guy a lot. For the life of Todd, he couldn't seem to figure out why he was allowing Grant to peep into just a small part of his life. He was careful to not allow Grant to look too deep into his heart.

Truthfully, he was ashamed of his upbringing. After all, who wouldn't be? What was he to say? Was he to admit he was raised by a prostitute? Not hardly. At least not in this lifetime. Sure, he shared with Grant he was raised in a dysfunctional home, and he had no idea who his dad might be. But that was about it.

Todd was still a little shocked he agreed to attend Mags's wedding. He supposed it was the right thing to do. At least he felt right about it. So why should he be trying to analyze his decision to go? He knew exactly why—because that was the way he operated. He had always been an analyzer, and he supposed he always would be. He guessed he was happy for Maggie even if he was a little apprehensive. Could she really change? He supposed time would tell.

"You seem to be in deep thought," Grant commented.

Todd started rapidly blinking his eyes, and he cleared his dry throat. He took a drink of his water and wished it was Jack Daniel's. He felt his hands starting to shake the way they did when it was time for his evening drink of JD. Although he had to give himself a little credit, he had cut back to just one drink of Jack in the evening just before going to bed.

"Actually, I guess you could say I was in deep thought."

"Care to talk about it?" Grant asked.

Todd picked at his food for a beat as he pondered on how much he should share with Grant. He wasn't used to having someone to talk to, and he most certainly wasn't accustomed to having a man to show him so much interest. After allowing a few moments to slip by, Todd decided he would tell Grant about Maggie's wedding.

"It's my mom, she's getting married."

"Hey, that's great. Isn't it?" Grant asked with a hint of concern.

Todd tugged at the collar of his shirt. He hoped Grant wasn't able to detect just how nervous he felt. Why did his life have to be so darn complicated? Better yet, why was Maggie so darn complicated? He wished he could calmly answer Grant's question without sounding like he was trying to defend Maggie. It seemed he defended her his entire life. Maybe, just maybe, it was high time he stopped. She was an adult, and he was not responsible for the dark paths she chose in life. He could only hope she was about to go down the right path.

"Well, you don't know Mags . . . my mom."

"Do you care to enlighten me?"

Grant silently prayed he was not prying too much. He felt this overwhelming desire to help Todd, but to help him, he needed to better understand him. However, he could sense Todd had a wall built around his heart. Grant was sure he had been through a lot. Probably more than Grant dared to even dream of. Why did life have to be so tough? Grant's only consolation was knowing God had a plan.

He allowed his mind to go back to the conversation he had a short time ago with Nick. He could remember Nick assuring him God had a plan. Grant prayed he wouldn't blow it. In his lifetime, he had led a few folks to the Lord, and there was only one other person who touched that special place in his heart—his wife, Jenna.

Sure, his relationship with Todd was by far different than his relationship with Jenna. But somehow, he felt this connection with Todd. It was as if he wanted to shelter him from pain. To Grant, it all seemed so outlandish. Mainly because Todd was a grown man. Yet Grant could detect there was a young boy locked up deep within Todd's heart crying, maybe even screaming to be released from the dark prison of pain.

Todd pushed his plate away and let out a slow sigh. He was starting to feel closed in and the weight of the world upon his shoulders. He really needed a drink and Misfit. Yes, that's it, he could tell Grant he needed to get home for Misfit. He wasn't really lying. It was time for Misfit's evening walk. Perfect excuse to avoid talking about his complicated life.

"Look, Grant. I really need to get going. I'm sure Misfit is barking like crazy. I really appreciate the dinner." Todd felt cold sweat bead up on his forehead. He needed to blow this joint before he blew a fuse. "We'll have to do it again sometime." Todd stood to his feet and then added, "Why don't you let me pay for the dinner?"

Grant shook his head as he replied, "Nope, my treat. You're right, I suppose it's past time for me to head home. I really enjoyed myself. I hope we can do it again."

For a brief moment, Todd felt a blanket of awkwardness sweep over him. Is this what it's like to have a dad? He shook his head as soon as the question formulated in his mind. Why was he thinking such an idiotic thought? He shoved his hands in the pockets of his jeans and spoke in a hush tone. "Only if you let me treat you next time."

Grant felt a peace wash over him as he released the air he had been holding in his lungs. He looked Todd in the eyes and playfully said, "You got yourself a deal. See you at work."

"Yeah, see you at work." With that said, Todd slipped out of the diner.

Grant could hardly wait to get home to share with Jenna the progress he made with Todd.

Jenna held on to every word Grant shared with her about Todd. Suddenly she saw Todd with compassion and love. No doubt, he lived a rough life, but she believed wholeheartedly his life was about to do a turnabout. Like lighting flashing across the sky, a thought flashed through her mind. She didn't want to even think the thought, much less voice it. But she recognized the still small voice of God, and He was asking her to share it with Grant.

"Grant, I need to share something with you."

Silence.

After what seemed to be hours but were just a few fleeting seconds, Grant asked, "Well, are you going to share your thought?" He could tell by the look on her face she didn't care to. In fact, he was sure she was even trying to push the thought out of her mind.

Jenna laced her fingers between Grant's thick fingers and started making small circles on the palm of his hand. She took a deep breath and bit her bottom lip as she contemplated how she should tell Grant what God had placed on her heart. She was still relatively new with discerning the voice of God. Maybe she didn't really hear from God. Maybe it's just her human emotions playing tricks on her. No, she was sure God spoke to her. She laid her running thoughts aside and dove straight into the warning God had spoken into her spirit.

"Baby, I believe the Lord warned me that Todd was going to experience something very painful before he completely surrendered over to him." She looked into Grant's eyes searching for something—anything that would indicate alarms going off in his spirit. "Grant, did you not hear what I said?"

"Yes, I heard you, and I say praise God!"

"Praise God?" Jenna asked with a hint of apprehension.

"Yes, baby, you heard me correctly."

"Wait a minute here, Grant. You're praising God for Todd busting his backside?"

Grant chuckled and then pulled Jenna into his arms. He captured her lips and kissed her in a way that caused her knees to go limp. He held her tight and whispered in her ears, "I love you."

She melted in his arms and purred, "I love you too . . ." She trailed off for a heartbeat and then pulled back just far enough that she could look into his grey eyes. "Wait a minute, I'm still trying to understand your reasoning." She allowed her hand to rest on his chest as she waited for him to explain.

"Baby, I'm praising God for Todd's salvation. Don't you get it? God has entrusted us with this small piece of Todd's future so we can start praying for his recovery. The important thing is he will come to God."

Jenna placed her hand over her mouth, and then she started jumping up and down. "Oh my, you're right. He's going to come to God. Oh, Grant, I want to meet him . . . No, wait, we need to pray."

"You'll meet him in God's timing. You're right, we need to pray, and there's no better time than the present."

The two fell on their knees and started praying for Todd.

☾☽

It was Wednesday Bible study, and Moe sat in the back of the storefront church clinging to every word that flowed out of the pastor's mouth. It was as if he knew Moe's every secret. The pastor spoke on new beginnings, and his text was taken out of the book of Jeremiah. His voice was calm yet powerful. He was unlike any pastor he had ever met. Not that he had been around many pastors because he hadn't. But there was something different about this pastor. It was as if he had a special connection with God.

Moe also noticed the people seemed different. They seemed to be so down-to-earth, so loving, and genuine. Moe allowed the pastor's word to play over in his mind.

Jeremiah 29:11—"For I know the thoughts that I think toward you, saith the Lord, thoughts of peace, and not of evil, to give you an expected end."

Yes, this was the peace he longed for. He felt God's peace flow through his soul, and with the peace came hope. Could God have a special plan for a guy like him? Was he able to have an expected end? Moe felt hot tears trickle down his cheeks. They weren't tears of heartache, but the tears made him feel refreshed and even cleansed from the filthy lifestyle he led.

Before he knew it, the pianist was playing soft music on the piano, and the pastor was inviting those who needed prayer to come forward. There was a hand full of street folks that made their way to the front, and a few church members met them. Moe noticed they began to pray, and he saw one fall on his knees at the altar. And then Moe heard his song. The lady singing looked to be about his age. She had the voice of an angel.

"Amazing grace! How sweet the sound
That saved a wretch like me!
I once was lost but now am found,
Was blind but now I see."

Moe wouldn't be able to explain it if he tried, but for whatever reason, he found himself at the altar crying refreshing tears. He emptied out years of guilt, shame, and remorse. He was completely unreserved. He knew he had nothing to lose but everything to gain. The angel's voice continued to sing, "I once was lost but now am found . . ."

Yes, he found his way home. He felt the Spirit of God wash over him. He was so undeserving of this amazing grace, yet God saw fit to offer it to him. He knew there would be no turning back. He planned to serve God for the rest of his living days. Yes, there would be some bumps along the way, but he found the peace he had been longing for. He found Jesus. Moe felt a hand on his shoulders and heard the voice of the pastor praying for him. Every word uttered out of the pastor's mouth was like sweet honey to Moe's ears. It was as if every part of Moe was alive. He was no longer dead, but he was a new person in Christ Jesus.

After Moe spent a few moments speaking with the pastor and a few other church members, he decided it was time to go home and pray some more. He was ready to walk into God's perfect plan. Just as he was about to walk out the door, the lady with the angelic voice put her hand out to shake his. At first Moe felt a little awkward, but once he placed his hand in hers, the awkwardness vanished.

"Hello, my name is Angie. I'm so glad you were able to be with us tonight."

"Hello, Angie. It's nice to meet you. I'm Hermon."

"Well, Hermon, I do hope we see more of you."

"I'll be here Sunday morning."

29

Maggie's Wedding

Maggie glanced at the clock that hung just above the choir loft. Todd should be here by now. Where was he? Her mind reeled in a thousand directions. Did he change his mind about attending her wedding? She hoped not. How she longed to see him. Surely he would show up. Todd was not one to back out on his word. If he says he's going to do something, then he complies. That's simply how she raised him. Lord knows she wasn't perfect when it came to parenting her son, but she taught him to keep his word and to be honest.

The short elderly pastor looked from Trent to Maggie. He cleared his throat and hesitantly remarked, "We really need to get started. I have a two o'clock appointment."

Maggie held Yorkie close to her heart as she looked into Trent's eyes. For a heartbeat, she allowed herself to swim in his chocolate-brown eyes. She knew the pastor was right. They had already taken up enough of his time. She supposed Yorkie would be their only guest outside of the pastor and his wife. She was about to nod in agreement when she heard a motorcycle drive up. She felt her heart soar to the sky. She knew it; she knew Toddy would come to her wedding. "Pastor, I think our guest has arrived."

Everything within Maggie wanted to run to her son and throw her arms around him. But she knew better than to do that. Why? Because he would more than likely walk out of the church. He looked the same yet so different. She supposed he looked more like a man. He was so handsome.

He looked just like his dad, Drake. She felt a pang in her heart at the thought of his dad. Maggie realized she needed to tell Todd about Drake, and she would when the timing was right.

How long had it been since she last saw him. She remembered the day all too well. She was busy entertaining one of her former customers. Maggie could still see the pain in Todd's ice-blue eyes as she tried to explain why she didn't have much time to visit. She felt her heart ache as she allowed her past to creep up on her. She had to put a halt on her running thoughts. She was no longer the woman she used to be. She was about to become Trent Wesley Anderson's wife.

Trent didn't want to appear to be staring at Maggie's son, so he sneaked a few quick glances. One of the first things he noticed was how nervous Todd seemed to be. Trent wanted to assure him he had nothing to be nervous about. After all, they were about to become family. However, the more Trent thought about the whole scenario, the more nervous her felt.

No, he wasn't nervous about marrying Maggie. Everything within him knew she was his destiny. He simply wished they would have done things a little differently. He would have liked to be more prepared. He should have taken her to Macomb and hunted Todd down so they could have gotten all of the formalities out of the way. Oh well, what's done is done. All of that can't be changed now. He was making Maggie his bride.

Trent also took note that Todd looked nothing like Maggie. Which meant he looked like his dad. Todd had fair complexion and ice-blue eyes. There was a coldness about Todd that Trent felt from across the sanctuary. Trent could almost see the wall Todd had built around him. He was no man's dummy, and he knew he had his work cut out for him if he planned to have any type of relationship with Todd. And he planned to; it would just take time. He would find a way to cause that wall to crumble at Todd's feet. He would do it for Maggie.

The pastor spoke with a hint of somberness. Maggie wanted to remind him this was a wedding and not a funeral. But instead she allowed herself to stay focused on the man who stood before her, and Todd, and of course, Yorkie. "Have all of your guests arrived?" he slightly turned his head to get a view of the dog.

Trent smiled and replied, "Yes."

The pastor opened his small black book and began the ceremony. "We are gathered here today to witness Trent and Maggie uniting in the bonds of marriage. The Lord saw it was not good for man to be alone. So

He made woman from the rib of man, and He gave her to him. The Lord said," the pastor paused as he looked from Trent to Maggie, and then he continued, "Genesis 2:24, 'Therefore shall a man leave his father and his mother and shall cleave unto his wife, and they shall be one flesh.'

Now, my thought for the two of you would simply be leaving, cleaving, and weaving. On this day, before God and your guests, the two of you are vowing to leave all other relationships and cleave to one another. Now, this does not mean God is asking you to shut out all of those who are dear to your lives, but God is asking you to place one another before others and cleave to one another. The Bible instructs the husband to love their wives even as Christ loved the church. Jesus gave himself for the church, and He expects us men to do the same for our wives. As you start your new life, you will begin to weave many different memories."

Todd sat in the back of the stuffy church feeling a lot like a fish out of water. He couldn't believe what he was witnessing. Did this man really know what he was getting himself into? Todd figured him to be in his late thirties or early forties. Therefore, he should have enough sense to know it's near impossible to teach an old dog new tricks. Not that he was comparing Maggie to a dog because he wasn't. But he knew her all too well. She had a lot of silly quirks that could drive a sane man crazy. Which is why when he lived with her, Todd choose to stay locked up in his room. But then again, maybe Trent was cut from the same cloth Mags was cut from. You know, two peas in a pod.

He listened to the elderly man go on and on about leaving, cleaving, and weaving. Todd couldn't help but wonder if Trent knew Maggie's whole story. Like how she left her family to live a life of prostitution? And there's the fact she allowed her son to witness the crazy lifestyle. Did he even realize just how many men she cleaved too? Not to mention how many memories she had weaved to the dark corners of her heart. Todd felt resentment surfacing from the dark places of his heart, places he tried to avoid. But somehow, being here and watching Maggie pledge to love, honor, and cherish one man made him infuriated and sick to his stomach.

Todd wondered how he could have gone from longing to see Mags to desperately wanting to run as far away from her as he possibly could. He supposed the answer was obvious. He wondered why she waited so long to make the changes in her life. He would have loved to be raised by a normal family. Like lightning, Grant's face flashed across the screen of Todd's mind. He knew in his heart of hearts that everything about Grant's life was normal, and Todd longed to spend more time with him.

Todd was brought back to matters at hand when he heard the elderly man say Trent could now kiss his bride. The way Todd saw it, that was his cue to hit the road.

Maggie heard the door to the humble church close. Somehow, she knew in her heart it was coming to this. She refused to allow Todd's selfish behavior to put a damper on her mood. She knew in time, Todd would come back around. He just had some things he needed to work through. Maggie felt her heart skip a beat as her husband whispered sweet words of consolation in her ear. Trent handed the pastor an envelope, picked her and Yorkie up, and then carried them off into the sunset.

Part Three

1994

30

For Todd, the winter months were long and cold, but he kept himself occupied with his job, Misfit, and his time with Grant. The snow had melted away, much like his life had melted away from Maggie. He hadn't heard from her since he walked out of the church on her wedding day. Well, he supposed he didn't exactly walk out. He did, after all, stay around long enough to hear the preacher tell Trent he could kiss his tainted bride.

In all honesty, Todd hoped Maggie had truly changed, and he reckoned he missed her just a little. His emotions were all over the place where she was concerned. He would never forget the way she tried to show him the proper love. She did teach him to always be honest with others and, most importantly, himself.

But on the other hand, he would never forget the life she subjected him to. And it was her choice. She could have choose a different path, but she chose the darkness. Now that Todd lived away from the darkness, he was able to clearly see she lived a life of contradiction.

Todd really didn't want to be eaten away by the bitterness in his heart, but he couldn't seem to stop the poison. He knew he would never be able to trust women . . . or people in general. What annoyed Todd the most was the fact Maggie waited until he was out of her way to make positive changes. He was sure she had plenty of opportunity to tie the knot with other men. Like Moe. Not that Todd thought too highly of Moe because he didn't. But Moe would have been better for her than the lifestyle she freely subjected them to.

Todd's mind went back to Grant and the peace he seemed to obtain. It was a peace Todd would like to have. So yes, he put an element of trust in Grant but not much. Grant was of the frail human species that was subject to inflicting pain upon others. Sure, Todd would continue spending time with Grant. Mainly because it helped him to fight off the loneliness, and it was somewhat therapeutic. Todd liked feeling a sense of normalcy in his life, and that's exactly what he felt when he was with Grant.

He still couldn't believe he agreed to go have dinner at Grant's. After all of these months, he was going to meet Grant's family. To Todd, it was as if he was about to step into a new chapter. In many ways, he expected he was. He questioned if he was ready for the next chapter. He was comfortable with living his life predictable. Or was he? He decided he was about to find out the answer tonight.

Todd wished his hands would stop shaking. He was craving a JD on the rocks. Maybe if he just had one shot of the dark liquid, his hands would stop shaking. No, he couldn't. When he met Grant's family, he didn't want to smell like Jack Daniel's. Todd glanced at the clock that ticked away in his living room and saw he still had an hour to waste. He knew he needed to get out of his apartment, or he would break down and give his body what it craved. He looked at Misfit and said, "Come on, boy, let's go for a walk."

As Todd walked Misfit, he felt his hands tremble and cold sweat come out of his pores. He was losing the battle. He needed just one shot of JD. There was no way he could face Grant and his family in this condition. Just one shot would stop the shakes and cold sweat, and once he returned home, he would have one drink on the rocks before calling it a night.

"Come on, boy, let's head back to the house." Misfit's ears perked up as he looked at a running rabbit. "Oh, no you don't. Misfit, now is not the time to play chase the rabbit." Todd tightened his hold on the leach as he walked back to his lonely house.

He was grateful to be moved out of the small apartment he had rented for serval months. He supposed the house made him feel like he was starting life anew. He used some of the money to buy Misfit and to pay for odds and ends for the house, his down payment on his truck, and all of his moving expense. He kept telling himself he needed to open an account at one of the banks in town, and deposit the money. But somehow, the thought of admitting to a banker he had never had a back account didn't set well with him. So he simply did what he did best. He hid his money in a safe place and paid cash for everything.

Once Todd got Misfit settled with food and water, he went to the kitchen and poured himself a shot of JD. He quickly downed the shot, and then without second-guessing, he downed another. He felt the warm liquid flow through his blood stream, and the shaking ceased. He took a deep breath and looked at the bottle. He contemplated if he should do just one more shot. For him, three shots were nothing. Heck, that was just enough to loosen him up a tad. In the end, he decided on one more shot.

Todd braced himself against the kitchen counter as he allowed his body to relax. He felt the built up tension dissolve away. How long had it been since he did three shot of JD in a row? Too long. He liked how he felt. He was more than ready to face Grant and his family. He was ready to face the world. The sound of the ticking clock brought him back to matters at hand. He took note that he had only twenty minutes to spare. That gave him just enough time to wash his mouth out with Scope and stop by the supermarket for flowers. He planned to make a real good first impression.

31

Jenna was beyond excited. She was finally meeting Todd. She had spent many hours praying for this young man. She glanced at the clock and thought Todd should be arriving any minute. She wanted the evening to be perfect. Grant had asked her not to go overboard. He assured her Todd would be easy to please. She decided to stay with happy medium. Not to fancy but not too casual.

Jenna prepared roasted chicken, rice pilaf, garden salad, key lime pie, and homemade brownies. She seriously considered using her fine china and lighting a few candles to set the atmosphere for a cozy evening. But Grant gave her his look that indicated "Let's not" and say we did. She was grateful Tessa was free for the evening. Tessa always had a way of lighting up the atmosphere. Jenna was just about to call for Tessa when she came running in from outside.

"Yummy, it smells good. When will . . . oh, what's his name?"

"Todd."

"Yes, that's right. When will Todd be here?"

"He should be here any moment."

"Well, I'm going to run up and take a quick shower. I just came from my run, and I feel a little grungy."

Jenna waved her out of the kitchen and shook her head. "Tess, make it a quick one. You know how important this is to Grant."

"Sure, Mom. See you in a few."

Grant came waltzing into the kitchen. He gave Jenna a kiss and then turned to Tessa and remarked, "Yes, make it quick. We wouldn't want your mom's dinner to get too cold. I think I just heard Todd pull up." On that note, Tessa ran upstairs for a shower.

It wasn't too late was all Todd could think. He could easily get back in his truck and go back home. Yes, he should. He needed another drink. What was he doing here? But his feet wouldn't seem to comply with what his brain was screaming. *Leave, idiot! You don't belong here!* He felt his hand make a fist, and the smell of roses wafted through the evening air. Why on earth did he buy roses? He was setting himself up to look completely ridiculous. At least the roses were yellow.

Grant appeared in the shadows just when Todd was about to run to his truck. Todd stopped dead in his tracks as Grant approached him. He felt like one of those manikins that one would find in a department store. "Hello Todd, come on in. Hey, how did you know my wife loved roses?"

Todd shrugged his shoulders and took a deep breath. He wished he still felt the effect of the JD, but he didn't. He felt nothing but complete dread. He could only hope dinner was on the table so he could eat and run because he sure didn't see himself staying around long. "I don't know, I just assumed women like them is all."

"Well, I suppose you're right. Most women do like flowers. Come on and meet the family."

"Okay." Todd couldn't seem to think of anything else to say.

As soon as he stepped across the threshold, there were two things Todd noticed: one, the serene feeling that swept over him, and two, the smell of home-cooked food. A beautiful woman came from the kitchen with a smile and glow on her face. She had confidence, but she also possessed the same peacefulness Grant had. Grant brought Todd back to matters at hand when he started making the introduction.

"This is my beautiful wife, Jenna. Our daughter, Tessa, should be coming down soon. Jenna, I would like for you to meet Todd."

Todd awkwardly placed his hand in Jenna's and quickly shook her hand. He then handed her the roses. All the while, he kept trying to place where he heard the name Tessa. "It's nice to meet you, ma'am."

Jenna instantly felt a connection with Todd. Even though she could detect he was edgy, she wanted him to feel at home. She felt her heart soften as she took in the smell of the beautiful roses. She was rather shocked he took the time to purchase them, but she was glad he did. Yes, the roses spoke volumes about the young man who stood in front of her. He has a heart of gold. "Please, Todd, call me Jenna. Thanks so much for the beautiful roses. Let me get a vase to place them in."

"You're welcome, ma'am—or I mean Jenna." Todd stuffed his hands deep into his pockets. *I can do this. The evening will be over soon. Just not soon enough.*

Grant couldn't believe the scene playing out in front of him. God was good. No doubt, this was the beginning of a new beginning for Todd. Grant knew for some time Todd never experienced what it was like to have a real family. But as of today, all of that was about to change because as far as Grant was concerned, Todd was a part of their family.

Yes, he knew very little about Todd's background, but that too was okay. He felt the Spirit of God in the midst of this, and he learned a long time ago not to question the Almighty. Grant realized there was a time and place for everything. One day, when the time and place was right, Todd would open up to him. Grant was about to ask Todd if he would like to take a seat in the living room when Tessa appeared.

Tessa recognized Todd as soon as she laid eyes on him. She couldn't believe he was standing in her home, and this was the young man Grant had mentioned countless times. She had thought of him on more than one occasion, but she never dreamed she would see him again. Now she was about to have dinner with this mysterious guy. Boy, she could hardly wait to tell Hunter about this. Surely this was all fate.

Todd felt his mouth turn dry and his hand sweaty. It was her. The one he had seen at the park. At that moment, he couldn't decide if he wanted to run or stay. How was he going to keep his composure? Why was this happening to him? He wanted to be back home. He didn't like the emotions this girl stirred in him. He needed to keep his guard up. He planned to repeat one thing in his mind for the entire evening: *she is no different from any other woman.*

Grant was able to tell by the expression on their face they had already met. But he decided to ignore the vibes he felt and play like he didn't discern a thing. "Tess, I would like for you to meet Todd. Todd, I would like for you to meet our daughter, Tessa."

It was Tessa who took the initiative to first speak. She felt a little giddy but not at all nervous. "Wow! This is way cool! It's good to see you again, Todd."

I can't believe this. Why, is she sounding so darn excited?

"Yeah . . . huh, it's good seeing you again."

"How's Misfit?" Tessa asked.

What? She remembers my dog's name? "Good, real good."

"So I see you two have met," Grant stated.

Tessa was quick to reply, "Yes, at the park a while back ago."

Todd was so relieved to hear Jenna call them to dinner. He shyly nodded his head and smiled at Tessa. "Yes, at the park." *Was that smile really necessary, Jenkins?*

Everything looked scrumptious, and Todd was more than ready to dig in. But then Grant calmly asked they all join hands and say grace over the feast. Really? Join hands? Talking about awkward. Todd couldn't remember ever praying over his food or even praying, period. Yeah, sure, Maggie prayed with him a few times, but he never held her hand or shut his eyes.

"Father, we thank you for this food that we're about to partake. Lord, we pray your blessing be upon . . ."

Why does her hands have to be so soft? I'm about to pass out, Todd thought.

Aw, he's so cute. Kinda like a shy schoolboy, Tessa thought.

"Lord, I ask that you bless the hands that prepared this food. And, Lord, please bless our special guest . . ."

She's beautiful. She really is beautiful, but I would never let her know I think so. Not in this lifetime.

"In the wonderful name of Jesus, amen."

"Amen," Jenna and Tessa repeated.

Todd felt his face turn red, and his eyes start to blink rapidly fast. Why now? He wanted so badly to crawl under the table. But instead, he looked at his plate and the eating utensils. Where did he start? He wasn't used to all of this. There were two of everything. Even two plates. He decided he would be polite and wait for the ladies to start eating so he wouldn't look like a complete moron.

Tessa could tell Todd was about to have a meltdown, so she decided it was time to liven things up a little. She felt so drawn to him, and she really couldn't explain why. Yes, he was good-looking, but it went deeper than the outer appearance. She noticed his eyes were rapidly blinking, and his face was red as fire. Why? Maybe he wasn't accustomed to meeting new people, which is why she needed to get his mind on something funny. But what? It took her a moment, but then it came to her.

She first put salad on her plate, and then she playfully picked up his plate. "Around here, we believe in serving our guest." She put a generous amount of salad on his plate and then placed his salad fork on the plate.

Todd didn't know what to think. Was she poking fun at him? Surely not. She was just being kind is all. "Thanks."

Tessa smiled and then took a big bite of her salad. "You're welcome. Yummy, good salad, Mom."

"Why, thanks, Tess."

"Yes, my wife is quite the cook."

"Hey, Mom, do you remember our first pet?"

"Oh my, how could I forget? You called Max a dog, but I say he was more wolf than dog."

"Okay, Mom. If you say so. Anyway, remember the first time I walked Max by myself?"

"How could I forget?"

Grant looked from Jenna and Tessa and then asked, "Well, Tess, are you going to tell us about it?"

Tessa started laughing, and then she proceeded to tell her story. She was so vibrant and colorful. Todd decided he could sit and listen to her tell stories for hours. Why, within no time, even he joined in with the laughter. He felt relaxed. He completely forgot about his own little world of loneliness. Todd marveled at how they all interacted and shared in laughter. He couldn't help but wonder if this is what he had been missing all of his life. Was this how a real family really acted? Or was it just this family? He really didn't know, but he liked it. Maybe he didn't say much, but he loved the way he felt inside. It was as if he was a part of something special. He supposed he was, and he knew he would never forget this night.

Grant couldn't believe the change in Todd's demeanor. It was as if he went from being a nervous wreck to being downright calm. He owed it all to his fun-loving stepdaughter. He was beginning to question if maybe he made a mistake by inviting Todd. But now, he could plainly see Todd fit right in with the family. Yes, Todd was a little different. But who wasn't? After all, how many people sit around the dinner table eating a wonderful meal listening to someone relay how their dog messed all over a grouchy old man's front porch?

32

Later that evening, Todd found himself in complete disbelief. He wanted to pinch himself to see if he was dreaming. He actually agreed to walk Misfit around the park with Tessa. She indicated she would meet him there at eight o'clock. It was three minutes until eight when he noticed headlights from a distance. As the car approached, he recognized the Toyota Tercel. Todd chuckled as he watched Tessa whip the small car into a parking space. He couldn't picture himself feeling comfortable with such a small car, but he had to admit, it suited Tessa.

He felt his breath catch and his heart hit the payment when she exited the car. She donned a WIU jersey, and her hair was pulled up in a simple ponytail. To Todd, she was perfect. She was beyond beautiful. Fact was he doubted there was a word found in all of the dictionaries that would adequately describe her. He realized he needed to gain his composure, so he casually placed one hand in his pocket as he led Misfit toward her.

Without hesitation, Misfit went straight to Tessa. "Hey, boy. Do you remember me?" Misfit softly barked and licked Tessa's hand. "I guess that's a yes." Tessa playfully rubbed behind Misfit's ear and then looked up at Todd. "Do you mind if I walk him?"

Todd chuckled as Tessa's little story replayed in his mind. "I guess it'll be okay. I mean, it's not like there are any houses around."

"Well, actually there's a neighborhood just behind those trees." She laughed. Her laughter danced in the night air and caused a chill to run down Todd's back. He was sure the chill wasn't from the coolness in the air. Nope, it was from her. Tessa placed her hands on her hips and playfully chided, "Well?"

"Well?"

"Are you going to allow me to walk him?"

Suddenly Todd felt a little giddy. He wasn't used to feeling this way, and he couldn't decide of he liked the fact he enjoyed the way she made him feel. After all, she was a woman. He needed to be careful. He suppressed his feelings and painted a serious look on his face. He handed Tessa the leash and coldly stated, "I told you yes, didn't I?"

Tessa took the lead. She refused to allow Todd's behavior to put a damper on a pleasant evening. She could handle this. She knew without a doubt she did nothing wrong. Whatever his problem was, he would just have to get over it. In her studies, she read about people with multiple personalities. Maybe this was the case with Todd.

He did after all seem a little nervous earlier this evening. At least until she penetrated through the wall he had carefully built around his heart. So the way she saw it, she did it once, and she could most certainly do it again. She was up for the challenge. She could look at her relationship with Todd as a project. Yes, of course, he could be her first unofficial patient. She simply needed to figure out a way to get into his brain. And she would, she was sure of that.

Todd felt bad for being so cold, but he couldn't seem to shake Maggie and Donna out of his head. He couldn't—no—*wouldn't* place his trust in her. He simply wasn't up to the sure pain that would come with trusting Tessa. He would have to keep his distance. But what if she was different? What if he was throwing away the only positive relationship in his life? What would Grant think if he started treating his daughter cold? Grant was good for him. He was solid, positive, stable, and caring. Todd finally reached the conclusion he would be nice to Tessa but would keep his guard up. He could do this. He was a master at hiding his true emotions. After all, he had done it most of his life.

Todd had to admit Tessa wasn't even remotely like Maggie. The two were like day and night. As for Donna, well, he wasn't given the opportunity to get to know her. Yes, she stirred his emotions, but there was still alarms that sounded loud and clear in Todd's spirit. In the beginning, he wasn't able to pinpoint why, but it didn't take him long to learn why. Donna was about as unstable as Maggie. Sure, as far as he knew, she wasn't a prostitute. But then again, maybe she was.

Tessa breathed in the clean scent of the night air. She loved spring. All of nature was waking from her long winter nap. The leaves on the trees were starting to bud, and the flowers were starting to pop up from the earth. Soon, they would be getting the April showers, and the farmers were cumbered about planting there fields. From the distance she heard a night owl, and the crickets were singing to their Maker. There were a few stars shining in the heavens, and the moon seemed to be just a reaching distance away.

She was able to hear the sound of their footsteps as they walked side by side. Why, if she was someone passing by, she would more than likely think what a lovely couple. But she wasn't just passing by, she was in the here and now moment, and she planned to add a little spice to the evening.

"Come on, Misfit, let's run." With that said, Tessa took off running like someone had lit fire to her backside.

How in the world could he keep his guard up around someone like Tess? She was as free as a bird, and he was about to catch her. Todd allowed her to get a little ways down the road, and then he charged after her.

After running until they were completely out of breath, they decided they needed to rest. Misfit was laying on the cement block close to Todd. Tessa and Todd were laying side by side on a large picnic table, stargazing. The air was cool but not too cool. Nature was singing as the stars shone down upon them. Tessa felt such a peace. It was almost as if she was locked away in her own little fantasy world. She loved it, and she didn't want to come back to reality. Nonetheless, she knew she had to.

Tessa loved the way Todd felt next to her. She could feel his shoulder brushing against hers and the warmth of his masculine body. She was sure heaven could hear the drumming sound of their heartbeats. Everything about the evening seemed so right. Well, almost everything. She couldn't dismiss the way Todd had shut down on her earlier. She wanted to know more about him, and she decided there was no better time than the present.

Todd kept reminding himself to breathe. The closeness of Tessa made him feel emotions he was sure he had never felt. He tried to keep his attention on the stars, but with Tessa next to him, it was hard. He could smell the light scent of mint coming from her breath. The clean scent of Tessa mingled in with the fresh outdoor scent. He wanted to be her friend—really, he did—but he had fear hovering over him like a hazy cloud. It was as if the fear was keeping him from pursuing happiness.

In his mind, he questioned what it was like to be happy. His answer came quick. Happiness was family. He experienced enough happiness tonight to give a longing for more. He related to the first time he felt numb from the JD. Once he felt that place of ecstasy, he knew there would be no turning back. He had been drinking the dark liquid since.

But being with Tessa was a different type of ecstasy. Already, she made him feel special, peaceful, and thirsty. Yes, that's correct—thirsty. She caused him to thirst after life whereas the Jack Daniel's made him thirst after darkness. Todd was quite baffled how one woman could make such a deep impression on his life. He only became acquainted with her tonight. Crazy. Absolutely crazy was all Todd could think. At the sound of Tessa's soft whisper, he was brought back to earth.

"So we all have a story. Do you mind if I share mine with you?"

If she thinks I'm going to share my story, she is disillusioned. It will be a cold day in, well, my lips will remain sealed. Although it would be nice to taste her lips. "Yeah, sure, I would love to hear your story." Todd had to refrain from chuckling. He knew without a shadow of doubt that her life had been a bed of roses.

Tessa proceeded to tell Todd every single detail about her childhood and all the way up to her adulthood. She was sure she felt hidden doors start to open. Doors she kept locked for so many years. As far as she knew, she hadn't even shared with Hunter the true battle that raged within her when she was younger. The war of bitterness toward her mom. Yes, she had shared with Hunter how she felt about her dad and maybe some about her mom. But not the secret details she was ashamed to admit, even to herself. Yes, her mom was and always had been one of her best friends. But there was still that secret war that raged within Tessa's heart which she kept suppressed.

"The thing is," her voice was just above a whisper, "I'm so ashamed I battled with such feelings." Tessa paused for a brief moment and then continued.

"I realize my mom did everything she could to provide for me, and she did such a wonderful job. But it's like she became a robot, and well, she never really seemed happy. At least not until Grant came along. I will forever be grateful for Grant. He has done so much for my mom."

There was silence for a beat. It was almost like a holy hush. Todd was trying to process everything that Tessa had shared. Tessa took a deep breath and then continued.

"I guess in the beginning of Mom and Grant's relationship, I was a little jealous. I know that sounds so ridiculous, but I was. I supposed it was because he was able to give her something that I couldn't. He gave her joy.

Anyway, that's all water under the bridge. We're a happy family. The now moment is what counts. Right?"

Todd merely nodded. He was lost for words. He tried to recall if Grant had shared with him that Tessa was his stepdaughter. For some reason, he believed they had always been a happy family. Maybe Tessa had no idea what it was like to live the crazy life he lived, but she had a story. And her life wasn't exactly a bed of roses.

"Cat got your tongue?"

"Uh, no," Todd replied.

"Oh, sorry. Anyway, at least Hunter has always been there for me. He's been with me through thick and thin."

"Hunter?" *He must be the guy she was with when I saw here a while back.*

"Yep, my bestie, Hunter. He's been like a rock for me. I love him like a brother. I can tell he would like for our relationship to go deeper than friendship level. But that's not happening." Tessa felt a pang of guilt as soon as the words tumbled out of her mouth. She chided herself and wished she could take them back. She didn't want Todd to get the wrong impression. After all, she was trying to gain his trust, and he was sweet on the eye.

"I don't know, I guess I wouldn't want my relationship with Hunter to be any other way. I love him like family."

"No, you're good. I think I understand."

"Good. Hey, I would love for you to meet him. I think the two of you would hit it off."

Number one, Todd had no desire to meet Hunter, and number two, he had no right to be feeling jealous. What Tessa did with her life was her business, not his. She was not his girlfriend. Heck, they weren't even really friends. Fact was they were just mere acquaintance. "Maybe one day." *Why did I just say that? Idiot!*

"That would be great. Now, it's your turn to tell me your story."

They both turned their heads and allowed their eyes to lock. Todd wanted so badly to kiss her, but he wouldn't. Not now, anyway. He felt his defenses come down a notch or two. Maybe he should share just a small portion of his childhood. Like the fact that he had never met his dad and had no idea where he might be. But instead he whispered, "It's late. You should be getting home. Your parents will be worried." Todd could hear the sound of Misfit breathing, and he could tell by his steady breathing he was sound asleep.

"I'm a big girl . . . and they trust me. Do you?"

Everything within Todd wanted to trust her, but he couldn't. At least not yet.

"I love classical music," Todd whispered.

"Well, that interesting."

33

"Hunter, do you believe in love at first sight?" They were at their private spot, the train tracks. There was one thing Tessa knew for sure: she would never share this place with another. This was where she and Hunter shared some very personal moments. Maybe she never shared with Hunter the demons she fought with over her mom, but that was okay. She had learned to trust Hunter with a lot of her dark secrets. She figured the main reason she never told him about how she battled with unhealthy emotions about her mom was because she didn't want to taint her mom's reputation. Hunter always admired her mom, and Tessa didn't want to say anything that would cloud Hunter's image.

After all, she had overcome those silly childhood-teenage emotions. Tessa still considered her mom to be one of her best friends. Seemed to Tessa her best friend list was growing. She decided to add Todd to her list of best friends. Yes, she had only officially known him for a few days. Yes, she was trying to sort through the way he made her heart flutter, her knee turn into rubber, and her brain cells melt.

There were two things she knew for certain: One, they had a kinder spirit. Two, she wanted to help him out of his shell. The one thing she wasn't quite sure of was love at first sight. She felt like she fell in love with him when she first locked eyes with him at Glenn Wood Park a while back ago. But she gave up on ever seeing him again. What really blows her mind away was the fact she had been praying for Grant's troubled friend for weeks.

Hunter had no idea where this crazy question came from. Had Tessa met someone on campus? They were about to start spring break, so maybe she was thinking about going on a trip with the mystery guy. But then again, maybe he was reading too deep into her question. Maybe her off-the-wall question had something to do with one of her studies. After all, she was studying to be a psychiatrist. No doubt she studied on human behavior, and love was definitely a touchy subject.

He allowed his mind to travel back in time when he first met Tessa. He could still see the sparkle in Tessa's blue eyes. He could still feel the way his heart skipped a beat, and his mouth went dry. He was sure he had met his forever love, but he learned real quick like that Tessa's heart was not easily won over. Yes, he managed to get into her heart, but only as one of her best friends. One thing Hunter knew for sure was that he believed in love at first sight because he fell head over heels in love with Tessa when he first laid eyes on her.

"Yes, I do."

"Really, Hunter?"

"Yes. Why do you ask?"

Tessa pondered in her heart if she should tell Hunter about Todd. She was sure he wouldn't be in agreement with her new-found relationship. But she wasn't living her life for Hunter. She was a grown woman, and she was ready to follow her heart. She simply couldn't pass this opportunity up. Why? Because Todd was her soul mate. She just knew he was. Tessa refused to allow Hunter's or anyone else's opinion to hinder her future.

She decided to spill the beans. "Do you remember Todd?"

"I can't say that I do."

"Remember, I met him at the park with his dog, Misfit, some time ago."

This can't be happening. Why, God? "Oh, yes, I remember."

Silence.

"Tess, have you been seeing him?"

"Well, kinda. Sorta."

"What is that supposed to mean? Tess, have you prayed about this?"

"Well, actually, yes, I have . . . kinda sorta, prayed."

"Again, what is that supposed to mean?" Hunter asked with a hint of frustration.

"Chill, Hunter. Allow me to explain."

After a heartbeat of complete silence, Hunter whispered, "Okay, I'm all ears." He could do this. He could listen to the woman he had loved forever tell him about her love-at-first-sight experience. He willed himself to focus on the positive aspects of his relationship with Tess. He was grateful she was being honest. He was thankful for their friendship. He would treasure all of the private moments they have shared . . . moments like tonight. Hunter started to feel his racing heart slow down a tad. He whispered a prayer to Jesus, asking for strength where he was weak. Only the good Lord knew just how weak he was when it came to Tessa.

Tessa was able to detect Hunter wasn't too happy about her feelings for Todd. She figured he would have a hard time with the news. She loved Hunter dearly, but he would just have to get over it. It's time he accept the fact she was not his happy ever after. Yes, she found him to be attractive, but she could never imagine the two of them being like peas and carrots. They simply were not meant to be soul mates. Tessa felt certain that in time, Hunter would come to see things her way. At least she prayed he did because the last thing she wanted to do was hurt him.

"Well, you already know about the park incident, so I'll just fast forward. I'm sure you remember me asking you to be praying for Grant's coworker. Right?"

"Yes. What does he have to do with Todd?"

"Well, Hunter, he is Todd."

Hunter allowed Tessa's comment to sink in. This whole time he has been praying for Tessa's lover boy? Okay, maybe "lover boy" is over doing it a bit, but still. "You mean the guy Grant has felt such a burden for is your Todd?"

"Yes, that's correct. Well, maybe not totally correct. He's not 'my Todd' as you put it. But I don't know, Hunter. I believe one day, he will be 'my Todd' . . . not that I'm trying to sound possessive. Oh, you know what I'm saying. Right?"

"No, I'm not sure I do." Hunter noticed Tessa shivering. The night air was getting a little cool. It was late March, and the last of winter still lingered in these parts of Illinois. "You cold? Why don't we go someplace where it's a little warmer?"

"I came prepared," Tessa replied. "I have some hot chocolate in a thermos. We could sit in my car and drink our creamy hot chocolate."

"That sounds good."

"Wait, Hunter! Do you feel the vibration?"

"Yep, I do."

"A train's coming. Let's wait until it gets closer."

"Okay, Tess."

After a short while, they sat nice and cozy in Tessa's Tercel sipping hot chocolate. In Hunter's opinion, they were maybe too cozy. He could smell the light scent of her minty shampoo and the Baby Soft body spray that she had used since he had known her. He wondered if Todd knew this about Tess. Surely not. They had only met. Sure, maybe he had smelled the smell of her sweetness, but he did not know her like Hunter knew her. No man knew her like he knew her.

Tessa looked at Hunter all dreamy eyed, and she smiled. "You know, Hunter, you're my bestie. Right?"

"Yeah, sure, of course." He looked deep into her eyes and whispered, "Always and forever. Now, tell me about Todd." *Not that I want to hear how you're falling for another man.*

"Oh, where do I start? I guess I'll start with dinner. Well, Grant invited this mystery guy over for dinner, and Mom was beside herself to finally meet him. I guess I was just a little curious. Anyway, I went up to take a shower, and when I came down, there he was. I couldn't believe it. I actually thought my eyes were playing tricks on me. I never thought I would see him again, but there he was, standing in my living room. Well, as soon as he looked, I knew he recognized me."

Tessa paused for a moment as she allowed her mind to reflect back on the look in Todd's eyes. "Well, I could tell he was a little nervous. But you know me, I kinda have that special touch."

Hunter chuckled and replied, "Yes, you sure do. So what did you do to calm his wayward nervousness?"

"I simply shared with him my first experience of walking my dog, Max."

"No, you didn't?"

"Yes, I did."

"You do mean the one when Max messed on Mr. Grouch's front porch?"

"Yes, I do."

"Well, I'm sure he felt right at home after hearing that story."

"Yes, he did. Anyway, later that evening, I met him at Glenn Wood. We walked Misfit around the park."

I knew "later that evening" would be coming up soon. "You mean he actually trusted you with his dog?"

"Hey, watch it, Buddy," Tessa teasingly remarked.

"Okay, okay, continue with your story."

"Hunter, to put it plain and simple, it was at the park that I realized the first time I laid eyes on Todd, I had fallen in love with him. He makes me feel different. I feel emotions I never felt, and I tell ya, I believe he feels the same about me."

At that moment, Hunter realized he went into the wrong vocation. He should have gone into the field of acting. He was sure Tessa had no idea the war raging within his heart. One thing he knew for sure, he would be here for when her heart was broken. Because he was sure she was about to get burned. He playfully tapped her on the nose. "That's great. I'm happy for you. What do you say we call it a night?"

CR&CO

Todd tossed and turned wishing for sleep. He needed to be up in just seven short hours. While on the job, he wanted to be well rested and fully alert. He was coming up for his evaluation and was hoping for a promotion. The extra money would be nice. He thought about taking a few courses at Spoon River. Who knows, he might work at getting at least an associate degree. He wouldn't mind earning a degree in business.

Todd couldn't seem to get Tessa out of his mind. It was as if her shadow was following him everywhere he went. Her smile was engraved upon his heart, and her eyes captured his soul. She had given him her phone number and asked that he call. He could see the look in her eyes when she asked him to call. She seemed so sincere. Maybe if he called and spoke with her for just a few moments, he would get some rest. Without second-guessing, he picked up his phone by his nightstand and dialed her number.

One ring, two rings, three rings, and four rings. Just when he was about to hang up, he heard the sweetest voice on earth.

"Hello, Hunter, what's up?"

Silence.

Todd contemplated hanging up. She thought he was Hunter. Didn't she say they were only friends? He felt the wall around his heart go up, yet for whatever reason, he couldn't bring himself to hang up.

"Hello? Who is calling?"

"Tessa, it's me, Todd."

Breathe, Tess, breathe. "Todd?" *Okay, now sound intelligent!*

Todd had to stifle a laugh, and he felt his wall coming down just a notch or two. "Yes."

"Oh my goodness. I can't believe it's you. I mean, I'm glad it is, but I thought it was my friend Hunter . . . and I'm rambling."

"You're good. You asked me to call. I hope I didn't wake you."

"Oh no, I was just getting out of the shower. So how are you?"

"I'm doing well. I just wanted to tell you good night."

"Okay, well, good night, Todd."

"Hey, Tessa, how would you like to go out for dinner?"

"I would love to. When?"

"I was thinking maybe tomorrow evening around six?" *What in heaven's name am I doing?*

"Yeah, that sounds great. You know, I am on spring break, so maybe we can hang out some."

"Yeah, sure," Todd replied.

Silence for a heartbeat.

"Okay, well, sweet dreams, Tessa."

"Sweet dreams, Todd."

34

Moe had grown accustomed to being called Hermon. He actually liked it. He was also growing quite fond of Angie. It seemed the two of them shared a lot in common. She understood what it was like to be backed against the wall. She had shared with him during one of their lunch dates, when she came to Jesus, she had nothing to lose but everything to gain. Moe felt exactly the same way the first time he stepped foot in the storefront church.

Moe was learning more and more about God's amazing grace, and he was falling in love with Jesus. He only wished he had learned of God's grace before he made so many mistakes. Angie assured him he would have never become the powerful man of God that God intended for him to be if he had not made so many mistakes. She simply indicated while he was out there making mistakes, he was being trained to work for God. At first, Moe had a real hard time understanding her concept. But in time, he understood what she meant.

How would he have compassion for other brokenhearted people if he himself never experienced pain? How could he passionately speak of God's amazing grace if he himself had not tasted the goodness of God's mercy? How could he tell other's there were no mistakes Jesus would not forgive if he had not made mistakes? How could he explain to other's God specialized in cleaning up messes if he never witnessed the hand of God clean his own life? Yep, Moe realized Angie was right; he was simply being trained for God's perfect plan.

Just the other day, Angie had shared Luke chapter 7 with Moe. He could visualize the entire scene playing out as Angie read to him about the sinful woman that came to Jesus. Moe picked up his new Bible and started rereading the scriptures.

Luke 7:36-50—"And one of the Pharisees desired him that he would eat with him. And he went into the Pharisee's house and sat down to meat. And, behold, a woman in the city, which was a sinner, when she knew that Jesus sat at meat in the Pharisee's house, brought an alabaster box of ointment, And stood at his feet behind him weeping, and began to wash his feet with tears, and did wipe them with the hairs of her head, and kissed his feet, and anointed them with the ointment.

Now when the Pharisee which had bidden him saw it, he spake within himself, saying, This man, if he were a prophet, would have known who and what manner of woman this is that toucheth him: for she is a sinner. And Jesus answering said unto him, Simon, I have somewhat to say unto thee. And he saith, Master, say on. There was a certain creditor which had two debtors, the one owed five hundred pence and the other fifty. And when they had nothing to pay, he frankly forgave them both. Tell me therefore, which of them will love him most?

Simon answered and said, I suppose that he, to whom he forgave most. And he said unto him, Thou hast rightly judged. And he turned to the woman, and said unto Simon, Seest thou this woman? I entered into thine house, thou gavest me no water for my feet, but she hath washed my feet with tears and wiped them with the hairs of her head. Thou gavest me no kiss, but this woman since the time I came in hath not ceased to kiss my feet. My head with oil thou didst not anoint, but this woman hath anointed my feet with ointment. Wherefore I say unto thee, her sins, which are many, are forgiven, for she loved much, but to whom little is forgiven, the same loveth little. And he said unto her, Thy sins are forgiven. And they that sat at meat with him began to say within themselves, who is this that forgiveth sins also? And he said to the woman, Thy faith hath saved thee; go in peace."

In the eyes of Moe's mind, he could imagine the religious rulers trying to pick the mind of Jesus. And then all of the sudden, in came this sinful woman, more than likely a lady of the evening. No doubt her reputation was tainted, but she didn't allow that to stop her from getting to the feet of Jesus. She was more than likely tired and broken. She didn't care what the Pharisees thought of her. She simply knew she needed a change. It amazed Moe how she pushed her way past the porter and all of the dignitaries.

She allowed her hair to come down and opened her alabaster box, and she anointed the feet of Jesus.

Moe loved Jesus's responses to the Pharisees when they tried to reprimand him. He simply reminded them what they did not do. Here they were trying to find fault in this poor woman who fell at the feet of Jesus, when all the while, they were at fault. What touched Moe's heart the most was the one little quote, "Wherefore I say unto thee, her sins, which are many, are forgiven, for she loved much, but to whom little is forgiven, the same loveth little." Wow! Amazing grace!

So in many ways, Moe and Angie identified with this little sinful woman who captured the heart of Jesus. They were both broken vessels in need of God's amazing grace. But there was another woman Moe thought of as he meditated on the passage. Maggie.

He wondered how she was doing and if she had married Trent. He hoped so. Maggie deserved happiness. She had a heart of gold, but she was dealt a bad hand of cards. Moe could see God using Maggie to touch a lot of lives. No doubt she would serve Jesus with much passion. A lot like the sinful woman he just read about.

But there was someone else who came to Moe's mind. Todd. Moe felt a pang of guilt stab at his heart as he recalled the way he poked fun at Todd. He wondered what the young man may be up to. No doubt he was still fighting the demons that came from childhood pain. Not that Maggie was abusive to Todd because she wasn't. It was just the life she exposed him to. She wasn't at all discreet about her lifestyle. Moe felt tears sting the back of his eyes as he allowed images of Todd to replay. Without wasting another moment, he fell on his knees and began to pray for Maggie, Todd, and Trent. Moe had a made up mind that he would pray for them daily.

ᏯᎦᏋᎧ

Maggie lay in bed relishing the feel of her husband's masculine body. She loved watching him sleep. He looked so adorable with his dark thick eyelashes fanning across his cheeks and his mouth slightly opened. He was breathing so peacefully. She watched his broad chest slowly rise up and down. She was careful not to disturb him. She simply wanted to look at him a while longer before she went to cook a nice hearty breakfast.

To Maggie, life was almost perfect. If only her son would come to see her or at least call. Maggie hadn't heard from him since the day of her wedding. She still felt the sting of his rejection. How could he have done such a thing? To Maggie, it seemed he came only to create pain. Well, she refused to allow his inconsiderate behavior to cause her to slip into darkness. She would continue to hold on to the tiny thread of hope that he would return home.

Trent never ceased to stop encouraging her. He assured her he saw a look of longing in Todd's eyes, and he saw something else. He saw love radiating in her son's ice-blue eyes, and that love was for her. Maggie knew she made more mistakes as a mom than she could ever make up for, but she also knew she tried to show Todd love. She refused to live in a world of guilt. God had blessed her, and she planned to spend the rest of her days thanking Jesus for giving her a second chance.

Maggie couldn't resist her husband's sweet lips any longer. She gently brushed a kiss across his lips and then another. Trent responded with a soft groan, and then he captured her lips and deepened the kiss. He kissed her cheeks, her nose, and her neck, and he again captured her luscious lips. All he could think was surely he was experiencing a piece of heaven on earth. Maggie was his sweet angel. He loved her more with each passing day.

Trent paused and looked into hazel eyes. "Good morning, baby."

"Good morning. What do you say we go cook up some breakfast?"

"Hmmm, that sounds almost as good as you."

Later that day, they sat out on the back porch with Yorkie lying at Maggie's feet snoring away. They had just come from a five-mile walk, and poor little Yorkie was all tuckered out. There was a slight nip in the air, but Maggie liked the coolness. She never was too fond of extremely hot or cold weather. She preferred spring and autumn over summer and winter, any day.

The birds were flying about and chirping away. The insects were starting to come up from beneath the earth. There were a few white fluffy clouds in the sky. The fresh scent of nature flooded Maggie's senses. She heard laughter from the neighborhood children. Maggie gathered they were on spring break. She cringed at the hours Todd spent alone when he was on school breaks. She couldn't remember taking him on one vacation. He simply entertained himself in his small prison. *Lord, I failed in so many ways.*

Trent could see Maggie from his peripheral vision. He was learning her body language, and right now she was telling him she was thinking of Todd. He longed for her to realize how special she was, but he too realized she had made her share of mistakes. Heck, they all had. For his Maggie, it was all about survival. The one that needed a good swift kick in the backside was Drake. For the life of Trent, he couldn't see how a man could do such a thing. He supposed he came to the simple conclusion that Drake could not have been a man. At least not a man in his right mind. Sure, he was man enough to get Maggie pregnant, but he wasn't man enough to face the responsibility that came with a child.

And then there was her so-called Christian parents. For Trent, it was folks like them who turned him away from religion. He felt his heart tighten as he recalled Maggie informing him she didn't believe in religion, but she believed in having a relationship with Jesus. It still baffled him she could still believe in a God who threw her under the bus. Of course, she's determined her situation had nothing to do with God but had everything to do with the choices she made.

The way Trent saw it, his Maggie was just a teenage girl looking for attention when she settled on the choices she made. She didn't deserve to be thrown out to the wolves. She deserved happiness, support, and love, which she did not receive. But that was then, and this is now. He planned to shower her with all of the love and happiness she deserved.

Trent reached for her dainty hand and intertwined his callused fingers with hers. He felt a rush of love surge through his heart as he noticed the spark in her eyes as she looked up at him. There was no questioning her love for him. "Baby, I love you."

"I love you more, babe," she whispered.

And then the moment was quenched at the sound of Yorkie's yap. "You do know we should have named her Yappie?"

"Aw, you be nice. Come here to Momma, girl." Yorkie jumped up in Maggie's lap and started licking her cheeks.

"Hey, Yorkie, you're stealing my kisses."

35

"That was Hunter," Jenna commented as she walked back out to the patio. "He was calling for Tess." She hated the disappointment in Hunter's voice. She had been praying about this situation for a few weeks. Jenna could easily see the attraction between Todd and Tessa, and she supposed they made a fine couple. Her heart simply bled for Hunter. He was a good guy, and he deserved happiness. But Jenna realized his heart was set on Tessa. Maybe she should start praying that God would send a young lady Hunter's way.

"Did you tell him she was with Todd?" Grant asked with a hint of apprehension.

"No, of course not. I simply told him she was out. It's not for me to share Tessa's love life." Jenna and Grant had invited Cindy and Bob over for a BBQ. After the long winter, they were all ready to enjoy the outdoors. To Jenna, the weather was perfect. There was a slight breeze and just a few fluffy clouds in the sky.

"Yes, I totally agree." Grant felt bad for Hunter, but he kind of liked the way God was using Tessa for Todd. "You know, they're all young. Why, by the time next year rolls around, who knows who they may be dating."

Cindy perked up. "Ahh, I think I'm confused. Who is Todd? Bob, did you forget to tell me about this?"

Bob shrugged his shoulders as he responded, "I have no idea what's going on."

"Jenna, you want to fill me in?"

"I'm sorry, Cindy, I meant to talk to you about Todd before now. Well, I guess I kind of did already mention him to both of you. Do you recall the young man we requested prayer for?"

"You mean the one Grant works with?"

"Yes. Well, it seems Tessa met him some time ago at the park. And they have hit it off remarkably well."

Grant jumped in, "Babe, you need to back up. You're not telling the whole story."

"Well, babe, I'm still trying to process everything."

"I understand. Why don't I fill them in, and then we'll get the grill fired up, Bob."

"Yeah, yeah, that sound good. I hope the story isn't too long. I am getting a little hungry."

"Why, Bob, I cooked you a big breakfast. I can't believe you're already hungry."

"Cindy, that was a few hours ago. I am a growing guy, you know."

Grant proceeded to explain how everything fell into place. From the beginning to the end.

୧୬୨୭

Tessa had taken Todd to Argyle Lake. They spent a few hours hiking and had just finished up a late lunch. Tessa had packed a picnic basket full with all kinds of goodies. She found Todd was an easy person to spend time with even if he was quiet as a mouse. She had done most of the talking. She had tried to pick his brain, but it was to no avail.

So Todd was a private person. At least their relationship was coming along quite well. They were about to try out paddle boating, and Tessa planned to use the opportunity to get in Todd's head. She supposed she could have taken advantage of the hours they had already spent together and pulled out information about his upbringing. But instead, she simply enjoyed just being with him. She was sure he knew about everything there was to know about her, and the odd thing was she wanted him to know her secrets.

They were drifting a ways out on the lake when Todd noticed Tessa was unusually quiet. He questioned if he had done something to upset her. He was beginning to become accustomed to her body language, and right now she was telling him something was heavy on her mind. He decided it was time he opened to her just a tad, but before he did, he wanted to lighten up her downhill mood swing.

Tessa was relaxing with her fingertips making small ripples in the water. She loved coming to Argyle. The park was so peaceful. She was about to ask Todd if he planned to utter one single word when her thoughts were interrupted.

"Tessy, does a cat have your tongue?"

Tessa loved it when he called her Tessy. It was the special nickname he gave her. Not one other living person called her Tessy. "Actually, I'm thinking a tiger has yours."

"Nah, Tessy, it's more like a tiger has me by the tail."

"Hahaha. Whatever, Toddy."

At the sound of the name that only Maggie called him, Todd felt a thousand emotions storm through his soul. Why did Tessy have to go and call him Toddy? She could have called him any name but that name. But Todd knew all too well why. It was because *Toddy* sounded a lot like *Tessy*.

"Hey, Todd, are you okay."

Silence hovered over them like a thick cloud for what seemed to be eternity. Todd was searching for the right words and at the same time trying to calm his racing heart. He didn't want to think about Maggie. He wanted to enjoy his time with this woman who kept him captive.

He cleared his throat and looked squarely into her beautiful sky-blue eyes. At that very moment, he felt this overwhelming serge of emotion. He felt butterflies in his stomach, and his knees went weak. He was grateful he was sitting because he was sure he would have fallen. Heck, he had fallen. He was head over heels in love with Tessy.

"Tessy," he tenderly asked, "please never call me Toddy again."

Tessa looked into his ice-blue eyes. He was looking at her with such intensity that she felt the need to look away. Suddenly, she wished she had never opened her mouth. She longed to be back on one of the hiking trails. She didn't know this side of Todd, and she wasn't sure if she liked how he was making her feel. It was as if the paddle boat shrank a few feet, and the air was so thick that one could cut it with a knife.

Yes, his voice was tender, but his eyes conveyed differently. It was almost as if there was an element of hate in his eyes. Tessa was able to see a dark side of him she had never seen before. Sure, she detected a lot of apprehension when she had first met him, but this was different. It was like a door that led to a dark place in his heart was opened, and he wanted desperately to slam the door shut. However, Tessa wanted nothing more than to enter into every dark chasm of his inner being. She wanted to know the Todd that was locked away from the outside world.

Todd slightly shook his head as he willed his thoughts to come back to the moment at hand. Back to Tessy. "I'm sorry, Tessy . . ." he drifted off for a beat, "it's just Mags calls me Toddy." My, how he craved a drink. Just one shot of JD would calm his racing heart and running emotions.

Tessa felt her heart slip all the way to her feet. Who was Mags? Was this mystery woman one of his old flames? Somehow, she had never pictured Todd dating. Not because he wasn't sweet to the eye, but he simply didn't seem like the dating type. She even allowed herself to believe she was his first girl. Even his first love. Who was she fooling? Only herself, that's who. Why wouldn't he have a girl waiting for him in Peoria?

Todd could literally see the wheels spinning in Tessa's mind. He sensed he needed to clarify Mags was his mom. The last thing he wanted to do was misinform Tessa, which was why he neglected to share much with her. Come to think of it, he had shared very little with her. She on the other hand had freely allowed him to peep into every area of her life. He felt a pang of guilt stab away at his heart.

He didn't want to blow what had been established in their relationship. She deserved to know the truth. But could he share his upbringing with her? To put it plain and simple, no, he couldn't take the chance of losing her. As sure as his name was Todd Jenkins, he knew he would lose her if she knew about his demons. Yet he didn't like seeing her so vulnerable, so he decided to keep things short and simple.

"I'm sorry, Tessy, I guess I should clarify that Mags is none other than my mom." When he saw the smile play on her face and the sparks flying out of her eyes, he so badly wanted to pull her in his arms and kiss her.

Bingo! Jackpot! So his mom is one of his demons? "Makes perfect sense to me."

"What?" Todd asked.

"That you would call your mom Mags. Hey, nowadays, who calls their mom *mom*?"

Todd could detect a hint of playfulness in the tone of her voice. He decided it was time to have some fun. He gently started rocking the paddle boat, and to his surprise, Tessa started rocking it with a little more force than him. She sure was a feisty little lady, but he wouldn't want her any other way.

"Whoa, careful. We're about to cap this—" Too late. Before Todd could complete the sentence, they were both in the lake.

Tessa spit and spattered as she swam above the water. She was thankful she decided on wearing dark T-shirt with her jeans. The cold water felt exhilarating. She felt charged, alive, and freezing cold all at the same time. She loved this feeling, but most importantly, she loved the look in Todd's ice-blue eyes. And his laugh was amazing. He was laughing from deep within his soul.

Todd couldn't stop the laughter. In all of his life, he had never felt so free, and he had Tessy to thank for the joyous occasion. He knew they needed to get out of the lake because there were "No Swimming" signs posted everywhere. He easily tipped the lightweight paddle boat upright.

"Here, let me get in, and then I'll give you a hand."

"Aw, come on. I was hoping we could swim a little while."

"You're freezing, and I don't want to be responsible for you catching a cold."

"Actually, I'm getting use to the water." Tessa disappeared under the water and came back up with a mischievous smile. "Come on, just for a while longer."

How could he resist? He breathed in deeply and then added, "You do realize we are violating the law?"

Tessa dipped her head back in the water to get her hair out of her face. She absently glanced around and then replied, "There's not a soul around. Come on. Only for a little bit. Trust me, I have done this before."

"Oh? With who?" Why was he feeling a pang of jealousy?

"Hunter."

The mention of Hunter's name was all it took. Before Tessa could swim away from him, he jumped into the lake and had her in his arms. She placed her arms around his neck and pulled herself closer to his body. Every male hormone within him came alive. She felt so soft. She smelled so delicious. She fit so perfect in his arms. It was as if she was made for him. There was a drop of water dripping from her nose, and droplets on her eyelashes. He wanted to savor the moment. It was so serene. So this is what love felt like? Without second-guessing, he voiced his heart.

"I believe I love you, Tessy."

"I believe I love you too, Todd."

He kissed her nose and her forehead, and then he captured her lips. He was gentle, and he silently wondered where his proper mannerism came from. Surely not Maggie. He treated Tessa like a china doll. To Todd, she was his prized possession. He didn't want to harm her. She was priceless, and he planned to love her with the love she deserved. But could he? What did he know about love? One thing he knew for certain was that he loved his Tessy.

Tessa allowed him to continue kissing her in a chaste way for about as long as she could take it. She took matters in her own hands as she deepened the kiss. Oh, was she ever glad she followed her heart because she loved his response.

36

Hunter lay in bed tossing the idea back and forth in his mind about calling Tessa. When did calling her become such an issue? The answer was quite obvious. His friendship with Tessa, his best friend, did a nosedive when Todd became a part of her life. There were three things that troubled Hunter the most: one, His friendship with Tessa; two, the way Tessa fell for Todd; and three, Todd's background.

Hunter analyzed this whole situation and concluded what troubled him the most was knowing very little about Todd. The guy was a mystery, even to Grant. When Hunter casually questioned Grant about Todd's background, Grant simply shrugged it off. He tried to assure Hunter there was nothing to worry about because God was in the midst of their paths crossing.

He understood Grant's theory, but to assume Tessa was perfectly safe with the character was unrealistic. For all they knew, Todd could be some lunatic. Of course, that would be right up Tessa's ally. She was always drawn to people who carried tons of baggage. Not that that was a bad thing because it wasn't. She had a heart of gold, and she would be willing to lay her life on the line for any poor lost soul trying to find their way in life.

Hunter felt heartburn coming on. He couldn't decide if it was from worry or his mother's meatloaf that she cooked for ten-plus hours in the crockpot. He came to the conclusion it was a combination of both. He met his mother as he was on his way to the restroom for some Tums.

"Hunter, are you okay?" she asked with a hint of concern.

"Yeah, sure. Why do you ask?"

"I don't know. I guess you seem a little lovesick. Did you and your girlfriend have a fallout?"

Girlfriend? It took Hunter a moment to remember the night he introduced Tessa to his folks as his girlfriend. At the time, he believed in his heart that in the near future, she would be. "No, we're fine." He still refused to give up hope that one day she would be his girl.

"Are you sure? Here lately, I noticed you've been staying home a lot—"

"Mom," he rudely interrupted, "I said we're fine. We both have a lot on our plate with school and all."

"Okay, if you say so. I'm going to bed. Your father's staying up to watch *Johnny Carson*. Good night, Hunter."

"Good night, Mom."

Later that evening, Hunter picked up his phone to call Tessa. He simply needed to hear her voice.

Her phone didn't even put out one complete ring. "Hey, baby, I'm glad you called."

Hunter felt his face turn beet red. He couldn't believe what his ears was hearing. *Baby? Really? Calm it down. She can't know you're upset.* "Well, baby, I'm glad I called too."

"Oh, Hunter, it's you."

"I'm sorry to disappoint you, but yes, it's me."

"No, no, Hunter, I'm glad you called. You're not going to believe the amazing day I shared with Todd."

"Oh, try me." *Spare me!*

By the time Tessa finished relaying every little detail about her day with lover boy, Hunter needed more Tums.

Just across the hall, Grant and Jenna were deep in their own conversation.

"I don't think we have a thing to worry about, sweetie."

Jenna loved the way Grant was able to calm her nerves with his soothing voice. However, tonight the calming effect she longed for wasn't coming near as quickly as she would like. Everything within Jenna wanted to believe him, but she couldn't seem to shake the uneasiness that set off internal alarms. Was she just being overly protective? Probably.

"I want to believe you're correct, but I just can't seem to shake this gut feeling . . ." she trailed off for a beat. "Maybe it's just my motherly emotions slipping into fifth gear."

Grant placed his arm around her and started wrapping strands of her hair around his index finger. He loved these quiet times with his wife. It seemed he lived for these moments. He didn't like seeing her in such turmoil, and he desired to find out what troubled her so about Todd and Tessa.

"Why don't you help me to understand how you're feeling?" he tenderly asked.

"Well, for starters, there's the fact Tessa has been missing a lot of church."

"True. But mostly because of school. She's still going to her group Bible study. Correct?"

"Well, yes. And I suppose you're right about her missing church because of her studies. But what about tomorrow? She said she would only be attending Sunday school because she was spending the day with Todd. And haven't you noticed the way they look at each other?"

"At least she's going to Sunday school. I suppose they look at each other the same way we look at each other. So they're falling in love. Is that such a bad thing?"

"Grant, they're so young."

"Yes, this is true. But we have to allow Tess to find her way in life. She's no longer a teenage girl, but she's a young woman. I can assure you Todd has good intentions."

"Oh?" Jenna asked.

"Let's just say we've had a few man-to-man talks. I don't believe he has it in him to hurt Tess. Yes, his background is a little complicated. But we all have skeletons in our closet, so to speak."

"That's just it, Grant. I mean, we know very little about him. Other than the fact he comes from a dysfunctional home. For all we know, he may be running from the law . . . or . . . or worse yet, a—"

"Hey, slow down there. I think you're jumping the gun. Have you forgotten the words of advice you spoke to me?"

"What?"

"That God has placed him in our life to guide him to salvation."

"Yes, but I also remember God speaking that he would fall hard before coming to salvation."

"Shhh, shhh, like I said, you're jumping the gun—"

"But did you see the shape they were in when they came home from Argyle?

"Yes. So they fell in the lake?"

Jenna relished in his touch and the low tone of his sexy voice. Maybe he was right. She was just overreacting. Todd was a good guy, and she needed to trust her daughter's judgment. She looked up at Grant, and their eyes locked for a beat. She whispered, "I could really use a kiss."

"I think I can arrange that."

He kissed her once, twice, three times, and then he reached over to turn off the lamp.

Meanwhile across town, Todd was wrestling with his demons. He was trying to lay off from the JD. But tonight, his body craved a good stiff drink. He was starting to feel cold chills as the members of his body craved the dark liquid. Just one shot flowing through his bloodstream would stop the chills.

He tried to focus on the novel he was reading, but he couldn't seem to get into the story. He laid the book aside and looked over at Misfit all curled up on his blanket. He loved his dog, but it was nothing like he loved Tessy. He felt his heart skip a beat at the thought of her. He never knew love could be so beautiful. Today at the lake was magical. If heaven was real, he tasted a piece of it today. Only God knew how much hell on earth he had tasted.

God was another topic he had been avoiding with Tessy. But come tomorrow, he planned to share some of his dark past with her. He had the day planned out. He was going to get up early and go for his run with Misfit, and then he was going to head to town in search of a gift for his girl. He would pick her up at noon and then take her someplace special. Heck, the middle of Timbuktu would be special as long as he was with her.

Todd felt a warmth spread through every fiber of his body as he recaptured every detail of their kiss. It was as if he could still feel her soft lips and smell the sweetness of her hair. He noticed that the chills had passed, and the craving for JD was quenched. His soul was filled with his sweet Tessy. Todd drifted off to a peaceful sleep with one thought on his mind. Tessa's lips.

CB&O

"Wow, this is so cool! I didn't know you owned a motorcycle."

"Correction, I own a Harley." Todd looked around for a beat and then asked, "Is Grant and your mom around?"

"No, they're still at church. I slipped out of church after Sunday school." Tessa could tell by the reaction on his face that she needed to divert the topic. "I could hardly wait to look into your ice-blue eyes." She took a few steps closer to him, and he took one toward her. They were so close their noses were practically touching. She wanted to taste his lips once again, but she was determined to allow him to make the first move. She had no problem with nudging him a tad, but she refused to throw herself at him.

Todd wanted to kiss her more than anything he ever wanted his entire life, but he planned to wait. He wanted her to know him. The true him. He loved her too much to keep his whole story from her. He was going to do exactly what Mags taught him. He was going to be completely honest with her. Would it be easy? No, but she deserved to know the truth. He would kiss the living daylights out of her if she still wanted to give him her time of day after hearing his story.

He tapped her on the nose and whispered, "Tessy, I have something for you." He reached for his oversized backpack and pulled out a helmet.

She felt her breath catch as he placed the helmet on her head. His touch set her on fire and caused her brain to turn into scrambled eggs.

"There, you look beautiful." He couldn't believe he just told her she was beautiful, but it felt right. Everything about her felt right. "I was thinking maybe we can stop by KFC for lunch."

"I love KFC." She was thankful for the helmet because she was blushing like a silly teenager. She couldn't believe he told her she looked beautiful, but she was glad he did.

Todd strapped his backpack on his Harley and then placed his helmet on. She couldn't help but notice how nice his jeans fit, and there was something about the helmet that added to his manhood. She jumped on and placed her hands on his narrow waist, and off they rode with the wind.

Later that afternoon, after Todd had literally spilled his guts out, they walked hand in hand around the lake. Todd had taken her to Spring Lake. Tessa had almost forgotten just how peaceful Spring Lake was. She hadn't been there for a few years. She supposed she allowed this beautiful lake to slip from her memory.

The campers were already out setting up camp, some for just a few days and some for the spring/summer months. Tessa could remember coming here as a child with her mom. They would set up their tent and rough it for the weekend. She felt a pang of guilt in her heart for ever feeling bitter toward her mom. Especially after hearing Todd's story. She couldn't imagine living such a life. One thing she knew for sure was that his transparency only made her love him more.

Tessa could sense he was feeling somewhat insecure, and she didn't like it. He was a good guy who survived a life she feared she could have never lived. She felt the need to say something to break the silence that threatened to suffocate them. Something that would lift up his ego and lighten the mood at the same time.

"Well, you do know that your childhood does not define your true character?"

Silence for a beat.

"I'm learning that."

"Good. Just so you know, I'll be writing a thesis on your life. Of course, I'll change names and all that good stuff."

"You wouldn't. Would you?"

"Well, that depends."

"On what?"

"If you give me a big kiss."

He kissed her forehead, her cheeks, and finally her lips. The kiss was raw and passionate. My, how she assured him she still loved him.

37

August

How long should one remain passive to avoid confrontation? That was the question that continued to tumble around in Maggie's mind. She didn't deserve the way Todd was treating her. He was being selfish. He was the one calling the shots in their relationship. Everything had to be at his terms. Like her wedding. He showed at the last minute and then left without even saying hello or goodbye.

She had called and left him several messages, practically begging him to return her calls. She had been praying for God to soften his heart and knit their relationship back together. But her prayers were only hitting a brass ceiling. It seemed to her Todd was purposely trying to make her miserable. Maggie had apologized over and over for her many mistakes. A day did not pass without her regretting the life she subjected her son to.

Trent was her only peace of mind, but even he was growing weary of the entire situation. He was ready to take a trip to Macomb and look Todd up for himself. Maggie struggled with the idea. A part of her believed Trent to be correct; they should hightail it to Macomb and have a little family meeting. On the other hand, she wasn't sure if that was such a good idea. Mainly because she knew her son. He was able to shut people out as easy as the sun rises and sets.

She would love to share with Todd the progress she had made in the past several months. Who would have ever thought she would be driving? Heck, she even passed the GED test and was looking into taking a few night classes. She was right proud of herself. Trent had assured her she had every reason to be proud. Most importantly, he assured her day and night that he's proud of her.

She pondered on the idea of driving herself to this town, but she wasn't confident enough. And there was the fact she wasn't so sure she was strong enough to face Todd alone. But the unknowing was about to drive her crazy. She had to at least see the town, and maybe, just maybe, God would see fit for her to see her son.

Maggie sighed as she looked around the room Trent fixed up for her. He was so good to her. She never dreamed love could be so enchanting. He had carefully framed Todd's pictures and hung them where she asked. He purchased a small desk, daybed, two beautiful wicker wingback chairs, a small television, and stereo for her room. Of course, she enjoyed sharing her safe haven with him. They had already started some wonderful memories in her room.

As Maggie looked at Todd's senior year picture, she felt a prick of guilt in her heart. He looked so much like Drake. She should have told him about his dad. She could have at least showed him pictures. Maggie felt a peace sweep over her, and the still-small voice of God assured her that it wasn't too late. She knew what she needed to do.

She was brought back to the moment when she heard Yorkie scratch at the door. She jumped up out of her chair feeling a little surer about herself. "Hey Yorkie-Poo. Come here to Mommy. Daddy should be coming home soon." Yorkie yapped as Maggie swept her into her arms. "You wanna go for a walk?" She yapped one more time. "Aw, I guess that's a yes."

Later that evening, after they completed their dinner, Maggie decided to talk with Trent about her decision. "Baby, how about we sit outside under the stars for a while?"

All evening Trent was able to detect something was troubling his wife, or more like someone. Todd. He took it upon himself to do a little fishing. It paid to have friends in high places. His head supervisor just happened to be friends with one of the supervisors at Bowers. With a little persuasion, Trent was able to find out Todd's home address. He had a good mind to make a trip to Macomb and kick the kid in the backside. However, Trent realized that would upset Maggie. He also realized Todd was not a kid even though he was acting like one.

"That sounds great. Why don't I pour us a glass of wine?" Trent asked.

"Yes, wine sounds wonderful." Maggie eased over to her husband and placed her arms around his thick neck. She kissed him once, twice, and three times. His lips moved over her neckline and then back to her lips. He deepened the kiss as she ran her soft fingers through his thick hair. She was performing her magic on him, and he knew if he didn't slow down, they wouldn't make it to the front door, much less outside to the patio.

His voice was husky, and desire was written all over his face. "Why don't I go pour the wine?"

"That sounds good. I'll just slip out back."

"All righty, but you do know we will be picking back up . . . a little later tonight."

"Why, baby, I wouldn't have it any other way."

Maggie sat on the patio loveseat enjoying the peace her soul cried for. Somehow, Trent's touch calmed her nerves. He was her lover, best friend, therapist, and husband all wrapped up in one beautiful package. She looked up at the stars and whispered a prayer of thanks. Maybe she wasn't where she should be with God, but she refused to stop talking to him. She longed for Trent to make steps back to God. It would be nice if they could find a small church, maybe the one where they married, and live the all-American life.

But then there's Toddy. Maggie felt her heart rate speed up as she pictured her son alone in a dark apartment drinking his life away. *Lord, please keep your hand upon him.* One word continued to tumble around in her mind. Trust. She realized God was asking her to trust him. She could do that. Right? Sure she could.

"Here you go." Maggie jumped and let out a little yelp. "I'm sorry, baby, I didn't mean to startle you."

"No, it's okay, babe. I was just enjoying God's beautiful creation.

Trent placed their wine on the small table that was positioned in front of them and draped his arm around her. His touch was like a whisper, and he spoke in a low tone, "Yes, His creation is very beautiful." Trent allowed himself to get lost in her hazel eyes for a beat. "You're His prized creation."

She was so thankful he never made her feel rushed. He allowed her to open up in her time. She could see a mixture of love and concern in his beautiful chocolate eyes. "Well, I believe that's a matter of opinion. I happen to think you're His prized creation."

Trent kissed her nose and whispered, "Okay, we both are."

She pressed her forehead against his and playfully scrunched up her cute nose. "I knew you would see it my way."

"Oh, always."

"Always?"

"Yes, always," he softly muttered.

"Let's go to see Toddy."

Trent pulled back just a fraction. He traced his index finger around her neck. His touch was as soft as a feather and smoother than butter. He lightly kissed her lips, and his kiss was as sweet as honey. He gave her his heart melting smile, and she was sure she had slipped into a fairytale. He was her prince charming, and she was his princess. But she was brought back to reality at the sound of his deep voice.

"I think I can arrange that small request."

She blinked once, twice, and three times. She parted her mouth to speak, but she found herself completely lost for words. She was sure he would try to persuade her to leave well enough alone. "I-I didn't think you would agree."

Trent loved her childlike character. He only wished she would come to forgive herself. He hoped this little trip would bring restoration. She was relentless as a wife, mother, and friend. She put her entire heart into everything she did. He had never met a person that obtained the passion Maggie possessed. She had come a long way in the short time they had been together. But Trent was no man's fool. He knew Maggie needed her son back in her life. Yes, he was able to fulfill her womanly desires, but he would never be able to fill the void in her heart that was caused by Todd.

"Baby, I have his address."

"Really?"

"Yes, really."

"B-but how did you get his address?"

"Let's just say I have friends that know a lot of folks. I think we should go this weekend."

Maggie didn't know if she wanted to laugh or cry, so she did both. She couldn't believe Trent had Todd's address. When did he get it? Was he planning to tell her he had it? Or was he waiting for the right moment? In the end, she decided that all of the unanswered questions didn't matter. What mattered was come this weekend, she would see her son. Suddenly, it dawned on her she should maybe call Todd. No, if she called he might insist they not come. She didn't think her heart could handle more rejection.

She was tired of swimming in an ocean of guilt. She needed to look in his ice-blue eyes and tell him she loved him. She needed to see where he lived and know he was taking care of himself. Surely once he saw her, he wouldn't turn her away. Yes, their relationship had been strained, but Todd never flat out shunned her. Well, maybe he did somewhat on her wedding day. She felt doubt try to slip into the recesses of her mind, but she shoved it back as soon as she felt it try to creep in. Maggie refused to believe anything but positive. Her Toddy would be happy to see her.

"I think this weekend would be great."

She was about to say something else when Trent placed his index finger over her mouth. He tenderly picked her up and spoke with a hint of desire. "I think it's time we finish what we started earlier this evening."

03 80

Angie and Moe, who now preferred to be called Hermon, were sitting in a small coffee shop on River Street, enjoying a late night latte with a piece of pie. She was downright proud of Hermon. He was growing leaps and bounds in his Christian walk. She loved the way his faced lit up every time he talked about Jesus. She loved the many questions he asked. She loved the way they prayed together. To put it plain and simple, she had fallen in love with him, and she was sure he had with her.

She was grateful God had allowed her to play a small part in helping Hermon get back on his feet. She referred him to a job opening at Saint Frances Hospital. They needed help in the janitorial department, and Angie was quick to tell him about the position. Once he completed the job application, she also put a good word in for him. She had been working as a nurse there for over ten years. It also helped that one of her dear friends worked in the human resources department. God was working everything together for the good. Why? Because they loved Him.

"Hey, what do you say we go for a walk along the riverfront?" Hermon asked.

"I think that sounds delightful."

Hermon paid the ticket and escorted Angie out of the small café.

For a long while, they walked in a comfortable silence under the moonlit sky. The air was a little thick from the hot summer days, but soon summer would be behind them, and cool evenings would be just around the corner.

Hermon easily slipped his hand in hers and pulled her a tad closer. He loved the feel of her soft skin against his rough hands. She was a true Christian lady, and he felt so undeserving of her time. Yet Angie continued to remind him they were all sinners saved by grace, and she too made her share of mistakes. He was in love with her, and he desired to shout it from a mountaintop. But instead he simply whispered ever so softly, "Angie, I love you."

Angie laid her head on his strong shoulder as her heart turned flips. "I love you too, Hermon."

38

"Come on Hunter, you can do this for me. Please, I want you to get to know him. Besides, he's a piece of work I have been perfecting. I might add, my work is coming along quite well."

For the love of heaven, why couldn't Tessa see how hard this was for him? He loved her for crying out loud. She was supposed to be his happy ever after. Everything in their relationship seems to be going downhill. But still, it was too hard for him to say no. He came to the conclusion that he was fool enough to jump off a bridge for her. Now, this was true love.

Hunter still felt uneasy about Todd. Maybe going to Peg's for a bite to eat with them would help him better understanding why he felt this overwhelming uncertainty about the guy. He needed to know if it was his intuition setting off alarms or if it was jealously on his behalf. He was thinking it was more than likely a little of both.

"Okay, I'll go. What—"

"Hunter, I can't believe you'll do this for me." Tessa threw herself in his arms. "I love you, my sweet friend."

Hunter really had very little choice but to wrap his arms around her and pull her closer. She felt oh so good. She fit perfect. She smelled of Love's Baby Soft. He resisted the desire to run his hand threw her soft hair. He needed some space before he did something he would come to regret. So he pulled back just a fraction and tenderly whispered, "I love you too, sweet friend. Now, what time am I to meet you guys?" He playfully tapped her on the nose.

"Six." With that said, Tessa pulled away and added, "And I still need to get ready!"

"Okay, I'll see my way out. I know how long it takes you girls to get ready."

"Whatever, Hunter."

"Remember, Tess, we're now adults."

CR&

Why was Todd feeling so uptight? He was only going to meet nitwit. It was really no big deal. He could do this for Tessy. Maybe if he just downed one shot of JD, the shakes would subside. After all, he had cut way back. What harm would one shot do? He was about to go to the kitchen to retrieve the bottle of dark liquid when the sound of the ticking clock stopped him dead in his tracks.

He looked at the clock to see that he only had ten minutes to make it to Peg's. He didn't want to be late. He simply couldn't. So he retrieved his keys and looked at Misfit lying peaceful in front of the television. Todd was glad he took him for a good run because he should be tuckered out for a good while. Todd turned on the stereo to a classical radio station and headed out the door.

CR&

By the time Todd reached Peg's, his mouth was dry, and cool sweat beaded on his forehead. He spotted Tessy and what's-his-name right away; however, he realized he needed to make a quick trip to the restroom. He was in dire need of water to help wet his mouth and wash his face.

Todd was thankful he managed to slip into the restroom completely unnoticed. After all, a man still had his pride. He could kick himself in the backside for not downing a shot of JD before his little dinner date. He continued to remind himself he was doing this for Tessy.

Within no time, he was sitting across from nitwit. His only consolation was that Tessy was at his side. They had placed their order, and Todd had to resist the temptation of ordering himself a cold beer. Granted, he wasn't a big beer drinker, but at least it would help calm his nerves. One thing he knew for sure was that this evening would not end fast enough. Hunter's ridiculous question brought him out of his private world.

"So, Todd, what college did you attend?"

Todd could feel Tessy stiffen, so he casually slipped his arm around her. "Actually, *Harry*, I didn't attend college. But I have been thinking about taking a few classes at Spoon River." He loved the sound of Tessy's giggles. She was like a breath of fresh air, water in a dry desert, and sunshine after a rain. "What are you giggling about?" he asked her.

"Baby, his name is Hunter."

"Oh, I'm sorry, Hunter—"

Hunter interrupted, "It's okay, really." *If these two think I'm going to sit here and be their laughingstock, they are wrong.*

"Besides, Toddy, I'm sure you and Tessy don't spend a lot of time talking about little old me."

"No, actually we spend very little time talking about you, Hunter."

Tessa could tell Todd was getting mad because of the way his eyes were rapidly blinking. She could also tell that Hunter was about to blow a gasket because his ears were red as fire. She was beginning to wonder if this was such a good idea. She merely wanted her best friend to come to know the man she had fallen in love with.

"Hey, guys, why don't we just drop it? Okay?"

Todd nodded his head in agreement, and Hunter was about to counteract with his expertise opinion when the waiter arrived with the pizza. Tessa was never so happy for the timely interruption. Needless to say, dinner seemed to crawl.

CB EO

"Thanks for tonight. I don't know what got into Hunter. He's normally not so rude," Tessa shyly commented as Todd pulled into her driveway. Her mom had dropped her off at Peg's mainly because Tessa couldn't see driving her car when she was sure she would be leaving with Todd. They had just come from walking Misfit, and now she was about to say good night.

Todd pulled her closer to him and whispered in her ear, "It's okay. If I were in his shoes, I would be jealous too." He then captured her lips. She melted in his arms as he deepened the kiss. He knew he needed to be going, but it was difficult to pull away. "I love you, Tessy."

"I love you too, baby." She looked into his eyes and saw nothing but raw desire. She wanted him. All of him. Yes, she was taught to save herself for the wedding night, but she wasn't sure she would be able to. She felt her heart rate speed up as he pulled her on his lap. His kisses were unlike any he had ever given her. Her breathing was short. She ran her hands through his thick hair and then down his back.

Todd felt his entire body burn with desire. His brain was telling him to stop, but his heart would not allow him to comply. Suddenly, the image of Grant flashed through the screen of his mind. He released his hold on her and spoke with a husky voice, "I should go. I have to get up early for work, and you have school."

She slipped off his lap and tenderly kissed his lips. "You're right. Thanks again, and sweet dreams."

"Anything for you, Tessy. And sweet dreams to you too."

CB 80

"Hunter, why did you act so rude?" Tessa hissed over the phone.

"Rude? Really? I think you have it all backwards. Toddy was the one who acted downright rude."

"First of all, his name is Todd. Please never call him Toddy—"

"Whatever, Tess. Does it not matter that he called me Harry?"

"Hunter, you're jealous, aren't you?"

"Yes, you darn straight I am! I'm jealous that you have allowed this guy, who we hardly know, to come between us. I mean, look at us, Tess. We have never argued like this. Come on, it's me, your best friend. Can't you see I love you, Tess?"

Tessa didn't want to hear this. She wanted Hunter and Todd to be buddies. But who was she fooling? She could see the hurt in Hunter's eyes tonight. And she guessed deep in her heart, she hurt for him.

"You're right, Hunter. I'm sorry. You're still my best friend, and I love you. Really, I do. It's just that I love you with a different kind of love. Look, maybe it would help if you found yourself a girlfriend—"

"Look Tess, I gotta go. Good night."

Click.

39

Todd was on his way to pick up Tessy when he heard the knock at the door. He planned to take her to a special place he found in Bushnell called Timberview. He was sure she had already been there, but nonetheless, she had not been with him. All that mattered to him was he would be spending time with his woman. Todd also planned to take Misfit with them. He could tell Misfit was ready for some fresh air.

Misfit barked at the sound of the second knock. "Come on, boy, let's see if it's Tessy." At the sound of Tessy's name, Misfit wagged his tail. "You miss her too, boy? I know I sure do."

Todd took a step back when he opened the door to see Mags and her husband standing at the threshold. He wasn't sure if his eyes were playing tricks on him. How did she find out where he lived? Why was she here? This wasn't supposed to be happening. It should be Tessy standing at the door, smiling back at him.

"Two questions. What are you doing here? And how did you find out where I lived?" Todd felt his blood start to boil as his eyes blinked rapidly fast.

Trent had to restrain himself from plowing into his punk of a stepson. Who did he think he was? One thing for sure, he would not tolerate no one talking to his wife with such disrespect. "Hey, you need to watch how you talk to my—"

"Todd, aren't you going to at least ask us in? I mean, we are here and—"

"No, I'm not inviting you in because I didn't invite you here!" As Todd raised his voice an octave or two, Misfit started barking. Todd continued, "You're not welcome. So just hightail it on down the road."

Todd quickly stepped across the threshold and slammed the door, keeping Misfit in the house barking away. He was nose to nose with Trent as he hissed through clenched teeth. "Don't you ever again bring her here." Even he couldn't believe the bitterness that spewed out of his mouth. He wouldn't dare look at Mags. Mostly because he wasn't sure if he could handle the pain that would be in those beautiful hazel eyes.

Maggie saw the whole thing happening. She knew Todd had crossed the line. Her husband grabbed Todd's T-shirt and yanked him off the ground. She wanted to scream stop, but her mouth was glued shut.

"Look here, son, if you ever speak to my wife . . . your mom, with that tone of voice, I will personally turn you into a man."

Maggie felt her heart slam against her chest as she watched her husband manhandle her son. She simply couldn't stand back and watch. She had already made more mistakes than she even she cared to admit. "Trent, please . . . Stop!"

Trent jerked Todd a few times and then shoved him against the door. "We'll be going. Nice meeting you." He took Maggie by the hand. "Come on, baby, I'm taking you home."

"Hey, Mags, aren't you happy you finally got rid of me? Now life has really started for you. Right?"

Maggie twisted her head to get a clear view of her son. In her mind, she was certain this would be the last time she looked into his ice-blue eyes. "Toddy, I'm so sorry, and I love you." Her tears started falling like rain.

CB&ED

Trent felt the bad vibes coming from Maggie as soon as his anger simmered down. He knew he was wrong for his little outburst. But he simply couldn't stand back and allow him to treat his wife in such a way. Son or not, he had no right talking to Maggie like she was a worthless piece of dirt. Her days of being a doormat came to a halt when she became his bride.

Okay, man, say something to bring down this mountain that has been thrown between us.

"Baby, I'm sorry—"

"Don't you sorry me! How dare you take it upon—"

"How dare me, darling? Look, you're my wife. I. Will. Not. Tolerate. You. Being. Talked. To. Like. That!"

Maggie saw the raw pain in his chocolate-brown eyes. She knew he was right. It was time that Todd become a true man. He couldn't blame her for the rest of his life. He needed to learn the beauty of forgiveness. Maybe this would be his wakeup call. She needed to believe this. She needed to trust God. Yes, God would work everything together for the good. Maybe if she continued to remind herself, she would come to believe it.

She looked over at her husband and felt the air squeeze from her lungs when she saw the tears running down his cheek. She did this to him. She made him cry. "Baby, I'm sorry. You're right. Toddy had no right to treat us that way. I love you," she reached for his hand, "really, I do."

Trent tenderly kissed her palm. "I know you do, baby."

"I guess we've had our first official argument."

"Yep, I guess so. You wanna know what's fun about little arguments?" Trent asked.

"Yes, please enlighten me."

"The making up."

"Oh, well then I can hardly wait until we get home," Maggie whispered.

Cಶಐ

Todd had put Misfit out back. He was thankful he had fenced in the backyard because he didn't want Misfit to see him this mad. He must have hit the living room wall a hundred times. How dare them show up unannounced. Who did Trent think he was? Todd felt his blood start to boil each time he replayed the episode.

One thing he knew for sure, he was in no condition to meet with Tessy. He would simply call her and explain something came up, and then he planned to spend time with Jack.

Cಶಐ

It had been three days since Tessa heard from Todd. The last time she spoke with him on the phone, he was distant. There was something amiss, she could feel it in her heart. Grant had shared with Tessa that Todd had not been at work all week. This was very unlike Todd. Come hell or high water, he would be at work. Well, Tess planned to find out what was going on. She didn't care if she had to barge in his house. Her gut told her he was hiding something.

Todd slipped out of his house long enough to make a quick trip to the package store for some more of the dark liquor that flowed through his veins like hot fire. The store manager looked at him in a query way when he saw Todd was purchasing five bottles of Jack. Todd could still hear the old guy's question tumbling around in his mind.

"So, kid, what or who are you running from?" Todd badly wanted to tell the guy to shut up, or it was none of his business. But instead he simply paid for his JD and walked out.

Before Todd poured himself a stiff drink, he turned on his stereo. He was in the mood for Mozart. The music soothed his nerves. As he walked to the kitchen, he noticed Misfit in the backyard sprawled out under an oak tree. "You got it made, Misfit."

With shaking hands, Todd opened the bottle of JD. He downed two shots before pouring himself a drink on the rocks. He placed four bottles in the fridge and took the opened bottled with him to the couch. He rubbed his whiskered face, and he allowed his mind to get lost into the classical music. After pouring himself another glass of whiskey, he felt his eyes grow heavy. Before he realized it, he was drifting off into a peaceful sleep.

The first thing Tessa noticed when she pulled into Todd's driveway was the front door was cracked open. She could hear the sound of classical music from her car. As she approached the house, she heard Misfit scratching at the fence. Tessa felt alarms of warning go off in her spirit.

"Hey, boy, why has Daddy got you out here in the hot sun?" She tried to open the gate, but it was locked. In the end, she decided to go in the house and check on Todd. "Let me go get Daddy." Misfit looked at her with sad eyes. Tessa's heart fell to the ground. She had never seen Misfit look so sad. "I'll be back, boy."

Tessa walked up the breezeway to Todd's quaint little house. She could easily see herself living there as his wife. She quickly chided herself for thinking such a thought. She was nowhere near ready to become someone's wife. She still had at least four years of schooling to complete.

She easily opened the door and stepped across the threshold. Tessa felt the air leave her lungs when she caught a glimpse of the man who held her heart in the palm of his hand. He was passed out with a bottle of Jack Daniel's between his legs. The floor creaked, causing Todd to move as she slowly walked toward him. She paused for a brief moment in hopes he would settle back into a deep sleep.

Tessa worked hard to steady her heart. She was sure the thud of her heartbeat was capable of waking the dead. She needed to get the bottle of whiskey from between his legs. Why? Because she simply couldn't bare seeing him like this. This man before her was not the man she fell so madly in love with. She didn't even recognize this man passed out before her.

The music was so loud. She wondered how he was able to sleep so soundly, but then her eyes dropped to the bottle that rested between his masculine legs. Just when she was only a whisper away from him, the phone rang. She jumped and frantically glanced around for the phone. Surely it had to be nearby. Before she took another step, Todd sat straight up and opened the bottle of JD. He took a big swallow, shook his head, and then attempted to stand.

Todd fell back, causing the opened bottle to tumble onto the floor. The dark liquid oozed onto the stained carpet. Tessa instantly went to retrieve the bottle, but when she did, she tripped over a piece of the carpet. She landed at Todd's feet.

Todd felt his eyes start to rapidly blink. How could this be? His woman here at his feet. Was he dreaming? He tried to speak, but it seemed his lips were sealed shut. Until finally he managed to say her name. "Tessy?"

Tessa felt her heart beating in her throat, and her eyes cloud with tears. She felt a fear wash over her and the need to leave. Why did she come? Once again, her curiosity got the best of her. "Hey." She tried to sound calm as she attempted to stand to her feet. She was on her knees when Todd grabbed her arm and pulled her onto his lap. Her intellect told her to get up and run out the door, but her heart told her to stay.

Todd pulled her closer. His breath smelled of sour whiskey, his eyes were bloodshot, and his touch was cold as ice. He traced her lip with his index finger. His eyes traveled the length of her body. She felt a cool chill run down her spine. Who was this man? She felt her defense want to go up but knew she needed to keep calm. His voice was filled with lust as he whispered, "Are ya finally ready to do what you women do best? Hmmm?"

He pulled her closer and started kissing her neck, her ears, and then her lips.

Tessa pulled back and managed to speak with firmness, "Todd, you need to go take a shower and sober up. And Misfit needs to be brought in the house." She felt her heart restrict and tears sting the back of her eyes. No, she refused to give into her fear. This was Todd. Her man. Surely she was okay. He wouldn't hurt her. He loved her.

"No, what I need is you. Now come here." Todd pulled her onto the couch and forcefully started removing her clothing. This was all a bad dream. Surely, she would wake up in her own bed. But it wasn't a dream. She had so freely given him her love. Only so he could freely take from her what she was saving for her husband. The next thing she knew, her entire world turned completely black.

40

The box, Todd had to find the shoe box. After searching the entire house, he found it tucked away in the most obvious place, his desk drawer. He opened it to count the money, but the letter Maggie wrote stood out life a sore thumb. With shaking hands, he retrieved the letter. He sat at his desk and started reading his mom's heart to him.

As he read the letter, he felt his heart soften. For the first time in a while, Todd cried. He allowed his hot tears to fall completely unreserved as he took in her tender words. How could he have been so hateful? Heck, she did the best she could. It wasn't like she beat on him or verbally abused him. She did teach him some good morals such as honesty. One paragraph really caused his heart to rip out of his chest. He read it over and over again.

> Toddy, I really am concerned about your personal life . . . meaning, your love life. You're a very nice-looking man, and you deserve happiness. Yes, you're young, but still, time stops for no one. I mean, it seems only yesterday, I was your age. I want you to promise me you will allow your heart to be opened to love. Okay?

He buried his face in the letter and allowed his tears to soak up the ink. He couldn't take reading another word. What had he done? He only remembered fragments of the awful nightmare. Why could he not tune out the sound of Tessy's cry? Did he harm her? He was sure she had come by to see him, and she even sat on his lap. But the rest was like a faded memory. He had tried calling her private line, but she refused his calls. Surely he didn't harm her? But the sound of her cries. Why else would she cry? Maybe because of the sight of him. He must have looked like a mess. One thing he knew for certain was that if he did harm her, he would never forgive himself.

He looked at the telephone. Maybe he should try calling her at least one more time. At the moment, he felt twenty years older than his age. He was so young yet so old. If only he could turn back time, but he knew all too well that wasn't possible. Why did he have to allow his mind to be so weak? He should never have given into his craving for JD.

Images of Mags's face flashed through his mind, and he felt his heart slam in his chest. He needed to call her and apologize for his rude behavior. But first he was going to try calling his girl, just one more time.

With trembling hands, he dialed Tessa's number. Just as he was about to hang up on the forth ring, he heard the sound of her sweet voice. "Hello." She sounded so vulnerable. What had he done to her?

Todd cleared his throat and moistened his lips. He was barely able to think much less speak. "Tessy, it's me Todd. How are you? I miss you."

She wanted to slam the phone down so hard that his ears would ring for days. Surely he didn't forget what he had done to her? Maybe he did. He was after all pretty wasted. Should she remind him? No, she refused to humiliate herself. She simply wanted to put that dark day far behind. She needed to break off this relationship so she could go forward. Tessa figured it was now or never.

"Look, Todd." She paused for a beat. "I've been thinking that it would be best if we call this relationship off. It's time for me to put everything into my studies." As hard as she tried, she wasn't able to keep the tears at bay. She didn't want him to hear her cry. She was ready to cry her last tear over him. He was a fraud. She could kick herself for falling for the jerk.

Todd wanted to reach through the phone and touch her. This can't be happening. She was his sunshine, his rock, and his next heartbeat. He harmed her. He felt it in his heart and heard it in her voice.

"Tessy, did I harm you?" He found it difficult to breathe. This was too much. He needed a drink to calm his nerves. But it's the whiskey that caused him to hurt Tessy. The pause was too long. She needed to say something. "Tessy—"

"Look," she interrupted, "like I said, it's best that we go our separate ways." She received her answer. She knew without a doubt he had no idea he raped her. She did the only thing she knew to do. She hung up the phone, leaving her broken heart forever in his hands.

Todd was sure his world had just come to an end as he listened to the dial tone. He must have harmed her badly. He could only pray he didn't do what he feared. If he took her purity away from her, he would never forgive himself. He needed to hear Mags's voice. He longed to express his heart. She had taught him honesty. He needed to tell her that he hurt his girl.

"Hello."

Her voice brought comfort to his shattered heart. "Maggie-pie." His voice cracked and the tears fell.

"Toddy?"

"I'm so sorry, can I come home?" He glanced at Misfit asleep without a care in the world. He would need to ask about his friend. "With Misfit?"

"Of course you can, Toddy. You're always welcome to come home." Maggie held on to a thread of hope that God was about to do a miracle for all of them.

Overview for

A Thread of Hope

Maggie Jenkins felt suffocated by the cold darkness of yesterday's mistakes. She silently wondered how she had allowed herself to slip into such a dark abyss. It mattered not which direction she turned, the shadows of yesterday lurked down every avenue. She had grown accustomed to the weight upon her shoulders that came from the heavy blanket of regret. So much so that she was able to venture out among "normal" people with her head held high. She learned to tune out the whispers and block out the cold sneers. But she would never learn to forgive herself for the life she had provided for the only ray of sunshine in her life. Her son, Toddy. You see, Maggie was a professional prostitute. Maggie simply held on to a tiny thread of hope that one day God would smile down upon her.

Todd was an introvert. He loved hiding away in his own prison. In his early teenage years, he started drinking Jack Daniel's regularly. He loved reading books that revolved around darkness, mainly because he related to the horror of thick darkness. He loved his mom, Mags, the best he knew how. About the only thing he could give her credit for was her honesty . . . even though her line of profession was about as dishonest as the day is long. He was determined to find a way out of the dark pit that he found himself sucked into. Deep in his heart, he knew there had to be something better for him. He was sick and tired of watching his only relative give herself to one man after another. He had no idea who is dad might be or where he lived. As for grandparents, they threw Mags under the bus when she got knocked up with him.

Jenna and Grant were two brokenhearted vessels who were destined to become one. They both suffered from a bad divorce, but they bounced back stronger than ever. After Jenna's ex-husband left her for a younger woman, she struggled with God and trust issues. Her only consolation was knowing that she had a beautiful daughter, Tessa, to look after. Grant, on the other hand, drew his strength from God when his ex-wife walked out on him. When God brought the two of them together, they became powerhouses for humanity.

Tessa and Hunter were best friends. Hunter desired to take their friendship to a more serious level, but Tessa is determined to maintain a healthy friendship. She had high ambitions and no time for a serious relationship. Tessa desired to become a psychologist, and she knew she would have to study hard in order for her dream to come true. Her whole world changes when a stranger moves to her cozy little town. Tessa falls head-over-heels in love, leaving Hunter brokenhearted.

ACKNOWLEDGMENTS

Well, first and foremost, I want give all glory and honor to my Savior, Jesus Christ.

I would like to personally thank Silas Abersold for proofreading my manuscript.

I thank God for entrusting me with two of the most beautiful young women in the world (okay, maybe I'm a little biased). I love you, Andrena and Eileen, to the moon and back. I thank God for all of my family members. I thank God for my special friend, Pappy, for encouraging me.

I thank Jesus for my wonderful church family at Shiloh House of Peace. I love each one of you dearly, and I thank you for your prayers. Your support has touched my heart in more ways than you could ever know.

I thank God for you, the reader, so much that I have also included a personal note to express my deepest gratitude.

And last but most certainly not least, I thank God for the fine staff at Xlibris for their help and support.

Dearest Reader,

I would like to personally thank you for your support. It means the world to me. Without you, my writing would be in vain. Please allow me to share my heart with you.

I immensely enjoyed writing *A Thread of Hope*. I became emotionally attached to every character, so I honestly can't say I have a favorite. I love the way God allowed me to include such a diversity of personalities. It amazes me how God directs my mind as I create my novels.

I wanted to address issues that many Christian writers wouldn't dare write on. We live in a world full of hurting people, and if only one life is touched by my novels, then my labor will be paid off.

I realize I left you hanging in this novel, but I promise to tie everything together in the next novel, *Secrets*. I do covet your prayers as I work on this novel. I promise I will be lifting all of you up in my prayers. Please stay sweet!

Hugs, XOXO
Melinda

The Kirkus Review For *The Crooked Path*

In her first novel, Abersold, who co-pastors an Alabama church with her husband, shows Christian prayer and faith at work in a small Missouri town.

As Christian romance, the book extends charity, love and forgiveness without stooping to vulgar sensationalism; think 50 tasteful shades of love. The story succeeds in portraying what the author imagines to be a simpler, cleaner life back in 1959.

A gentle romance peppered with homespun expressions of faith in action, which will satisfy readers who trust in the Lord.

The BlueInk Review for *Whispers in the Night*:

"Abersold has constructed an intriguing Christian-oriented romance . . . (and) cleverly introduces plot twists that keeps readers guessing. Abersold is sincere in teaching a godly lifestyle through her characters."

The Kirkus Review for: Hadassah's Cry

Final volume of Christian romance trilogy that solves all problems in a godly fashion, as characters from *The Crooked Path* and *Whispers in the Night* grow older but still resolve difficulties through prayer, love and fellowship. Everything fall into place for readers who enjoyed the pervious looks at small-town life . . .

Edwards Brothers Malloy
Thorofare, NJ USA
May 23, 2016